India and Investor-State Dispute Settlement

Prabhash Ranjan explores the two competing narratives of investor-state dispute settlement (ISDS) and focuses on the six ISDS cases India lost. On the one hand, ISDS is chastised for affronting the State's sovereign regulatory power – the Philip Morris narrative. On the other hand, ISDS allows investors to hold States accountable for abuse of public power – the Yukos narrative. This book argues that India's ISDS story resembles the Yukos narrative.

With a focus on six case studies, this book examines the reasons that led to foreign investors suing India and the following developments. These ISDS claims are divided into four categories: a case arising from judicial actions, claims brought because of the cancellation of a contract to lease spectrum, conflicts resulting from the imposition of retroactive taxes, and disputes arising from the actions of sub-national governments. Based on India's recent treaty practice, the book also contends that India is de-legalizing and de-judicializing international investment law. By telling India's ISDS story, the book drives home the point that rectifying the ISDS system's flaws requires both narratives' centrality. Excessive focus on the Philip Morris narrative will replace the existing imbalances with a new one where the scale tilts towards the States to the detriment of foreign investment.

This is a useful reference for scholars and practitioners interested in ISDS and its implications for India.

Prabhash Ranjan is Professor and Vice Dean, Jindal Global Law School, O P Jindal Global University, Sonipat, Delhi-NCR, India. He holds a PhD from King's College London and teaches and publishes in the area of international investment law and international trade law.

Routledge Research in International Economic Law

The Legality of Economic Activities in Occupied Territories
International, EU Law and Business and Human Rights Perspectives
Antoine Duval and Eva Kassoti

International Investment Protection within Europe
The EU's Assertion of Control
Julien Berger

Trade, Migration and Law
Free Movement of Persons in the South African Development Community
Victor Amadi

The Americanization of the World Trade Order
Asif H Qureshi

Reform and Regulation of Economic Institutions in Afghanistan
Haroun Rahimi

The Freest Market in the World
The Constitutional Logic of Economic Liberty in Hong Kong
Gonzalo Villalta Puig and Eric C Ip

International Trade Regulation
Evolving Dynamics and Shifting Foundations
Zhiqiong June Wang and Jianfu Chen

India and Investor-State Dispute Settlement
Affronting Sovereignty or Indicting Capriciousness?
Prabhash Ranjan

For more information about this series, please visit https://www.routledge.com/Routledge-Research-in-International-Economic-Law/book-series/INTECONLAW

India and Investor-State Dispute Settlement

Affronting Sovereignty or Indicting Capriciousness?

Prabhash Ranjan

Routledge
Taylor & Francis Group
LONDON AND NEW YORK

First published 2024
by Routledge
4 Park Square, Milton Park, Abingdon, Oxon, OX14 4RN

and by Routledge
605 Third Avenue, New York, NY 10158

Routledge is an imprint of the Taylor & Francis Group, an informa business

British Library Cataloguing-in-Publication Data
A catalogue record for this book is available from the British Library

Library of Congress Cataloging-in-Publication Data
Names: Ranjan, Prabhash, author.
Title: India and investor-state dispute settlement : affronting sovereignty or indicting capriciousness? / Prabhash Ranjan.
Description: Abingdon, Oxon [UK] ; New York, NY : Routledge, 2024. | Series: Routledge research in international economic law | Includes bibliographical references and index. | Contents: ISDS, India and the competing narratives : a primer—ISDS, white industries, and the Indian judiciary—The unending spectrum saga—The retroactive tax misadventure—The Nissan saga : ISDS claims due to the actions of subnational governments—Missing ISDS in India's new FTAs—Towards de-legalization and de-judicialization.
Identifiers: LCCN 2023051131 (print) | LCCN 2023051132 (ebook) | ISBN 9781032349046 (hardback) | ISBN 9781032349053 (paperback) | ISBN 9781003324379 (ebook)
Subjects: LCSH: Investments, Foreign—Law and legislation—India. | Investments—Law and legislation—India. | Arbitration and award—India.
Classification: LCC KNS971.5 .R37 2024 (print) | LCC KNS971.5 (ebook) | DDC 346.54/092—dc23/eng/20231108
LC record available at https://lccn.loc.gov/2023051131
LC ebook record available at https://lccn.loc.gov/2023051132

ISBN: 978-1-032-34904-6 (hbk)
ISBN: 978-1-032-34905-3 (pbk)
ISBN: 978-1-003-32437-9 (ebk)

DOI: 10.4324/9781003324379

Typeset in Galliard
by Apex CoVantage, LLC

Papa, Mummy, Shweta, and Aanjnay

Contents

Preface and acknowledgements

I have been researching international investment law (IIL) since 2006, focusing on India's experience with the IIL regime. A good part of India's experience with the IIL regime was documented in my first book, ***India and Bilateral Investment Treaties: Refusal, Acceptance, Backlash***, published by Oxford University Press in 2019. This book is a sequel to my first book. When I was writing my first book, many vital and high profile investor-state dispute settlement (ISDS) cases against India were yet to be decided. Even if they were decided, the decisions were not publicly available. Many of these high profile ISDS decisions have come into the public limelight in the last few years. This book, therefore, focusses on critically studying these decided ISDS cases involving India. This book's journey starts from where my first book ended and, thus, continues the scholarly and academic foray into India's experience with the IIL regime.

The IIL regime and ISDS are fields that are passing through a turbulent phase. Given the prolific pace at which developments take place in this field, there's never a dull moment in the life of an IIL researcher and teacher. However, an IIL researcher must face a major challenge. Often, the ISDS decisions are not made public. They are shrouded in secrecy, although they deal with public interest. While writing this book, the unavailability of the Vodafone and several other awards crippled my research. This is a challenge that researchers in other fields of international law do not face because most court decisions are publicly available. In the universe of ISDS scholarship, I have visualized my role as a storyteller of India's experience in international investment law. This book is an endeavour in that direction.

Many people have helped me in writing this book. First and foremost, I thank Professor C Raj Kumar, Vice Chancellor of O P Jindal Global University, for his generous support and his enduring faith in my abilities. I am also grateful to all my colleagues at the Jindal Global Law School. Pushkar Anand, my former student, co-author, and currently a PhD candidate at Macquarie University, has provided me with valuable materials for which I thank him. I extend my gratitude to Shantanu Singh of the Geneva Graduate Institute for his help. Aryan Tuslyan, Yoshita Sood, Akshat Jha of the Jindal Global Law School, and Zoya Zaheed of Gujarat National Law University provided valuable research assistance for this book. I am incredibly grateful to them for their assistance, without which this book wouldn't have been possible. My students have always been a constant source of inspiration to me. I thank them for their motivation and encouragement. I sincerely hope that they will find this book helpful.

I am ever grateful to my family. Without their support, I could not have written this book. I thank my parents, Shashi Ranjan and Prabha Ranjan, for their invaluable love and blessings. My father-in-law, R N Sharma, and mother-in-law, Gyan Sheela Sharma, have always backed me. I thank my brother, Shashank Ranjan, my brothers-in-law, Vivek Anand and Sujit Rai, and my sisters-in-law, Malti Ranjan, Shilpi Rai, and Supriya Sharma, for their support. My nephew, Savya Rai, who kept me on my toes by constantly asking about the manuscript's progress, deserves a special mention. Cheers to him, my niece Sakshi Ranjan and all the children in our family: Saisha, Anvi, and Amaya.

Whatever work I could do would not have been possible without the unwavering support of my wonderful wife, Shweta. I cannot thank her enough for her innumerable sacrifices, love, care, and motivation. This book is as much hers as mine for this and several other reasons. My son, Aanjnay, will hopefully be proud that his Dad has completed his second book. I dedicate my book to my family. Last but not least, I thank the Almighty for divine blessings.

New Delhi
28 September 2023

Table of cases

- 9REN Holding S.a.r.l v Kingdom of Spain, ICSID Case No ARB/15/15, 31 May 2019
- A.M.F. Aircraftleasing Meir (and others) v Czech Republic, PCA Case No 2017–15, Award, 11 May 2020
- A11Y v Czech Republic, ICSID Case No UNCT/15/1, Decision on Jurisdiction, 9 February 2017
- Addiko Bank AG v Montenegro, ICSID Case No ARB/17/35, Award, 24 November 2021
- Adel A Hamadi Al Tamimi v Sultanate of Oman, ICSID Case No ARB/11/33, Award, 3 November 2015
- Agroinsumos Ibero-Americanos and others v Venezuela, ICSID Case No ARB/16/23, Award, 23 March 2022
- Aguas del Tunari S.A. v Republic of Bolivia, ICSID Case No ARB/02/3, Decision on Respondent's Objections to Jurisdiction, 21 October 2005
- Al-Bahloul v Tajikistan, SCC Case No 064/2008, Award, 8 June 2010
- AMTO v Ukraine, SCC Case No 080/2005, Final Award, 26 March 2008
- Anglia Auto v Czech Republic, SCC Case No 2014/181, Award, 10 March 2017
- Ansung Housing Co Ltd. v People's Republic of China, ICSID Case No ARB/14/25, Award, 9 March 2017
- Antaris Solar GmbH and Dr. Michael Göde v The Czech Republic, PCA Case No 2014–01, 2 May 2018
- Antoine Abou Lahoud v Democratic Republic of Congo, ICSID Case No ARB/10/4, Award, 7 February 2014
- Antrix Corpn. Ltd. v Devas Multimedia (P) Ltd., 2022 SCC OnLine Del 2622
- Apotex v USA (III), ICSID Case No ARB(AF)/12/1, Award, 25 August 2014
- ARA Libertad (Argentina v Ghana) [2012] ITLOS Case No 20, ITLOS Rep 21
- Arif v Moldova, ICSID Case No ARB/11/23, Award, 8 April 2013
- Asian Agricultural Products Ltd. (AAPL) v Republic of Sri Lanka, ICSID Case No ARB/87/3, Award, 27 June 1990

- AsiaPhos Limited and Norwest Chemicals Pte Limited v People's Republic of China, ICSID Case No ADM/21/1, Award, 16 February 2023
- ATA Construction, Industrial and Trading Company v The Hashemite Kingdom of Jordan, ICSID Case No ARB/08/2, Award, 18 May 2010
- Bayindir Insaat Turizm Ticaret Ve Sanayi A.S. v Islamic Republic of Pakistan (Bayindir v Pakistan), ICSID Case No ARB/03/29, Decision on Jurisdiction, 14 November 2005
- Bear Creek Mining Corporation v Republic of Peru, ICSID Case No ARB/14/21, Award, 30 November 2017
- Belenergia S.A. v Italian Republic, ICSID Case No ARB/15/40
- Bernhard von Pezold and others v Zimbabwe, ICSID Case No ARB/10/15, Award, 28 July 2015
- Bharti Televentures Ltd. v DSS Enterprise Private Ltd. and Ors. [2005] IA Nos 9735, 923, and 9925/03 in CS(OS) No. 1769/2003 (Delhi HC)
- Big Sky Energy Corporation v Kazakhstan, ICSID Case No ARB/17/22, Award, 24 November 2021
- Biwater-Gauff v Tanzania, ICSID Case No ARB/05/22, Award, 24 July 2008
- Brazil-Measures Affecting Imports of Retreaded Tyres, WT/DS332/AB/R (WTO AB 17 December 2007)
- Burlington Resources, Inc. v Republic of Ecuador, ICSID Case No ARB/08/5, Decision on Liability, 14 December 2014
- Cairn Energy PLC and Cairn UK Holdings Limited v Republic of India, PCA Case No 2016–7, Award, 21 December 2020
- Casinos Austria International GmbH and Casinos Austria Aktiengesellschaft v Argentine Republic ICSID Case No ARB/14/32, Decision on Jurisdiction, 29 June 2018
- CC/Devas (Mauritius) Ltd, Devas Employees Mauritius Private Limited and Telecom Devas Mauritius Limited v India, UNCITRAL, PCA Case No 2013–09, Dissenting Opinion of David R. Haigh QC
- CC/Devas (Mauritius) Ltd., Devas Employees Mauritius Private Limited, and Telcom Devas Mauritius Limited v Republic of India (I), PCA Case No 2013–09, Award on Jurisdiction and Merits, 25 July 2016
- CC/Devas (Mauritius) Ltd., Devas Employees Mauritius Private Limited, and Telcom Devas Mauritius Limited v Republic of India, PCA Case No 2013–09, Award on Quantum, 13 October 2020
- CC/Devas (Mauritius) Ltd., Devas Employees Mauritius Private Limited, and Telcom Devas Mauritius Limited v Republic of India, PCA Case No 2013–09, Procedural Order No. 7 (Concerning the Respondent's Request for Suspension of the Proceedings), 21 December 2016
- Centre for Public Interest Litigation v Union of India (2012) 3 SCC 1
- Charanne and Construction Investments v Spain, SCC Case No V 062/2012, Final Award, 21 January 2016
- Chevron and TexPet v Ecuador (I), PCA Case No 2007–02/AA277, Award, 31 August 2011

- Chevron and TexPet v Ecuador (I), PCA Case No 2007–02/AA277, Partial Award on the Merits, 30 March 2010
- Clayton and Bilcon of Delaware Inc. v Government of Canada, PCA Case No 2009–04, Award on Jurisdiction and Liability, 17 March 2015
- CMS Gas Transmission Co. v Argentine Republic, ICSID Case No ARB/01/08, Decision on Annulment, 25 September 2007
- Compañia de Aguas and Vivendi Universal S.A. v Argentine Republic, ICSID Case No ARB/97/3, Decision on the Challenge to the President of the Committee, 3 October 2001
- Compañía de Aguas del Aconquija S.A. (formerly Aguas del Aconquija) and Vivendi Universal S.A. (formerly Compagnie Générale des Eaux) v Argentine Republic (I), ICSID Case No ARB/97/3 Award, 21 November 2000
- Consutel v Algeria, PCA Case No 2017–33, Final Award 3 February 2020
- Continental Casualty Company v Argentine Republic, ICSID Case No ARB/03/9, Award, 5 September 2008
- Copper Mesa Mining Corp. v Republic of Ecuador, PCA No. 2012–2, Award, 15 March 2016
- Cruz City 1 Mauritius Holdings v Unitech Limited [2017] EXP132/2014 & EA(OS) Nos. 316/2015, 1058/2015 & 151/2016 & 670/2016
- Crystallex International Corporation v Bolivarian Republic of Venezuela, ICSID Case No ARB(AF)/11/2, Award, 4 April 2016
- Desert Line Projects LLC v Yemen, ICSID Case No ARB/05/17, Award, 2008
- Deutsche Telekom AG v Republic of India, PCA Case No 2014–10, Final Award, 27 May 2020
- Deutsche Telekom AG v The Republic of India [2023] SGHC(I) 7
- Deutsche Telekom AG v The Republic of India, PCA Case No 2014–10, Interim Award – 13 Dec 2017
- Deutsche Telekom AG v The Republic of India, PCA Case No 2014–10, Decision of the Swiss Federal Tribunal 4A_184/2022, 8 Mar 2023
- Devas Employees Mauritius (P) Ltd. v Antrix Corpn. Ltd., 2021 SCC OnLine NCLT 484
- Devas Employees Mauritius (P) Ltd. v Antrix Corpn. Ltd., 2023 SCC OnLine Del 1608
- Devas Multimedia (P) Ltd. v Antrix Corpn. Ltd., (2023) 1 SCC 216
- Devas Multimedia (P) Ltd. v Antrix Corpn. Ltd., 2021 SCC OnLine NCLAT 448
- Devas Multimedia Private Limited v Antrix Corporation Limited, ICC Case No 18051/CYK, Final Award, 14 September 2015
- Devas Multimedia Private Ltd. v Antrix Corp., C18–1360 TSZ (WD Wash Nov. 4, 2020)
- Duke Energy v Ecuador, ICSID Case No ARB/04/19, Award, 18 August 2008
- Eco Oro Minerals Corp. v Republic of Colombia, ICSID Case No ARB/16/41, Decision on Jurisdiction, Liability on Quantum, 9 September 2021

- Eiser Infrastructure Limited and Energia Solar Luxembourg S.a r.l v Kingdom of Spain, ICSID Case No ARB/13/36, Award, 4 May 2017
- El Paso Energy International Company v Argentine Republic, ICSID Case No ARB/03/15, Award, 31 October 2011
- Eli Lily v Canada, ICSID Case No UNCT/14/2, Award, 16 March 2017
- Emilio Agustin Maffezini v Kingdom of Spain (Maffezini v Spain), ICSID Case No ARB/97/7, Decision on objections to jurisdiction, 25 January 2000
- EnCana Corporation v Republic of Ecuador, LCIA Case No UN3481, Award, 3 February 2006
- Enron Creditors Recovery Corporation (formerly Enron Corporation) and Ponderosa Assets, L.P. v Argentine Republic, ICSID Case No ARB/01/3, Award, 22 May 2007
- Enron Creditors Recovery Corporation (formerly Enron Corporation) and Ponderosa Assets, L.P. v Argentine Republic, ICSID Case No ARB/01/3 Decision on Jurisdiction, 14 January 2004
- Flemingo Duty-Free v Poland, UNCITRAL, Award, 12 August 2016
- Fouad Alghanim v Jordan, ICSID Case No ARB/13/38, Award, 14 December 2017
- FREIF Eurowind Holdings Ltd v Kingdom of Spain, SCC Case No 2017/060, Final Award, 8 March 2021
- Frontier Petroleum v Czech Republic, Final Award, 12 November 2010
- Fynerdale Holdings BV v The Czech Republic, PCA Case No 2018–18, Award, 29 April 2021
- Garanti Koza LLP v Turkmenistan (Garanti Koza v Turkmenistan), ICSID Case No ARB/11/20, Decision on the Objection to Jurisdiction for Lack of Consent, 3 July 2013
- Gavazzi v Romania, ICSID Case No ARB/12/25, Award, 21 April 2015
- GEA v Ukraine, ICSID Case No ARB/08/16, Award, 31 March 2011
- Glencore International v Colombia, ICSID Case No ARB/16/6, Award, 27 August 2019
- Gramercy v Peru, ICSID Case No UNCT/18/2, Final Award, 6 December 2022
- H&H Enterprises Investments, Inc. v Arab Republic of Egypt, ICSID Case No ARB/09/15, Award, 6 May 2014
- Hesham T M Al Warraq v Republic of Indonesia (Warraq v Indonesia), UNCITRAL, Final Award, 15 December 2014
- HICEE B.V. v The Slovak Republic, UNCITRAL, PCA Case No 2009–11, Partial Award, 23 May 2011
- Hochtief AG v Argentina (Hochtief v Argentina), ICSID Case No ARB/07/31, Decision on Jurisdiction, 24 October 2011
- I.C.W. Europe Investments Limited v The Czech Republic, PCA Case No 2014–22, Award, 15 May 2019
- Içkale v Turkmenistan, ICSID Case No ARB/10/24, Award, 8 March 2016
- Impregilo S.p.A. v Argentine Republic, ICSID Case No ARB/07/17, Award, 21 June 2011

- Ioan Micula, Viorel Micula and others v Romania (I), ICSID Case No ARB/05/20, Final Award, 11 December 2013
- Itisaluna Iraq and others v Iraq, ICSID Case No ARB/17/10, Award, 3 April 2020
- Ivan Peter Busta and James Peter Busta v Czech Republic, SCC Case No V 2015/014, Final Award, 10 March 2017
- Jan de Nul and Dredging International N.V. v Egypt, ICSID Case No ARB/04/13, Award, 6 November 2008
- Jan Oostergetel and Theodora Laurentius v Slovak Republic, UNCITRAL, Final Award, 23 April 2012
- Jayam and Company v Assistant Commissioner & Anr. (2016) 15 SCC 125
- Jin Hae Seo v Republic of Korea, HKIAC Case No 18117, Concurring Opinion of Dr. Benny Lo, 27 September 2019
- Joseph Charles Lemire v Ukraine (II), ICSID Case No ARB/06/18, Award, 28 March 2011
- Joshua Dean Nelson v Mexico, ICSID Case No UNCT/17/1, Award, 5 June 2020
- KCI v Gabon, UNCITRAL, Award, 23 December 2016
- Khaitan Holdings (Mauritius) Limited v Republic of India (PCA Case No 2018–50)
- Khan Resources Inc., Khan Resources B.V. and Cauc Holding Company Ltd. v the Government of Mongolia and Monatom Co., Ltd., PCA Case No 2011–09, Decision on Jurisdiction, 25 July 2012
- Krederi Ltd. v Ukraine, ICSID Case No ARB/14/17, Award, 2 July 2018
- LaGrand (Germany v United States of America), Judgment, ICJ Reports 2001
- LG&E Capital Corp. and LG&E International Inc. v Argentine Republic, ICSID Case No ARB/02/1, Decision on Liability, 3 October 2016
- Link-Trading Joint Stock Company v Moldova, UNCITRAL, Final Award, 18 April 2002
- Loewen v United States, ICSID Case No ARB(AF)/98/3, Award, 26 June 2003
- Lone Pine v Canada, ICSID Case No UNCT/15/2, Final Award, 21 November 2022
- Louis Dreyfus Armateurs SAS (France) v The Republic of India, PCA Case No 2014–26, Award, 11 September 2018
- Malaysian Historical Salvors v Malaysia, ICSID Case No ARB/05/10, Award on Jurisdiction, 17 May 2007
- Mamidoil Jetoil Greek Petroleum Products Societe SA v Republic of Albania (Mamidoil v Albania), ICSID Case No ARB/11/24, Award, 30 March 2015
- Manchester Securities v Poland, PCA Case No 2015–18, Award, 7 December 2018
- Manolium Processing v Belarus, PCA Case No 2018–06, Final Award, 22 June 2021

- Marvin Roy Feldman Karpa v United Mexican States, ICSID Case No ARB(AF)/99/1, Award, 16 December 2002
- Masdar Solar & Wind Cooperatief U.A. v Kingdom of Spain, ICSID Case No ARB/14/1, Award, 16 May 2018
- McCulloch v Maryland [1819] 17 US 316, 431
- Mercuria Energy Group Limited v Republic of Poland (II), SCC Case No 2019/126, Final Award, 29 December 2022
- Mesa Power Group LLC v Government of Canada, PCA Case No 2012–17, Award, 24 March 2016
- Metal-Tech v Uzbekistan, ICSID Case No ARB/10/3, Award, 4 October 2013
- Metalclad Corporation v The United Mexican States, ICSID Case No ARB(AF)/97/1, Award, 30 August 2000
- Micula v Romania (II), ICSID Case No ARB/14/29, Award, 5 March 2020
- MNSS and RCA v Montenegro, ICSID Case No ARB(AF)/12/8, Award, 4 May 2016
- Muhammet Çap and Sehil v Turkmenistan, ICSID Case No ARB/12/6, Award, 4 May 2021
- Murphy Exploration and Production Company International v Republic of Ecuador (II), PCA Case No 2012–16 (formerly AA 434), Partial Final Award, 6 May 2016
- Mytilineos Holdings SA v The State Union of Serbia & Montenegro and Republic of Serbia (I), Partial Award on Jurisdiction, 8 September 2006
- Naftogaz and others v Russia, PCA Case No 2017–16, Award on Liability, 22 February 2019
- National Aluminium Co. Ltd. v Pressteel & Fabrication (P) Ltd (2004) 1 SCC 540
- Nissan Motor Co. Ltd. v Republic of India, PCA Case No 2017–37, Decision on Jurisdiction, 29 April 2019
- Novenergia II – Energy & Environment (SCA), SICAR v Kingdom of Spain, SCC Case No 063/2015, Final Award, 15 February 2018
- OAO Tatneft v Ukraine (OAO Tatneft v Ukraine), UNCITRAL, Award, 29 July 2014
- Occidental Exploration and Production Company v Republic of Ecuador (I), LCIA Case No UN3467, Final Award, 1 July 2004
- OJSC "Tatneft" v Ukraine, UNCITRAL, Award, 29 July 2014
- Olin Holdings Limited v State of Libya, ICC Case No 20355/MCP, Final Award, 25 May 2018
- Oschadbank v Russian Federation, PCA Case No 2016–14, Award, 26 November 2018
- Pantechniki S.A. Contractors & Eng'rs (Greece) v Republic of Albania, ICSID Case No ARB/07/21, Award (July 29, 2009)
- Parkerings-Compagniet AS v Republic of Lithuania, ICSID Case No ARB/05/8, Award, 11 September 2007
- Petrobart v Kyrgyz Republic, SCC Case No 126/2003, Arbitral Award, 29 March 2005

- Siemens v Argentina, ICSID Case No ARB/02/8, Award, 6 February 2007
- Silver Ridge Power BV v Italian Republic, ICSID Case No ARB/15/37, Award, 26 February 2021
- Sistem v Kyrgyz Republic, ICSID Case No ARB(AF)/06/1, Award, 9 September 2009
- Spółdzielnia Pracy Muszynianka v Slovak Republic, PCA Case No 2017–08/AA629
- Stabil, Crimea-Petrol LLC, Elefteria LLC, Novel-Estate LLC and others v The Russian Federation, PCA Case No 2015–35, Final Award, 12 April 2019
- Stati v Kazakhstan (I), SCC Case No 116/2010, Award, 19 December 2013
- Strabag v Libya, ICSID Case No ARB(AF)/15/1, Award, 29 June 2020
- Supervision y Control S.A. v Republic of Costa Rica, ICSID Case No ARB/12/4, Award, 18 January 2017
- Swisslion v Former Yugoslav Republic of Macedonia, ICSID Case No ARB/09/16, Award, 6 June 2012
- Técnicas Medioambientales Tecmed, S.A. v Mexico, ICSID Case No ARB (AF)/00/2, Award, 29 May 2003
- Tethyan Copper Company Pty Limited v Islamic Republic of Pakistan, ICSID Case No ARB/12/1, Award, 12 July 2019
- The Board of Trustees of the Port of Kolkata v Louis Dreyfus Armatures [2014] GA 1997 of 2014 and CS No. 220 of 2014 (Calcutta HC)
- Togo Electricité et GDFSuez Energie Services v La Republique Togolaise, ICSID Case No ARB/06/07, Decision on Annulment, 6 September 2011
- Tza Yap Shum v PeruTza Yap Shum v Republic of Peru, ICSID Case No ARB/07/6, Award, 7 June 2011
- UAB Eenergija (Lithuania) v Republic of Latvia, ICSID Case No ARB/12/33
- Union Fenosa Gas, S.A. v Arab Republic of Egypt, ICSID Case No ARB/14/4, Award, 31 August 2018
- Union of India v Khaitan Holdings (Mauritius) Limited & Ors. [2019] CS (OS) 46/2019, I.As. 1235/2019 & 1238/2019 (Delhi HC)
- Union of India v Vodafone Group Plc United Kingdom & Anr [2018] CS(OS) 383/2017 & IA No 9460/2017 (Delhi HC)
- United Parcel Service of America Inc (UPS) v Government of Canada, UNCITRAL, Award on the Merits, 24 May 2007
- Valores Mundiales v Venezuela, ICSID Case No ARB/13/11, Award, 25 July 2017
- Vedanta Resources PLC v India, PCA Case No 2016–05
- Venezuela US, SRL v Venezuela, PCA Case No 2013–34, Interim Award on Jurisdiction, 26 July 2016
- Veolia Propreté v Arab Republic of Egypt, ICSID Case No ARB/12/15
- Víctor Pey Casado and President Allende Foundation v Republic of Chile, ICSID Case No ARB/98/2, Award, 8 May 2008

- Vincent J. Ryan v Poland, ICSID Case No ARB(AF)/11/3, Award, 24 November 2015
- Vivendi v Argentina, ICSID Case No ARB/97/3, Award, 20 August 2007
- Vodafone Group Plc and Vodafone Consolidated Holdings Limited v Government of India [II], UNCITRAL
- Vodafone International Holdings B.V. v Union of India (3 December 2008), WP No. 2550 of 2007
- Vodafone International Holdings BV v Government of India [I], PCA Case No 2016–35, Award, 25 September 2020
- Vodafone International Holdings BV v India (I), PCA Case No 2016–35, Award, 25 September 2020
- Vodafone International Holdings BV v Union of India (2012) 6 SCC 613
- Voltaic Network GmbH v Czech Republic, PCA Case No 2014–20, Award, 15 May 2019
- WA Investments-Europa Nova Limited v The Czech Republic, PCA Case No 2014–19, Award, 15 May 2019
- Watkins Holdings S.à.r.l. and others v Kingdom of Spain, ICSID Case No ARB/15/44, Award, 21 January 2020
- Westmoreland Holdings v Canada (II), ICSID Case No UNCT/20/3, Final Award, 31 January 2022
- White Industries Australia Limited v The Republic of India, UNCITRAL, Final Award, 30 November 2011
- Yukos Universal Limited (Isle of Man) v The Russian Federation, PCA Case No 2005–04/AA227, Final Award, 18 July 2014
- Yukos Universal Limited (Isle of Man) v The Russian Federation, PCA Case No 2005–04/AA227, Interim Award, 30 November 2009
- Zhongshan Fucheng Industrial Investment Co. Ltd. v Federal Republic of Nigeria, Final Award, 26 March 2021

1 ISDS, India, and the competing narratives

A primer

1.1 Introduction

Investor-state dispute settlement (ISDS) is one of the most contentious issues in international law today. The dominance of treaty-based ISDS[1] owes its origin to the increasing legalization of international investment relations whereby countries agree that their mutual relations be governed by the instruments of international law, like treaties.[2] Between 1959 – when the first modern-day bilateral investment treaty (BIT) was signed between West Germany and Pakistan – and 1 January 2023, 2830 such treaties have been signed.[3] While the legalization of international investment relations was slow from 1959 to 1989 – 385 BITs were signed during this four-decade period[4] – the 1990s witnessed countries putting the pedal to the metal. Propelled by the tailwinds of neoliberalism that swept the world after the Cold-War triumph of a capitalist America over a communist Russia, the number of BITs quintupled to 1857 by the end of 1999.[5] The universalization of the Washington Consensus model[6] saw several developing countries like India giving up their reticence on foreign investment and embracing the process of investment legalization with open arms by entering into BITs.

1 ISDS can take different shapes. For instance, foreign investors bringing arbitration claims against States under a contract for contractual breaches can also be called ISDS. However, in this book, the use of ISDS means disputes between investors and States under the BIT or the relevant agreement like the investment chapter in an FTA unless stated otherwise. That is, ISDS means treaty-based claims, not contract-based claims unless specified.

2 On legalization, see Kenneth W Abbott and others, 'The Concept of Legalization' (2000) 54(3) International Organization 401–19. See also Chapter 6.

3 UNCTAD, 'World Investment Report 2023' (2023) 71 <https://unctad.org/publication/world-investment-report-2023>.

4 UNCTAD, 'Bilateral Investment Treaties 1959–1999' (2000) <https://unctad.org/system/files/official-document/poiteiiad2.en.pdf> accessed 18 September 2023.

5 ibid. See also E Prieto-Rios, 'Neoliberal Market Rationality: The Driver of International Investment Law' (2016) 3 Birkbeck Law Review 55.

6 For more on Washington Consensus see John Williamson, 'The Strange History of the Washington Consensus' (2004–2005) 27(2) Journal of Post Keynesian Economics 195–206.

DOI: 10.4324/9781003324379-1

A ubiquitous provision in most BITs is an ISDS clause. Such clauses are also found in an investment chapter of free trade agreements (FTA); for example, the Comprehensive and Progressive Agreement for Trans-Pacific Partnership (CPTPP) – an FTA between 11 countries – contains an ISDS clause in its investment chapter.[7] A typical ISDS clause in a BIT or any other treaty, like an investment chapter of an FTA, empowers foreign investors to directly bring claims against host States if the investor considers that the host State's actions breach the treaty. Notably described as 'arbitration without privity',[8] ISDS borrows the adjudicative method from international commercial arbitration – a private law mechanism – to address questions and issues that typically possess a public law character.[9] Thus, an emblematic ISDS claim will involve a foreign investor alleging that the host State's sovereign regulatory action related to issues of general interest, such as health or environment, infringes the former's substantive rights guaranteed under the treaty.[10] This allows an ISDS tribunal to review the sovereign conduct of the host State under the respective investment treaty, akin to what national courts do when they undertake the judicial review of the executive's actions.[11] ISDS marks the 'judicialization' – a phenomenon of the increasing role of international courts and tribunals in global governance[12] – of international investment relations. By accepting ISDS clauses in their investment treaties, countries agree to delegate the power to an investor-state arbitration tribunal to interpret the treaty and resolve the disputes between the investor and the State.[13]

7 See Articles 9.18–9.30 of Comprehensive and Progressive Agreement for Trans-Pacific Partnership (signed on 8 March 2018). See also Prabhash Ranjan, 'Emerging Trends in Investor-State Dispute Settlement in New Free Trade Agreements' (2022) 17(7) Global Trade and Customs Journal 332–37.

8 Jan Paulsson, 'Arbitration Without Privity' (1995) 10(2) ICSID Review 232–37.

9 See Anthea Roberts, 'Clash of Paradigms: Actors and Analogies Shaping the Investment Treaty System' (2013) 107 American Journal of International Law 45; Jose Alvarez, 'Is Investor-State Arbitration "Public"' Institute for International Law and Justice <https://www.iilj.org/working-papers/is-investor-state-arbitration-public/#:~:text=ISDS%20is%20increasingly%20perceived%20as,are%20silent%20arbitrators%20exercise%20their> accessed 18 September 2023; Martti Koskenniemi, 'It's Not the Cases, It's the System' (2017) 18 Journal of World Investment and Trade.

10 A typical BIT provides various substantive protective rights to foreign investors like protection from unlawful expropriation, fair and equitable treatment, most favoured nation treatment, national treatment, etc.

11 See Roberts (n 9) 58–63. See also Giovanni Zarra, 'The Issue of Incoherence in Investment Arbitration: Is There Need for a Systemic Reform?' (2018) 17(1) Chinese Journal of International Law 138. This does not mean that ISDS performs the role of global constitutional adjudication – Valentina Vadi, 'Investor-State Dispute Settlement as Global Constitutional Adjudication?' in S Schill, C Tams and R Hoffmann (eds), *International Investment Law and Constitutional Law* (Edward Elgar 2019).

12 See KJ Alter, EM Hafner-Burton and L Helfer, 'Theorizing the Judicialization of International Relations' (2019) 63 International Studies Quarterly 449–63. See also Chapter 6.

13 Abbott and others (n 2) 401–19. See also Chapter 6.

The first BIT containing an ISDS clause was signed in 1969 between Italy and Chad.[14] However, it wasn't till 1987 – almost 18 years later – that the first treaty-based investor-state dispute was filed in a case known as *AAPL v Sri Lanka*.[15] The decision in this case was delivered in 1990. In the decade of 1990s, foreign investors started testing the ISDS waters and tasting success. Consequently, the 2000s, especially the 2010s, saw an avalanche of ISDS claims. In about three and a half decades, from 1987 till the end of 2022, 1257 publicly known ISDS claims have been initiated (see Figure 1.1).[16] In other words, an average of 34–35 ISDS claims have been undertaken annually during these 36 years. This number is unprecedented compared to dispute resolution in other areas of international law.

Put differently, formally, the process of judicialization of international investment law started in the late 1960s, but it took root only in the 1990s, 2000s, and 2010s. This phenomenal growth in the number of investor-state treaty claims amply exhibits that ISDS has emerged as a pivotal means of settling international investment law disputes and as the most dynamic type of international arbitration.[17] Over the last three decades, foreign investors have employed the ISDS mechanism to challenge an extensive range of sovereign actions of States as breaches of the investment treaty. For example, foreign investors have challenged a country's public health measures, such as Philipp Morris, a tobacco company, sued Australia and Uruguay for its plain packaging regulations.[18] Investors have contested a country's regulatory activities aimed at protecting the environment, including actions directed at combating climate change; for example, RWE – a German Company – opposed Netherland's measure aimed at phasing out coal-fired electricity plant[19] or the ISDS

14 International Institute for Sustainable Development, 'State-State Dispute Settlement in Investment Treaties – Best Practices Series' (2014) 1 <https://www.iisd.org/system/files/publications/best-practices-state-state-dispute-settlement-investment-treaties.pdf> accessed 18 September 2023.

15 *Asian Agricultural Products Ltd (AAPL) v Republic of Sri Lanka*, ICSID Case No ARB/87/3, Award, 27 June 1990.

16 UNCTAD (n 3) 77.

17 Yannick Radi, *Rules and Practice of International Investment Law and Arbitration* (CUP 2020) 262.

18 *Phillip Morris v Australia*, PCA Case No 2012-12, Final Award, 8 March 2017; *Philip Morris v Uruguay*, ICSID Case No ARB/10/7, Award, 8 July 2016. According to UNCTAD, more than 30 ISDS claims have been brought by foreign investors challenging public health measures – See UNCTAD, 'IIA Issues Note: International Investment Policies and Public Health' (2021) <https://unctad.org/system/files/official-document/diaepcbinf2021d5_en.pdf> accessed 18 September 2023. See also AM Thow, W Alschner and F Aljunied, 'Public Health Clauses in International Investment Agreements: Sword or Shield? (2023) 14 Global Policy 260–69.

19 *RWE v Netherlands*, ICSID Case No ARB/21/4, See also *Eco Oro Minerals Corp v Republic of Colombia*, ICSID Case No ARB/16/41, Decision on Jurisdiction, Liability on Quantum, 9 September 2021; *Westmoreland Holdings v Canada (II)*, ICSID Case No UNCT/20/3, Final Award, 31 January 2022; *Lone Pine v Canada*, ICSID Case No UNCT/15/2, Final

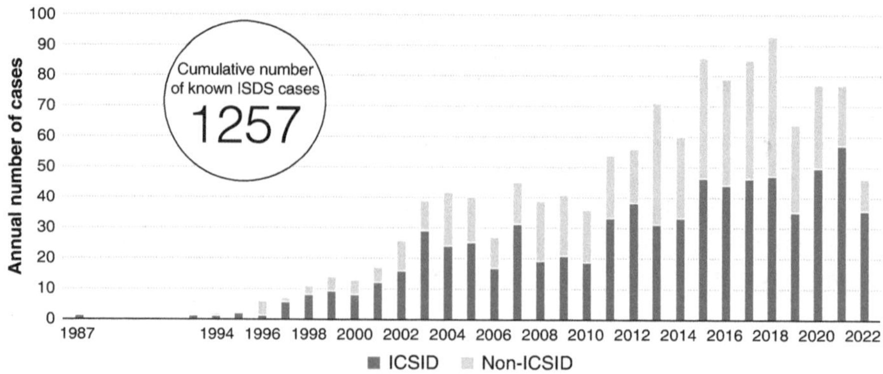

Figure 1.1 Trends in known treaty-based ISDS claims from 1987–2022

Source: World Investment Report, 2023

claims brought in the wake of country's renewable energy programmes.[20] Investors have attacked a country's taxation measures; for example, Cairn Energy brought an ISDS claim against India for imposing taxes retroactively.[21] ISDS has also been used to question a country's social policies; for example, Veolia Properte, a French firm, challenged Egypt for hiking its minimum wage rate,[22] and Italian investors brought an ISDS claim against South Africa for its Black economic empowerment programme.[23] Claims have also been brought

---

Award, 21 November 2022. According to UNCTAD, foreign investors have brought more than 170 ISDS claims against States challenging their environmental measures – UNCTAD, 'IIA Issues Note: Treaty-Based Investor-State Dispute Settlement Cases and Climate Action' (2022) <https://unctad.org/system/files/official-document/diaepcbinf2022d7_en.pdf> accessed 18 September 2023.

20 See Jack Biggs, 'The Scope of Investors' Legitimate Expectations Under the FET Standard in the European Renewable Energy Cases' (2021) 36(1) ICSID Review 99–128; Maximilian Schmidl, 'The Renewable Energy Saga from Charanne v Spain to The PV Investors v Spain: Trying to See the Wood for the Trees' (*Kluwer Arbitration Blog*, 1 February 2021) <http://arbitrationblog.kluwerarbitration.com/2021/02/01/the-renewable-energy-saga-from-charanne-v-spain-to-the-pv-investors-v-spain-trying-to-see-the-wood-for-the-trees/> accessed 19 September 2023.

21 *Cairn v India*, PCA Case No 2016-07, Final Award, 21 December 2020. See also Chapter 4. According to UNCTAD, foreign investors have challenged tax-related measures in 165 ISDS claims – UNCTAD, 'IIA Issues Note: Facts on Investor-State Arbitrations in 2021: With a Special Focus on Tax Related ISDS Cases' (2022) <https://unctad.org/system/files/official-document/diaepcbinf2022d4_en.pdf> accessed 19 September 2023. See also *Vodafone v India (I)*, PCA Case No 2016-35; *Voltaic v Czech Republic*, PCA Case No 2014-20, Award, 19 May 2019; *Photovoltaik v Czech Republic*, PCA Case No 2014-21, Award, 19 May 2019; Prabhash Ranjan, 'Investor-State Dispute Settlement and Tax Matters: Limitations on State's Sovereign Right to Tax' (2023) 31(1) Asia Pacific Law Review 219–34.

22 *Veolia Propreté v Arab Republic of Egypt*, ICSID Case No ARB/12/15.

23 *Piero Foresti, Laura de Carli & Others v The Republic of South Africa*, ICSID Case No ARB(AF)/07/01.

on the protection of cultural property.[24] A country's national security measures have also been targeted; for example, several American corporations initiated ISDS claims against Argentina when it adopted emergency measures to safeguard itself from a perilous economic crisis.[25] Such a wide range of claims has understandably made States jittery about the ISDS mechanism. Since States zealously guard their sovereign right to regulate, they consider these claims an affront to their sovereignty.

Another important fact is that if an ISDS tribunal rules in favour of an investor and against a State, the latter may have to pay compensation to the former, which has been more than US$1 billion on some occasions.[26] Seeing the momentous growth of BITs and ISDS, both quantitative and qualitative, over the last three decades, it would not be an exaggeration to state that the legalization and judicialization of international investment relations have outpaced similar endeavours in other areas of global governance.

The breathtaking growth in ISDS claims is accompanied by the swelling of its critics, who find the system unfair and biased.[27] It has triggered a backlash: dissatisfaction and bitterness about the ISDS regime.[28] The virulent critics chastise ISDS for maximizing investor protection and safeguarding the economic interests of neo-colonial powers, that is, of countries with high levels of economic development, to the detriment of poorer nations.[29] Arguably, overpowered foreign investors, ably supported by big law firms and arbitrators mainly from developed countries, use the ISDS mechanism to bring treaty-based claims against States, thus infringing upon their sovereign right to regulate in public interest like protecting public health and

24 *Malaysian Historical Salvors v Malaysia*, ICSID Case No ARB/05/10, Award on Jurisdiction, 17 May 2007.

25 See Jürgen Kurtz, 'Adjudging the Exceptional at International Investment Law: Security, Public Order and Financial Crisis' (2010) 59 International & Comparative Law Quarterly 325–71.

26 See *Agroinsumos Ibero-Americanos and others v Venezuela*, ICSID Case No ARB/16/23, Award, 23 March 2022 – amount awarded – US$1630 million; *Oschadbank v Russian Federation*, PCA Case No 2016-14, Award, 26 November 2018 – amount awarded – US$1111 million; *Tethyan Copper Company Pty Limited v Islamic Republic of Pakistan*, ICSID Case No ARB/12/1, Award, 12 July 2019, para 278 – amount awarded – US$4000 million.

27 See e.g. Gus Van Harten, 'Arbitrator Behaviour in Asymmetrical Adjudication: An Empirical Study of Investment Treaty Arbitration' (2012) 50 Osgoode Hall Law Journal 211.

28 See David Caron and Esme Shirlow, 'Dissecting Backlash: The Unarticulated Causes of Backlash and Its Unintended Consequences' in Andreas Follesdal and Geir Ulfstein (eds), *The Judicialization of International Law: A Mixed Blessing* (OUP 2018); Maria Laura Marceddu and Pietro Ortolani, 'What Is Wrong with Investment Arbitration? Evidence from a Set of Behavioural Experiments' (2020) 31 European Journal of International Law 405.

29 Thomas Shultz and Cédric Dupont, 'Investment Arbitration: Promoting the Rule of Law or Over-Empowering Investors? A Quantitative Empirical Study' (2014) 25 European Journal of International Law 1147.

the environment.[30] It is contended that the fear of ISDS claims has a chilling effect on a State's regulatory powers.[31] Thus, the argument goes that States exercise self-restraint over their regulatory powers, such as not enacting a law in the public interest, due to the worry of influential foreign investors suing them before ISDS tribunals demanding exorbitant monetary damages.[32] Critics also upbraid the ISDS mechanism for giving precedence to the interests of multinational corporations over the human rights of the local population and the indigenous communities.[33] ISDS is admonished for its failure to consider the international human rights law obligations of countries while deciding contentious claims involving issues like the human right to water.[34] ISDS tribunals awarding extensive monetary damages to foreign investors is also a lightning rod for criticism because of the exorbitant burden imposed on developing countries.[35]

The other reasons to criticize ISDS are that tribunals offer broader interpretations of investment protection provisions and, thus, radically reshape the notions of property favouring foreign investors;[36] inconsistent and incoherent

30 K Tienhaara, 'Regulatory Chill and the Threat of Arbitration: A View from Political Science' in C Brown and K Miles (eds), *Evolution in Investment Treaty Law and Arbitration* (CUP 2011) 606–28, at 615. See also Anil Yilmaz Vastardis, 'Investment Treaty Arbitration as Justice Bubbles' in Thomas Schultz and Federico Ortino (eds), *Oxford Handbook of International Arbitration* (OUP 2020) Chapter 26.

31 C Moehlecke, 'The Chilling Effect of International Investment Disputes: Limited Challenges to State Sovereignty' (2019) 64 International Studies Quarterly 1–12; A Schram and others, 'Internalisation of International Investment Agreements in Public Policymaking: Developing a Conceptual Framework of Regulatory Chill (2018) 9 Global Policy 193–202; P Ciocchini and S Khoury, 'Investor State Dispute Settlement: Institutionalising "Corporate Exceptionality"' (2018) 8(6) Oñati Socio-Legal Series 976–1000; M Sornarajah, 'International Investment Law as Development Law: The Obsolescence of a Fraudulent System' in M Bungenberg and others (eds), *European Yearbook of International Economic Law* (Springer 2016) 209, 212, 216.

32 Kyla Tienhaara, 'Regulatory Chill in a Warming World: The Threat to Climate Policy Posed by Investor-State Dispute Settlement' (2018) 7(2) Transnational Environmental Law 229–50; Gus Van Harten, *The Trouble with Foreign Investor Protection* (OUP 2020) 100–5.

33 See Nicolás M Perrone, *Investment Treaties and the Legal Imagination* (OUP 2021) 172–98; Nicolàs M Perrone, 'The International Investment Regime and Local Populations: Are the Weakest Voices Unheard?' (2016) 7(3) Transnational Legal Theory 383–405; D Schneiderman, *Resisting Economic Globalization: Critical Theory and International Investment Law* (Palgrave Macmillan 2016) 147–52; Ciocchini and Khoury (n 31).

34 S Deva and T Van Ho, 'Addressing (In)Equality in Redress: Human Rights-Led Reform of the Investor-State Dispute Settlement Mechanism' (2023) 24(3) The Journal of World Investment & Trade 398–436. See *Suez v Argentina*, ICSID Case No ARB/03/19, Decision on Liability, 30 July 2010.

35 Vera Weghmann and David Hall, 'The Unsustainable Political Economy of Investor – State Dispute Settlement Mechanisms' (2021) 87 International Review of Administrative Sciences 1.

36 See Gus Van Harten, 'Leaders in the Expansive and Restrictive Interpretation of Investment Treaties: A Descriptive Study of ISDS Awards to 2010' (2018) 29(2) European Journal of International Law 507–49; S Nichols, 'Expanding Property Rights Under Investor-State

interpretations;[37] the lack of transparency;[38] and the absence of an appellate mechanism.[39] For all these reasons, it is argued that the ISDS system suffers from a 'legitimacy crisis'.[40] A good example of public backlash against ISDS is that at the time of the COVID-19 pandemic, a demand was made that there should be a "permanent restriction on all arbitration claims related to government measures targeting health, economic, and social dimensions of the pandemic and its effects".[41] Given these criticisms, some argue for the abolition of the ISDS mechanism[42] or its radical transformation, such as by creating an investment court system.[43] The abolition of ISDS could lead to a return to the 19th-century world of Carlos Calvo where the host State courts would adjudicate the claims brought by foreign investors by applying the national law.[44] It could also trigger movement toward diplomatic protection or greater use of the state-state dispute settlement.

In sum, the critics of ISDS present the international investment law regime as an immoral arrangement that prioritizes corporate interests over the well-being of local populations.[45] If one were to employ the framework of populism, which the political scientist Cas Mudde describes as dividing the society into two antagonistic groups – the 'corrupt elite' and the 'pure people'[46] – critics of

---

Dispute Settlement (ISDS): Class Struggle in the Era of Transnational Capital' (2018) 25(2) Review of International Political Economy 243–69.

37 See Zarra (n 11) 137–85.

38 See George Kahale III, 'Is Investor-State Arbitration Broken?' (2012) TDM 7 <www.transnational-dispute-management.com> accessed 18 September 2023.

39 See Elsa Sardinha, 'The Impetus for the Creation of an Appellate Mechanism' (2017) 32(3) ICSID Review – Foreign Investment Law Journal 503–27.

40 For a debate on the perceived legitimacy crisis of ISDS see Malcolm Langford and Daniel Behn, 'Managing Backlash: The Evolving Investment Treaty Arbitrator?' 29(2) European Journal of International Law 551–80. See also C Giorgetti and others, 'Reforming International Investment Arbitration: An Introduction' (2020) 18(3) The Law & Practice of International Courts and Tribunals 303–13.

41 See Columbia Center on Sustainable Development, 'Call for ISDS Moratorium During COVID-19 Crisis and Response' (*CCSI*, 6 May 2020) <https://ccsi.columbia.edu/content/call-isds-moratorium-during-covid-19-crisis-and-response> accessed 18 September 2023. See also Prabhash Ranjan, 'Covid-19 and ISDS Moratorium – An Indiscreet Proposal' (*Opinio Juris*, 15 June 2020) <http://opiniojuris.org/2020/06/15/covid-19-and-isds-moratorium-an-indiscreet-proposal/> accessed 18 September 2023.

42 See M Sornarajah, 'Starting Anew in International Investment Law' (16 July 2012) 74 Columbia FDI Perspectives <https://academiccommons.columbia.edu/doi/10.7916/D8057Q6S> accessed 19 September 2023; Mattias Kumm, 'An Empire of Capital? Transatlantic Investment Protection as the Institutionalization of Unjustified Privilege' (25 May 2015) 4(3) ESIL Reflections 4; Deva and Van Ho (n 34).

43 See Marc Bungenberg and August Reinisch, *From Bilateral Arbitral Tribunals and Investment Courts to a Multilateral Investment Court* (European Yearbook of International Economic Law Series, Springer 2020).

44 Jose Alvarez, 'ISDS Reform: The Long View' (2021) 36(2) ICSID Review 253, 263–66.

45 See Ranjan (n 41).

46 See Cas Mudde, 'The Populist Zeitgeist' (2004) 39(4) Government and Opposition 541–63.

the ISDS mechanism would view it as a manifestation of the 'corrupt elite'. In the context of the ISDS regime, the purportedly 'corrupt elite' will comprise foreign corporations, the law firms who advise them, and the arbitrators. In contrast, the local population is the 'pure people' who empower their governments to represent and act on their behalf morally. Thus, in this scheme, the ISDS mechanism is the real villain of the piece that provides coercive legal firepower to the privileged and well-connected 'corrupt elite' who employ massive resources to further their interests at the cost of 'pure people'.[47]

On the other hand, the defenders of the ISDS mechanism argue that criticism against ISDS is not backed by evidence.[48] For instance, on the issue of the ISDS regime having a chilling effect on the host State's regulatory power, a study with a focus on environmental regulation finds no empirical support "for a general chilling effect on the regulatory activity relating to the environment in countries that face ISDS cases".[49] Also, it is essential to remember that most ISDS claims challenge executive or administrative acts like cancellation of licenses and permits; very few claims involve contesting the acts of legislatures.[50] This is significant because, arguably, the challenge posed to legislative actions, not administrative ones, would induce a chilling effect. Thus, most cases do not involve a Philip Morris or a Vattenfall-like situation. This does not mean that there have been no individual instances of such regulatory chilling.[51] Still, the key is whether one can propound a general theory of regulatory chill based on a few individual cases.

On the issue of the ISDS system being dominated by arbitrators hailing from developed countries, who, arguably, are biased against developing countries, Franck's research shows that statistically, the outcome of investment treaty arbitration is not reliably linked with the development status of the country of the presiding arbitrator.[52] Are all or most ISDS claims brought by

47 See Ranjan (n 41).

48 Gloria Maria Alvarez and others, 'A Response to the Criticism Against ISDS by EFILA' (2016) 33(1) Journal of International Arbitration 1. See also Stephan W Schill, 'In Defence of International Investment Law' in Marc Bungenberg and others (eds), *European Yearbook of International Economic Law* (Springer 2016) 309; Ylli Dautaj, 'Between Backlash and the Re-Emerging "Calvo Doctrine": Investor State Dispute Settlement in an Era of Socialism, Protectionism, and Nationalism' (2021) 41(3) Northwestern Journal of International Law and Business 273.

49 Tarald Laudal Berge and Axel Berger, 'Does Investor-State Dispute Settlement Lead to Regulatory Chill? Global Evidence from Environmental Regulation' <https://www.peio.me/wp-content/uploads/2019/01/PEIO12_Paper_78.pdf> accessed 18 September 2023.

50 Dautaj (n 48) 311–12. See also Jonathan Bonnitcha and others, *The Political Economy of the Investment Treaty Regime* (OUP 2017) 238–44.

51 See Van Harten (n 36) 105–23 who documents several such instances.

52 Susan D Franck, 'Development and Outcomes of Investment Treaty Arbitration' (2009) 50 Harvard International Law Journal 435. See also Prabhash Ranjan, 'Investor-State Dispute Settlement (ISDS) Cases and India: Affronting Regulatory Autonomy or Indicting Capricious State Behaviour?' (2022) 21(1) Journal of International Trade Law and Policy (Emerald) 42–64.

influential investors, such as giant transnational corporations belonging to the developed world, which the critics decry? Not quite. A study that examined ISDS claims from 1987 to 2017 finds that these claims have been brought by investors of a wide variety of sizes, including several small and medium companies originating from a diverse set of countries, including many from low-income countries.[53] As Paul Stephan argues, "none of the international oil and gas giants – British Petroleum, Chevron, Exxon, Royal Dutch Shell – shows up in the UNCTAD database as a successful claimant".[54]

As mentioned earlier, another critical concern in ISDS has been the hefty compensations that ISDS tribunals award to foreign investors, thus resulting in a fiscal hole in developing countries' pockets. Again, the reality is nuanced. When ISDS tribunals grant monetary compensation to foreign investors, they tend to do so by awarding less than 30 per cent of the compensation claimed.[55] There have indeed been some cases where heavy compensation has been granted to foreign investors. However, according to UNCTAD, in only 13 cases, out of a total of 240 where monetary compensation was awarded, payment was more than US$1 billion.[56] This comes to around five per cent of the total cases. In 178 cases, about 75 per cent of disputes, the compensation awarded is less than US$100 million.[57] If one were to take an average, the figure would be even smaller. A study that looked at all ISDS claims from 1990 to 2014 showed that the damages awarded were below US$16 million in half of the cases.[58] Moreover, it is critical to remember that there are examples of States not paying the monetary compensation that ISDS tribunals award, such as Russia and Venezuela, who haven't paid US$51 billion and US$15 billion, respectively.[59]

Another critical data point is that the ISDS tribunals have ruled more in favour of the host States as against foreign investors. According to UNCTAD, from 1987–2022, in 37 per cent of the total concluded 890 ISDS cases, the

53 Roberto Echandi, 'The Debate on Treaty-Based Investor – State Dispute Settlement: Empirical Evidence (1987–2017) and Policy Implications' (2019) 34(1) ICSID Review 32, 43–45.

54 Paul B Stephan, *The World Crisis and International Law* (CUP 2023) 230.

55 Sergio Puig and Anton Strezhnev, 'The David Effect and ISDS' (2017) 28(3) European Journal of International Law 731.

56 UNCTAD, 'Investment Dispute Settlement Navigator' <https://investmentpolicy.unctad.org/investment-dispute-settlement> accessed 18 September 2023.

57 ibid.

58 Rachel L Wellhausen, 'Recent Trends in Investor-State Dispute Settlement' (2010) 7(1) Journal of International Dispute Settlement 117. For a more recent take on this issue see Matthew Hodgson, Yarik Kryvoi and Daniel Hrcka, '2021 Empirical Study: Costs, Damages and Duration in Investor-State Arbitration' (*British Institute of International and Comparative Law*, 2021) 1, 28 <https://www.biicl.org/publications/empirical-study-costs-damages-and-duration-in-investor-state-arbitration> accessed 18 September 2023. See also J Bonnitcha and others, 'Damages and ISDS Reform: Between Procedure and Substance' (2021) 14(2) Journal of International Dispute Settlement 213.

59 Stephan (n 54) 230.

arbitration tribunal ruled in favour of host States.[60] The decision favoured foreign investors in 28 per cent of cases, whereas 19 per cent and 14 per cent of cases were settled and discontinued, respectively.[61] In two per cent of the cases, the tribunals found liability but did not award any damages.[62]

Based on the preceding discussion, the chapter presents the debate on ISDS as a tale of two competing narratives. This will set the tone and provide the background to tell India's ISDS story.

1.2 ISDS: A tale of two narratives

Given the polarized positions on ISDS, one can present the system as a tale of two narratives. The narrative that dominates the academic literature is one of powerful transnational corporations employing ISDS to hamstring powerless governments acting in the public interest. Typical examples of this will include a transnational tobacco corporation like Philip Morris challenging the public health regulations of countries like Australia and Uruguay; Vattenfall, a Swedish corporation challenging the German law aimed at phasing out the use of nuclear energy;[63] and other examples mentioned before. Although Phillip Morris lost both the cases against Australia and Uruguay, the very fact that an ISDS claim was brought for a public health measure has been problematized. One can call this the Philip Morris narrative for the sake of representation. The inherent and tacit assumption in this narrative is that States are innocuous actors in international investment law who act rationally and prudently to maximize public interest, and it is the foreign investors who throw a spanner in the works by bringing ISDS claims whenever their corporate profits plunge.

1.2.1 The Yukos narrative

As against the all-pervasive Philip Morris narrative, there is another competing narrative that perhaps does not get as much attention: the ISDS mechanism enables private powerless foreign investors to guard themselves against the arbitrary and capricious behaviour of powerful States, and against institutional inertia and governmental apathy that could prove detrimental to their rights.[64] Under this narrative, States do not always act sagaciously. There are

60 UNCTAD (n 3) 79.

61 ibid.

62 ibid.

63 Daniela Páez-Salgado, 'A Battle on Two Fronts: Vattenfall v Federal Republic of Germany' (*Kluwer Arbitration Blog*, 18 February 2021) <https://arbitrationblog.kluwerarbitration.com/2021/02/18/a-battle-on-two-fronts-vattenfall-v-federal-republic-of-germany/#:~:text=On%20May%2014%2C%202012%2C%20Vattenfall,energy%20under%20the%20Thirteenth%20Amendment> accessed 19 September 2023.

64 ibid. See also Puig and Strezhnev (n 55).

occasions when States abuse their public power or deliberately act to harm the interests of one or a group of foreign investors. For instance, States, using their public power, deploy all kinds of procedural tactics to thwart an investor's attempts to bring an ISDS claim. This could include States rushing to domestic courts to obtain an anti-arbitration injunction prohibiting an investor from pursuing an ISDS claim. States also use their public power to change the law when it is foreseeable that an investor might bring a claim or amend laws retroactively to overturn a decision favourable to a foreign investor, including in those instances where the State is a party to the dispute involving the foreign investor. There are occasions when States do not comply with the ISDS awards and drag their feet. It is also not uncommon to see States employ a plethora of means, including using State power to launch all kinds of investigations against the investor to create a situation of intimidation and coercion. States are also found to be acting in breach of due process and basic norms of transparency.

In other words, it would be incorrect to portray States as harmless actors in international investment law. Governments might work hard to create a situation where the legal 'process' becomes a 'punishment' for an investor. ISDS can be an essential instrument to hold governments accountable under international law in cases of abuse of public power or situations of lousy governance. There have been several instances where foreign investors used the ISDS mechanism because States abused their public power and behaved arbitrarily, chipping away at investor's legal rights.

For the sake of representation, this can be called the Yukos narrative emanating from a case known as *Yukos v Russia*.[65] The story of this case is of State arbitrariness and vindictiveness, and a lot has already been written about it. Russia arrested Mikhail Khodorkovsky, the Chairman of Yukos – a vast energy company with gigantic oil and gas reserves – in 2003, accusing him of tax evasion and fraud, forcing him to sell his company.[66] It is widely believed that the Russian government retaliated against Khodorkovsky for his political activism.[67] The assets of Yukos were assigned to a Russian State oil company.[68] Under the guise of taxation measures, Russia aimed at bankrupting Yukos and appropriating its assets.[69] In 2007, Yukos was struck off the registry of companies, and its assets were nationalized.[70]

65 *Yukos Universal Limited (Isle of Man) v The Russian Federation*, PCA Case No 2005-04/AA227, Final Award, 18 July 2014.

66 Puig and Strezhnev (n 55) 732.

67 ibid.

68 ibid 732.

69 *Yukos v Russia* (n 65) paras 756, 1579.

70 See Martin Dietrich Brauch, 'Yukos v Russia: Issues and Legal Reasoning Behind US$50 Billion Awards' (*IISD-Investment Treaty News*, 4 September 2014) <https://www.iisd.org/itn/en/2014/09/04/yukos-v-russia-issues-and-legal-reasoning-behind-us50-billion-awards/> accessed 18 September 2023.

Alleging that Russia expropriated Yukos's investment for political reasons, the shareholders of Yukos tried to recover damages from Russia in various domestic courts but to no avail. Finally, Yukos brought an ISDS claim against Russia under the Energy Charter Treaty before the Permanent Court of Arbitration. The ISDS tribunal held Yukos was the object of "a series of politically-motivated attacks by the Russian authorities", found Russia to be in breach of the Energy Chater Treaty's expropriation provision, and awarded a compensation of US$50 billion to the shareholders of a defunct company.[71] Assuming we were living in the world of Carlos Calvo where there was no ISDS, it would have been challenging to call out the arbitrariness of the Russian State.

Another critical case is *Bernhard von Pezold and others v Zimbabwe*.[72] The claims in this case arose from the expropriation of large properties held by the White people in Zimbabwe under the Robert Mugabe government.[73] In the name of land reform, the Zimbabwean government seized the lands held by the White people without paying compensation and clandestinely encouraged illegal settlement of some estates.[74] The measures adopted also included imposing restrictions on the sale of agricultural products, making it exceedingly difficult for the claimants to sell their produce. The measures in question were discriminatory in their application in so far as – in effect – once a person was identified as White, all the measures would almost always apply to them. The land owned by Bernhard von Pezold and other family members was acquired, their right to challenge the acquisition was revoked, and their occupancy of the land was criminalized.[75] All this was done through a Constitutional Amendment in 2005. Moreover, due to the popular uprisings in Zimbabwe, the land held by Whites was invaded.

The tribunal held that Zimbabwe illegally expropriated the investor's investment since it did not pay compensation.[76] The Constitutional amendment also denied due process to the investors and thus was illegal under the BIT.[77] As the tribunal correctly held, the investors were targeted for their skin colour; thus, the government's actions were discriminatory.[78] The tribunal also held

71 ibid. See also *Yukos v Russia* (n 65) paras 1253, 1888(a).

72 *Bernhard von Pezold and others v Zimbabwe*, ICSID Case No ARB/10/15, Award, 28 July 2015.

73 ibid. See also Jacob Greenberg, 'ICSID Tribunal Orders Zimbabwe to Return Expropriated Farms' (*IISD-Investment Treaty* News, 16 May 2016) <https://www.iisd.org/itn/en/2016/05/16/icsid-tribunal-orders-zimbabwe-to-return-expropriated-farms-bernhard-von-pezold-and-others-v-zimbabwe-icsid-case-no-arb-10-15-jacob-greenberg/> accessed 18 September 2023.

74 ibid.

75 ibid.

76 *Bernhard von Pezold v Zimbabwe* (n 72) para 497.

77 ibid para 499.

78 ibid para 501.

that the Zimbabwean government not only failed to prevent the invasions but also fostered and abetted them to hold on to power.[79]

Another case, *Olin v Libya*,[80] also demonstrates how the abusive use of public power left an investor high and dry. In 2005, the investor received multiple licenses to build and operate a juice and dairy factory in Tripoli.[81] At the end of 2006, once the claimants had finished constructing the factory and were ready to start production, they received a notice for eviction requiring them to vacate their premises ('Expropriation Order').[82] Subsequently, the Libyan Army destroyed the structures around the claimants' property and removed all occupants. The investors were directed to vacate the premises for public interest-related urban development reasons.[83] The Expropriation Order was declared unlawful by Tripoli Courts, yet it was sought to be enforced by the Executive, and the claimants were asked to liquidate.[84]

The tribunal held that Libya's conduct, including the Expropriation Order, the demolition around the claimant's factory (that caused electricity and water cuts) had an effect equivalent to expropriation.[85] The tribunal also held that Libya violated the national treatment obligation because exemptions from the Expropriation Order were granted to domestic companies but not to foreign investors.[86]

There are several other examples of foreign investors bringing ISDS claims because States abused their public power or acted in bad faith.[87] The genesis of these ISDS claims, which form part of the Yukos narrative, lies in the State's abuse of public power, not in adopting genuine public interest measures. These cases remind us that we live in an age of competitive authoritarianism.[88] The global political landscape today is dotted with populist leaders[89]

79 Greenberg (n 73).

80 *Olin Holdings Limited v State of Libya*, ICC Case No 20355/MCP, Final Award, 25 May 2018.

81 ibid paras 82–87.

82 ibid para 157.

83 ibid para 159.

84 ibid para 163.

85 ibid paras 178–81.

86 ibid paras 217–18.

87 *Manolium Processing v Belarus*, PCA Case No 2018-6, Final Award, 22 June 2021; *Joseph Charles Lemire v Ukraine (II)*, ICSID Case No ARB/06/18, Award, 28 March 2011; *Valores Mundiales v Venezuela*, ICSID Case No ARB/13/11, Award, 25 July 2017; *Glencore International v Colombia*, ICSID Case No ARB/16/6, Award, 27 August 2019; *Stabil LLC v Russian Federation*, PCA Case No 2015-35, Final Award, 12 April 2019; *Naftogaz and others v Russia*, PCA Case No 2017-16, Award on Liability, 22 February 2019; *Copper Mesa Mining Corporation v Ecuador*, PCA Case No 2012-2, Award, 15 March 2016; *Desert Line Projects LLC v Yemen*, ICSID Case No ARB/05/17, Award, 2008, para 186.

88 Steven Levitsky and Lucan A Way, 'The Rise of Competitive Authoritarianism' (2002) 13(2) Journal of Democracy 51.

89 See Jan-Werner Muller, *What Is Populism?* (U Pennsylvania P 2016).

and autocratic opportunists[90] who display blatant muscularity in claiming to defend their motherlands against foreigners – capital, goods, and people.[91] These populist leaders, including elected autocrats, leave no stone unturned to amass greater political control and power by weakening domestic institutions, including national courts and the rule of law.[92] At a time when institutional checks and balances are diminishing, a well-functioning ISDS system can prove to be a valuable instrument to hold populist governments accountable under international law for their actions that are precarious toward foreign investors.

At any rate, the discussion on these cases is not to argue that ISDS should be understood only through the prism of the Yukos narrative, or that this narrative is more important, or that the Philip Morris narrative does not exist or is not significant. The point is simply this: broadly speaking, ISDS is a tale of two competing narratives. On the one hand, there have been instances of overpowered and influential corporations suing hapless governments for the exercise of genuine regulatory powers. On the other hand, we have also witnessed cases of governments abusing their public power or displaying erratic behaviour against foreign investors. To fully grasp the ISDS system, including its strengths, deficiencies, and pitfalls, both narratives must get their due place in academic literature.

1.3 The purpose of this book

Given the Philip Morris and Yukos narratives that present the entire spectrum of debate on ISDS, this book is a modest attempt to focus on India's ISDS story. India's tale of backlash against ISDS and the investment treaty regime overall is well documented.[93] What is missing in the academic literature is a

90 Tom Gerald Daly, 'Democracy and the Global Emergency – Shared Experiences, Starkly Uneven Impacts' (*Verfassungs Blog*, 15 May 2020) <https://verfassungsblog.de/democracy-and-the-global-emergency-shared-experiences-starkly-uneven-impacts/> accessed 18 September 2023.

91 Ranjan (n 41).

92 Steven Levitsky and Daniel Ziblatt, *How Democracies Die: What History Reveals About Our Future?* (Penguin 2019).

93 Prabhash Ranjan, *India and Bilateral Investment Treaties: Refusal, Acceptance, Backlash* (OUP 2019); Prabhash Ranjan and Pushkar Anand, 'The 2016 Indian Model Bilateral Investment Treaty: A Critical Deconstruction' (2017) 38 (1) Northwestern Journal of International Law and Business 1–54; Prabhash Ranjan, 'India and Bilateral Investment Treaties – A Changing Landscape' (2014) 29(2) ICSID Review – Foreign Investment Law Journal 419–58; Josef Ostřanský and Facundo Pérez Aznar, 'Investment Treaties and National Governance in India: Rearrangements, Empowerment, and Discipline' (2021) 34(2) Leiden Journal of International Law 373–96; Biswajit Dhar, Reji Joseph and TC James, 'India's Bilateral Investment Agreements: Time to Review' (2012) 47(52) Economic & Political Weekly 113; Aniruddha Rajput, 'India's Shifting Treaty Practice: A Comparative Analysis of the 2003 and 2015 Model BITs' (2016) 7(2) Jindal Global Law Review 201–26; Grant Hanessian and Kabir Duggal, 'The Final 2015 Indian Model BIT: Is This the Change the World Wishes to See' (2017)

detailed discussion of India's individual ISDS claims tied together as a compelling narrative and placed within the broader global debate on investor-state disputes. This book aims to fill this gap. India has been one of the most frequent respondent States in the ISDS system, with 23 claims brought in the period from 2011 to 2022 (see Table 1.1). Of these 23 claims, ten cases have been decided (six favour foreign investors and four favour India). The outcome is pending in several cases (see Table 1.2). The decided cases involving India make a valuable contribution to the universe of ISDS. This makes India a gripping case study to understand the functioning of the ISDS regime from the point of view of the reasons that triggered these claims. It is critical to recall that although India signed the first BIT in 1994, it wasn't till 2011 that an ISDS award involving India was issued in a case known as *White Industries v India*.[94] Since then, India has seen an avalanche of ISDS claims. Thus, this book focuses on India's ISDS story from 2011. From 1994 till the end of 2010, nine ISDS claims were brought against India, all in 2004, and they pertained to one particular investment project in the power sector, about which much has been written.[95] All these nine claims were settled and didn't result in a publicly available ISDS arbitral award.[96]

From 2011 onward, did these claims originate because India adopted measures for protecting public health, safeguarding the environment, combating climate change, or pursuing social policies such as protecting labour rights or the rights of the indigenous communities (the Philip Morris narrative)? Or did these claims originate against India due to institutional slackness and inertia, abuse or misuse of public power, and poor regulatory governance (the Yukos narrative)? The core objective of this book is to show that India's ISDS story lies closer to the pole of the Yukos, not the Philip Morris narrative.

The book's methodology to accomplish this objective is to concentrate on the six ISDS disputes that India lost and whose decisions are available in the public domain. These disputes are divided into four categories. First, the dispute that arose due to the actions of the Indian judiciary, the *White Industries v India* case, is discussed in Chapter 2. Second, the disputes that originated due to the cancellation of the spectrum licenses by the Indian government,

32(1) ICSID Review – Foreign Investment Law Journal 216–26; Nish Shetty and Romesh Weeramantary, 'India's New Approach to Investment Treaties' (2016) 18(4) Asian Dispute Review 189; Azernoosh Bazarafkan, 'The (R)evolution of Indian Model Bilateral Investment Treaty: Escaping Liability Without Mitigating Risks' (2016) 7(2) Jindal Global Law Review 245–61; Deepak Raju, 'General Exceptions in the Indian Model BIT: Is the "Necessity" Test Workable?' (2016) 7(2) Jindal Global Law Review 227–43.

94 *White Industries Australia Limited v The Republic of India*, UNCITRAL, Final Award (30 November 2011) <https://www.italaw.com/cases/documents/1170> (accessed 25 July 2021).

95 See P Kundra, 'Looking Beyond the Dabhol Debacle: Examining Its Causes and Understanding Its Lessons' (2008) 41 Vanderbilt Journal of Transnational Law 908; Ranjan, *India and Bilateral Investment Treaties* 2019 (n 93).

96 Ranjan, *India and Bilateral Investment Treaties* 2019 (n 93) 130–33.

Table 1.1 ISDS Claims against India since 2011

No.	*Year of Initiation/ Award*	*Name of the Case*	*Outcome*	*Applicable BIT*
1.	2022	*Devas v India (II)* (PCA Case No 2022–34)	Pending	India-Mauritius BIT
2.	2021	*Earlyguard v India*	Settled	India-UK BIT
3.	2020	*GPIX LLC v The Republic of India* (PCA Case No 2020–36)	Decided in favour of State (award not publicly available)	India-Mauritius BIT
4.	2020	*Maxis and Global Communications v India*	Pending	India-Malaysia and India-Mauritius BIT
5.	2019	*Korea Western Power Co v India* (PCA Case No 2020–06)	Pending	India-Korea BIT India-Korea CEPA
6.	2017	*Carissa Investments LLC v India* (UNCITRAL)	Pending	India-Mauritius BIT
7.	2017	*Nissan Motor Co., Ltd. v Republic of India* (PCA Case No 2017–37, Decision on Jurisdiction, 29 April 2019)	Jurisdictional stage in favour of the investor. Reportedly settled	India-Japan CEPA
8.	2017	*Vodafone Group Plc and Vodafone Consolidated Holdings Limited v India (II)* (UNCITRAL)	Pending	India-UK BIT
9.	2016	*Astro All Asia Networks and South Asia Entertainment Holdings Limited v India* (UNCITRAL)	Discontinued	India-UK BIT, India-Mauritius BIT

No.	*Year of Initiation/ Award*	*Name of the Case*	*Outcome*	*Applicable BIT*
10.	2016	*Ras-Al-Khaimah Investment Authority (RAKIA) v India* (UNCITRAL, Award, 11 May 2022)	Decided in favour of State (award not available publicly)	India-UAE BIT
11.	2016	*Strategic Infrasol Foodstuff LLC and The Joint Venture of Thakur Family Trust, UAE with Ace Hospitality Management DMCC, UAE v India* (UNCITRAL)	Pending	India-UAE BIT
12.	2016	*Vedanta Resources PLC v India* (PCA Case No 2016–05)	Pending	India-UK BIT
13.	2015	*Capital Global and Kaif Investment v India*	Data not available	India-Mauritius BIT
14.	2015	*Axiata Group v India*	Data not available	India-Mauritius BIT
15.	2015	*Nokia v India*	Data not available	India-Finland BIT
16.	2015	*Cairn Energy PLC and Cairn UK Holdings Limited v The Republic of India* (PCA Case No 2016–7, Final Award, 21 December 2020)	Decided in favour of the investor	India-UK BIT
17.	2014	*Louis Dreyfus Armateurs SAS v The Republic of India* (PCA Case No 2014–26, Final Award, 21 December 2020)	Decided in favour of the State	India-France BIT

(*Continued*)

Table 1.1 (Continued)

No.	*Year of Initiation/ Award*	*Name of the Case*	*Outcome*	*Applicable BIT*
18.	2014	*Vodafone International Holdings BV v India (I)* (PCA Case No 2016–35, Award, 25 September 2020)	Decided in favour of the investor (award not available publicly)	India-Netherlands BIT
19.	2013	*Deutsche Telekom AG v The Republic of India* (PCA Case No 2014–10, Final Award, 27 May 2020)	Decided in favour of the investor	India-Germany BIT
20.	2013	*Khaitan Holdings Mauritius Limited v India* (PCA Case No 2018–50)	Pending	India-Mauritius BIT
21.	2012	*CC/Devas (Mauritius) Ltd., Devas Employees Mauritius Private Limited, and Telcom Devas Mauritius Limited v Republic of India* (PCA Case No 2013–09, Award on Jurisdiction and Merits, 25 July 2016)	Decided in favour of the investor	India-Mauritius BIT
22.	2012	*Maxim Naumchenko, Andrey Poluektov and Tenoch Holdings Limited v The Republic of India* (PCA Case No 2013–23, Award, July 2019)	Decided in favour of the State (award not available publicly)	India-Cyprus BIT, India-Russia BIT
23.	2011 (award was issued in this year, the claim was initiated in 2010)	*White Industries Australia Limited v The Republic of India* (UNCITRAL, Final Award, 30 November2011)	Decided in favour of the Investor	India-Australia BIT

Source: Author's compilation from UNCTAD and other sources

CC/Devas v India[97] and *Deutsche Telekom v India*,[98] are examined in Chapter 3. Third, claims that owe their origin to the imposition of taxes retroactively, *Vodafone v India*,[99] and *Cairn Energy v India*,[100] are the subject matter of Chapter 4. Fourth, the claims brought against India for the actions of sub-national governments, with a detailed focus on the *Nissan v India*[101] case, are explored in Chapter 5.

The book does not examine the pending ISDS disputes against India because very little formal or definite information about these cases is available. This makes any worthwhile analysis of these disputes arduous. Many of these disputes are shrouded in secrecy. Basic information such as the reasons for the origin of these disputes, at what stage these disputes are, who the arbitrators are, which arbitral institution is handling these claims, etc., is not officially available. This hamstrings the research on ISDS cases against India. The only reliable source that one can use is the data provided by UNCTAD, which has been tapped to collate information in Table 1.1. Even out of the ten decided ISDS claims, four awards are unavailable in the public domain. Of these four, India won three ISDS claims. India does not voluntarily make the ISDS awards publicly available. This is despite India stating in its 2016 Model BIT that arbitral awards shall be made publicly available subject to redacting any confidential information. Given this, one has to rely on private websites such as *italaw*[102] to read ISDS awards or use tools like the Right to Information Act. This Indian legislation allows citizens the right to seek information on public matters from the government. Pushkar Anand, an Indian academic, who has sought information on ISDS awards involving India from the government under the Right to Information Act, has experienced mixed results.[103] The *Nissan v India* award was made available when a request was filed under the RTI Act. However, the request to share the *Vodafone v India* award was denied.[104] The reason advanced not to make the *Vodafone* award public is that

97 *CC/Devas (Mauritius) Ltd, Devas Employees Mauritius Private Limited, and Telcom Devas Mauritius Limited v Republic of India (I)*, PCA Case No 2013-9, Award on Jurisdiction and Merits, 25 July 2016.

98 *Deutsche Telekom AG v Republic of India*, PCA Case No 2014-10, Final Award, 27 May 2020.

99 *Vodafone International Holdings BV v India (I)*, PCA Case No 2016-35, Award, 25 September 2020.

100 *Cairn Energy PLC and Cairn UK Holdings Limited v The Republic of India*, PCA Case No 2016-7, Final Award, 21 December 2020.

101 *Nissan Motor Co Ltd v Republic of India*, PCA Case No 2017-37, Decision on Jurisdiction, 29 April 2019.

102 Italaw is a very important resource to read several ISDS awards <https://www.italaw.com/>.

103 Pushkar Anand, 'India and Investment Arbitration: Transparency Abroad but Stonewalling at Home' (*The Wire*, 18 June 2021) <https://thewire.in/business/india-investment-arbitration-transparency-rti-act-section8> accessed 20 September 2023.

104 ibid.

the award is confidential under the UNCITRAL arbitration rules and that sharing the award, *inter alia*, would be prejudicial to the sovereignty and integrity of India.[105] The lack of actual information on many of the awards and cases is why the book restricts its analysis to the six ISDS claims that India has lost, whose awards are publicly available.

While discussing these decided ISDS claims that India lost, apart from understanding the reasons that triggered these disputes, the focus will also be on the jurisprudential developments that emerged in these cases, considering the burgeoning arbitral jurisprudence on investor-state disputes globally. Thus, the book aims to situate and contextualize the case law in these disputes against India in the larger normative world of international investment law jurisprudence. The attempt will be to shed light on the following issues through the Indian ISDS claims: meaning of effective rights and asserting claims clause in BITs, interpretation of essential security interest and fair and equitable treatment (FET) provision, the legality of imposing regulatory measures like taxation retroactively, and assessing the actions of sub-national governments in investment treaty law.

Notably, India's track record in compliance with ISDS awards is not very bright (see Table 1.3). There has been one instance, *White Industries v India,* where India complied fully and immediately. Fully and immediately means paying the entire amount ordered by the ISDS tribunal to the foreign investor without delay. In two cases – *Vodafone v India* and *Cairn Energy v India* – the compliance was delayed and partial, as will be discussed in Chapter 4. In the *CC/Devas v India* and *DT v India*, India hasn't complied with the ISDS awards, as deliberated in greater detail in Chapter 3. The delay in compliance in two cases and non-compliance in the remaining two led the foreign investors to start the attachment proceedings against India to recover the money.

After thoroughly discussing these six ISDS claims and how they contribute to the Yukos narrative and the body of international investment law case law, an additional objective of the book is to look at India's overall approach toward ISDS in the future. In this regard, the book, in the last substantive chapter, Chapter 6, will show India's averseness to ISDS and investment protection by examining India's recent FTA treaty practice. In recent years, India has signed a few FTAs with countries like UAE,[106] Australia,[107] and

105 'Vodafone FAA Reply, Dated 18 December 2020' (*Scribd*) <https://www.scribd.com/document/512160491/Vodafone-FAA-reply-dated-December-18-2020#download&from_embed> accessed 18 September 2023.

106 Comprehensive Economic Partnership Agreement between the Government of the Republic of India and the Government of the United Arab Emirates (signed on 18 February 2022) <https://commerce.gov.in/international-trade/trade-agreements/comprehensive-economic-partnership-agreement-between-the-government-of-the-republic-of-india-and-the-government-of-the-united-arab-emirates-uae/>.

107 India-Australia Economic Cooperation and Trade Agreement between the Government of the Republic of India and the Government of Australia (signed on 2 April 2022) <https://commerce.gov.in/international-trade/trade-agreements/ind-aus-ecta/>.

Table 1.2 Outcome of ISDS Claims against India, 2010 to 2022

Outcome	*Number of Claims*
Decided in favour of investor	6[108] (one award is not available in the public domain)
Decided in favour of State	4 (three awards are not available in the public domain)
Settled/Discontinued/Data not available	5
Pending	8
Total	23

Source: Author's compilation from Table 1.1

Table 1.3 India's Compliance with Adverse BIT Awards[109]

Case	*Immediate and Full Compliance*	*Partial Compliance*	*Initiation of Attachment Proceedings due to Non-compliance*
White Industries v India	Yes	Not applicable	Not applicable
Vodafone v India	No	Yes	Yes
Cairn Energy v India	No	Yes	Yes
CC/Devas v India	No	No	Yes
DT v India	No	No	Yes
Nissan v India (Jurisdiction)	Reportedly settled	Not applicable	Not applicable

Source: Author's compilation from various sources

Mauritius.[110] However, unlike India's previous FTAs, the ones signed in the 2000s, the new ones have decoupled investment protection from international trade. In its new FTAs, India has accepted international trade obligations but not investment protection and ISDS. This gives credence to the argument that India is moving towards de-legalizing (moving away from binding international law obligations on foreign investment) and de-judicializing (taking back control given to international tribunals to resolve investor-state disputes) its international investment relations.

108 The *Nissan v India* case is counted under 'decided in favour of investor' because India lost the case at the jurisdictional phase though later it was reported that the case has been settled.

109 See also Prabhash Ranjan, The Future of India's Investment Treaty Practice: An Important Parliamentary Intervention' (2022) 19 Manchester Journal of International Economic Law 112–25.

110 Comprehensive Economic Cooperation and Partnership Agreement (CECPA) between the Republic of India and the Republic of Mauritius (signed on 22 February 2021) <https://commerce.gov.in/wp-content/uploads/2021/08/India-Mauritius-CECPA-Text-for-Upload.pdf>.

Last but not least, the indispensable reason to study India's ISDS story is the significance of India in the global economy. India has emerged as one of the most important destinations for foreign investment.[111] It is not just now. India has been a prime destination for foreign investment even in the past.[112] As evident from Table 1.4, FDI inflow to India has increased significantly in absolute numbers in the last two decades, with the four years from 2004–2008 exhibiting the highest growth rate of 40, 48, 155, and 53 per cent, respectively.

While the absolute FDI numbers have increased, India's foreign investment net inflows as a percentage of India's Gross Domestic Product (GDP) have witnessed a see-saw trend (see Figure 1.2). It fluctuated from a high of 3.6 per cent in 2008 to a low of 1.3 per cent in 2012 and again rebounded to 2.4 per cent in 2020 before falling to 1.4 per cent in 2022.

The increasing FDI inflows show that India is deeply integrated with the global economy. This implies the presence of several foreign investors in India in diverse sectors, which, in turn, increases the propensity of disputes between foreign investors and the Indian State at all levels, including the sub-national governments. Thus, a careful study of ISDS claims against India becomes imperative to contribute to a fuller understanding of the ISDS regime. But before we examine ISDS claims against India, two other issues are critical to be flagged: India's backlash against ISDS and the investment treaty regime and what came out of it and a discussion on what role BITs have played in fostering FDI inflows to India.

1.4 India's backlash against ISDS

Although much has been written on India's backlash against ISDS and the investment treaty regime, including by this author,[113] it will be useful to briefly recall it here to provide a broader context for the readers. This will help in effectively understanding the discussion in the ensuing chapters. From 1994 till the end of 2010, India signed nearly 80 investment treaties consisting of BITs and FTA investment chapters. However, the year 2011 marked the turn of the tide. It was a watershed year in India's encounter with international investment law and ISDS when India lost the *White Industries v India* case, resulting in the first ISDS decision against India. The loss

111 'India Emerging as Preferred Destination for Foreign Investments: Govt' (*Business Standard*, 26 June 2022) <https://www.business-standard.com/article/economy-policy/india-emerging-as-preferred-destination-for-foreign-investments-govt-122062600035_1.html> accessed 20 September 2023.

112 'India Emerges Most Attractive Investment Destination: EY' (*The Economic Times*, 25 November 2023) <https://economictimes.indiatimes.com/india-emerges-most-attractive-investment-destination-ey/articleshow/26313801.cms?from=mdr> accessed 20 September 2023.

113 See Ranjan, *India and Bilateral Investment Treaties* 2019 (n 93); Ranjan, 'India and Bilateral Investment Treaties' 2014 (n 93); Ostřanský and Pérez Aznar (n 93). Also see the other works mentioned in note 93.

Table 1.4 Foreign Direct Investment in India

Financial Year	*Equity*		*Re-invested Earnings (millions of USD)*	*Other Capital (millions of USD)*	*FDI Inflow in India*	
	Government Route/ Automatic Route/ Acquisition Route (millions of USD)	*Equity Capital of Unincorporated Bodies # (millions of USD)*			*Total FDI Inflow (millions of USD)*	*%age Growth over the Previous Year (in USD terms)*
2000–01	2,339	61	1,350	279	4,029	–
2001–02	3,904	191	1,645	390	6,130	(+) 52%
2002–03	2,574	190	1,833	438	5,035	(-) 18%
2003–04	2,197	32	1,460	633	4,322	(-) 14%
2004–05	3,250	528	1,904	369	6,051	(+) 40%
2005–06	5,540	435	2,760	226	8,961	(+) 48%
2006–07	15,585	896	5,828	517	22,826	(+) 155%
2007–08	24,573	2,291	7,679	300	34,843	(+) 53%
2008–09	31,364	702	9,030	777	41,873	(+) 20%
2009–10	25,606	1,540	8,668	1,931	37,745	(-) 10%
2010–11	21,376	874	11,939	658	34,847	(-) 08%
2011–12	34,833	1,022	8,206	2,495	46,556	(+) 34%
2012–13	21,825	1,059	9,880	1,534	34,298	(-) 26%
2013–14	24,299	975	8,978	1,794	36,046	(+) 5%
2014–15	30,933	978	9,988	3,249	45,148	(+) 25%
2015–16	40,001	1,111	10,413	4,034	55,559	(+) 23%
2016–17	43,478	1,223	12,343	3,176	60,220	(+) 8%
2017–18	44,857	664	12,542	2,911	60,974	(+) 1%
2018–19	44,366	689	13,672	3,274	62,001	(+) 2%
2019–20	49,977	1,757	14,175	8,482	74,391	(+) 20%
2020–21	59,636	1,452	16,935	3,950	81,973	(+) 10%
2021–22	58,773	910	19,347	5,805	84,835	(+) 3%
2022–23 (P)	46,034	1,566	19,105	4,650	71,355	(-) 16%
2023–24 (up to June 23)	10,946	358	4,390	1,873	17,567	
	6,48,266	21,504	2,14,070	53,745	9,37,585	–

Source: Department for Promotion and Industry and Internal Trade, Ministry of Commerce and Industry, Government of India, available at <https://dpiit.gov.in/sites/default/files/FDI_Factsheet_June_23.pdf> accessed 18 September 2023

in the *White Industries* case was followed by a slew of other investor-state arbitration claims (see Table 1.1). These claims rattled India and caused a significant stir. Concerns were expressed on the floor of the Indian parliament about these claims.[114] Against the backdrop of these claims, civil society also raised alarm bells on India accepting international law obligations on foreign investment.[115] This led to a fundamental re-think and review of BITs

114 Ranjan, *India and Bilateral Investment Treaties* 2019 (n 93).

115 Forum Against FTAs, 'We Call Upon the Government to Review and Rescind Its Decision to Sign BIT/BIPA with the USA' (*Open letter to the Indian Prime Minister, Dr Manhoman*

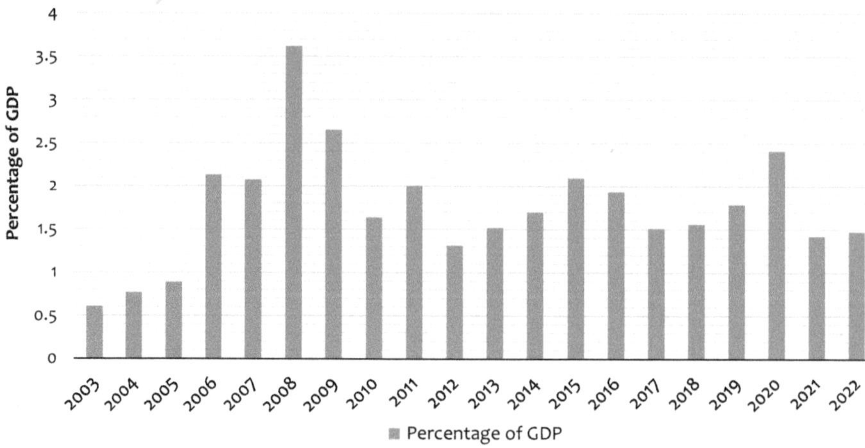

Figure 1.2 Foreign Investment Net Inflows to India (as a percentage of India's GDP)
Source: The World Bank, available at: <https://data.worldbank.org/indicator/BX.KLT.DINV.WD.GD.ZS?locations=IN>

and ISDS.[116] The review led to the following tangible outcomes. First, India adopted a new Model BIT towards the end of 2015, early 2016.[117] Second, India decided to terminate all BITs whose initial validity period had expired, that is, those BITs that were more than ten years old.[118] Let us discuss these outcomes one by one.

Singh, 26 September 2013) <http://www.bilaterals.org/IMG/pdf/lettter_forum_ag_ftas_us_india_bits_26_sept.pdf> accessed 17 July 2023.

116 Sonia Rolland and David M Trubek, *Emerging Powers in the International Economic Order* (CUP 2019) 56.

117 See 'Model Text for the Bilateral Investment Treaty' (2016) <https://dea.gov.in/sites/default/files/ModelBIT_Annex_0.pdf> accessed 20 September 2023 (hereinafter '2016 Model BIT). The Indian Model BIT was adopted by the Cabinet in December 2015 – Cabinet, Government of India, 'Model Text for the Indian Bilateral Investment Treaty' (*Press Information Bureau*) <https://pib.gov.in/newsite/printrelease.aspx?relid=133411> accessed 20 September 2023; and was published on 14 January 2016 – see Prabhash Ranjan and others, 'India's Model Bilateral Investment Treaty: Is India too Risk Averse?' (*Brookings India*, 2018) 9 <https://www.brookings.edu/wp-content/uploads/2018/08/India%E2%80%99s-Model-Bilateral-Investment-Treaty-2018.pdf> accessed 20 September 2023. In this book, the Model BIT is referred to as the '2016 Model BIT' although some authors refer to it as the 2015 Model BIT. Both the years refer to the same text. Many scholars refer to the Indian Model BIT as the 2016 Model; see for example Rolland and Trubek (n 116).

118 See Department of Economic Affairs and Ministry of Finance, 'Major Policy Initiatives/Achievements/Highlights of the Year 2016: Material for Year-End Review 2016–17' (2016) 16 <https://dea.gov.in/sites/default/files/Year%20End%20Review%20Final%20.pdf> accessed 18 September 2023.

1.4.1 The 2016 Indian Model BIT

India's new Model BIT, which has already attracted considerable attention and replaced the 1993 version, is unique.[119] It has moved away from an asset-based definition of investment to an enterprise-based definition of investment;[120] it does not contain the most favoured nation (MFN) and the FET provision;[121] it ousts the jurisdiction of an ISDS tribunal to hear investor-state disputes on taxation;[122] it excludes specific regulatory measures such as issuance of compulsory licenses from the ambit of the BIT provided such licenses are issued in accordance with the WTO Agreement;[123] and most importantly it contains a severely constrained ISDS mechanism.[124] The ISDS system is constrained and restricted primarily because of two features: exhaustion of local remedies and immunity of the decisions of national courts.[125]

Article 15.1 of the 2016 Model BIT provides that the foreign investor must exhaust local remedies for "the same measure or similar factual matters for which a breach of this Treaty is claimed". Furthermore, domestic remedies should be exhausted for a minimum period of five years from the date the investor first acquired knowledge of the measure in question.[126] Given the high pendency of cases in India – as of 15 September 2021 about 45 million cases are pending in all courts across India[127] – it is pretty unlikely that the foreign investor's dispute with the State will be resolved in just five years.

Suppose the dispute is not resolved or there is no domestic recourse to settle the conflict. In that case, the foreign investor can commence ISDS proceedings provided no more than six years have elapsed from when the investor first learned or should have learned about the measure in question.[128] To initiate the ISDS process, the investor must submit a notice of dispute to the State.[129] Once this notice is served, the investor must spend six months to resolve the dispute amicably with the State through consultation and negotiations.[130] Thus, it becomes five years of domestic remedies plus six months of

119 See Ranjan and Anand (n 93); Ranjan, *India and Bilateral Investment Treaties* 2019 (n 93) 310–50; Jarrod Hepburn and Ridhi Kabra, 'India's New Model Investment Treaty: Fit for Purpose?' (2017) 1(2) Indian Law Review 95–114.
120 See Article 1.4, 2016 Model BIT.
121 The 2016 Model BIT contains a provision titled 'Treatment of Investments' in Article 3.1.
122 See Article 2.4(ii), 2016 Model BIT.
123 See Article 2.4(iii), 2016 Model BIT.
124 See Alvarez (n 44) 266; Ranjan, *India and Bilateral Investment Treaties* 2019 (n 93) 333–48.
125 Rolland and Trubek (n 116) 116–17.
126 Article 15.2, 2016 Model BIT.
127 Omir Kumar and Shubham Dutt, 'Pendency and Vacancies in the Judiciary' (*PRS Legislative Research*, 11 October 2021) <https://prsindia.org/policy/vital-stats/pendency-and-vacancies-in-the-judiciary> accessed 18 September 2023.
128 Article 15.5(i), 2016 Model BIT.
129 Article 15.2, 2016 Model BIT.
130 Article 15.4, 2016 Model BIT.

negotiations. If the dispute is still unresolved, the foreign investor can submit the dispute to investor-state arbitration subject to a few more conditions.[131] Not more than 12 months should have elapsed from the date of the conclusion of domestic proceedings,[132] and the investor should issue a 'notice of arbitration' to the State at least 90 days before submitting the claim to arbitration.[133] In other words, this gives the foreign investor a window of a mere three months to submit the dispute to arbitration. Such a tight time frame is unnerving for foreign investors and might make it practically impossible to submit a dispute to arbitration.

On top of this, if the investor loses the case at the domestic courts and the opportunity to go before an ISDS tribunal is still available, she will be precluded from employing the ISDS mechanism. This is because Article 13.5(i) restricts the jurisdiction of an ISDS tribunal from reviewing the 'merits' of a decision made by a domestic judicial authority.[134] The word 'merits' is not defined anywhere. Arguably, the word, 'merits' is included to ensure that ISDS tribunals do not act as a court of appeal. However, 'merits' can also have an alternative interpretation. Since the investor will bring an ISDS claim on the same issue adjudicated by the domestic court, the State can plausibly argue that the case is on the 'merits' of the decision made by the domestic court. This will impede an ISDS tribunal from hearing it.[135] Assume that the investor brings a claim before Indian courts on the cancellation of a license by the executive, which the investor believes violates one of the substantive rights given in the treaty. Further, assume that the domestic court pronounces the said cancellation lawful. Suppose the investor now wants to take the license cancellation to an ISDS tribunal. In that case, the tribunal might be barred from examining the issue since it would invariably involve going into the 'merits' of the domestic court decision, even if the tribunal is not acting as a court of appeal. Moreover, what happens in situations when a domestic judicial decision violates treaty obligations? An ISDS tribunal will have to go into the 'merits' of the decision rendered by a domestic court to decide whether it violates the investment treaty obligations but will not be able to do so due to Article 13.5(i).[136]

Thus, as stated earlier, a combination of the exhaustion of local remedies requirements and the immunity of the domestic court decisions makes the ISDS system in the 2016 Indian Model BIT unfeasible for foreign investors. There are other pro-State parts in the 2016 Indian Model BIT. For

131 Article 15.5, 2016 Model BIT.
132 Article 15.5(ii), 2016 Model BIT.
133 Article 15.5(v), 2016 Model BIT.
134 Article 13.5(i), 2016 Model BIT provides: "In addition to other limits on its jurisdiction, a Tribunal constituted under this Chapter shall not have the jurisdiction to: (i) review the merits of a decision made by a judicial authority of the Parties".
135 Rolland and Trubek (n 116) 117.
136 See also Hepburn and Kabra (n 118) 104–7.

instance, Article 23.1 requires an ISDS tribunal to grant a "high level of deference" to the host State as regards decisions pertaining to their "development and implementation of domestic policies".[137] Terms like "development" and "implementation of domestic policies" are too broad and would cover almost most, if not all, regulatory measures a host State may adopt. This means that an ISDS tribunal shall have to confer high deference to the host State for virtually all regulatory actions. While ISDS tribunals should grant due deference to States, an across-the-board requirement of "high deference" tilts the scale too much in favour of the State against the interests of foreign investors.

Let us now discuss India's termination of BITs.

1.4.2 Unilateral termination of BITs

As already stated, a critical element of India's backlash against ISDS has been the decision to terminate its BITs unilaterally. After adopting the Model BIT, India started issuing notices of termination to its BIT partner countries. India wishes to renegotiate its BITs based on the 2016 Model BIT.[138] From 2017 till date, India has unilaterally terminated close to 75 BITs.[139] However, India's ambition of renegotiating its old BITs based on the new Model has not been realized. Since 2015–2016, when a new Model BIT was adopted, India has successfully signed BITs with only four countries – Belarus,[140] Kyrgyzstan,[141] Taiwan,[142] and Brazil.[143] Even of these four treaties, only two – India-Belarus and India-Taiwan BITs – have entered into force. India's BITs with Belarus, Kyrgyzstan, and Taiwan are almost carbon copies of the 2016 Model BIT. Thus, they contain the same ISDS provisions as the 2016 Model BIT discussed before. The India-Brazil BIT is very different from the 2016 Model BIT.[144] It mirrors Brazil's investment treaty practice and thus is more Brazilian

137 Article 23.1, 2016 Model BIT states: "This Treaty shall be interpreted in the context of the high level of deference that international law accords to States with regard to their development and implementation of domestic policies".

138 See Department of Economic Affairs and Ministry of Finance (n 118) 16.

139 Government of India, Ministry of Finance and Department of Economic Affairs, 'Bilateral Investment Treaties (BITs)/Agreements' <https://dea.gov.in/bipa> accessed 18 September 2023.

140 Treaty Between the Republic of Belarus and the Republic of India on Investments (entered into force 5 March 2020).

141 Bilateral Investment Treaty between the Government of Kyrgyz Republic and the Government of Republic of India (signed on 7 June 2019).

142 Bilateral Investment Agreement Between the India Taipei Association in Taipei and the Taipei Economic and Cultural Center in India (signed on 18 December 2018).

143 Investment Cooperation and Facilitation Treaty between the Federative Republic of Brazil and the Republic of India (signed on 25 January 2020).

144 Prabhash Ranjan, 'India-Brazil Bilateral Investment Treaty – A New Template for India' (*Kluwer Arbitration Blog*, 19 March 2020) <https://arbitrationblog.kluwerarbitration.

than Indian.[145] Most importantly, the India-Brazil BIT has abandoned ISDS. It uses a unique method of settling disputes through joint committees, failing which state-state dispute settlement (SSDS) will be activated.[146]

The fact that India has managed to sign BITs with just a handful of countries after adopting the Model BIT clearly demonstrates that the Model BIT has very few takers. The Parliamentary Committee on External Affairs, while reviewing India's BITs policy, expressed its displeasure at the slow pace at which India has been signing BITs.[147] The committee said that the number of BITs India has signed after adopting the Model BIT is "not commensurate with the growth of India's interest in this domain and [India's] rising stature in global affairs".[148]

In the last few years, India also signed a joint interpretative declaration/note/statement (JID/JIN/JIS) with a few countries like Colombia,[149] Bangladesh,[150] and Mauritius.[151] The purpose of issuing these JIDs is to complement the process of treaty interpretation by resolving the ambiguities and abstruseness in certain treaty terms.[152] For example, Article 9(1) of the India-Bangladesh BIT provides: "any dispute between an investor of one Contracting Party and the other Contracting Party in relation to an investment of the former under this Agreement". Several tribunals have interpreted "any dispute" between an investor and the State, in such

com/2020/03/19/india-brazil-bilateral-investment-treaty-a-new-template-for-india/> accessed 20 September 2023.

145 Ashutosh Ray and Kabir Duggal, 'Dispute Resolution in the India-Brazil BIT: Symbolism or Systemic Reform' (*Kluwer Arbitration Blog*, 9 April 2020) <https://arbitrationblog.kluwerarbitration.com/2020/04/09/dispute-resolution-in-the-india-brazil-bit-symbolism-or-systemic-reform/> accessed 18 September 2023.

146 ibid.

147 Parliamentary Committee on External Affairs, 'India and Bilateral Investment Treaties Tenth Report' (*Indian Government Ministry of External Affairs*, 2021) <http://164.100.47.193/lsscommittee/External%20Affairs/17_External_Affairs_10.pdf> accessed 18 September 2023 (hereinafter 'Committee Report').

148 ibid at 11. See also Ranjan (n 109).

149 Joint Interpretative Declaration Between the Republic of India and the Republic of Colombia Regarding the Agreement for the Promotion and Protection of Investments Between India and Colombia (signed on 10 November 2009) <https://dea.gov.in/sites/default/files/JID%20with%20Colombia.pdf> accessed 20 September 2023.

150 Joint Interpretative Notes on the Agreement between the Government of the Republic of India and the Government of the People's Republic of Bangladesh for the Promotion and Protection of Investments (signed on 4 October 2017) <https://dea.gov.in/sites/default/files/JIN%20with%20Bangladesh.pdf> accessed 20 September 2023.

151 Joint Interpretative Statement to the Agreement between the Government of the Republic of India and the Government of the Republic Mauritius (signed on 4 September 1998) <https://www.mea.gov.in/Portal/LegalTreatiesDoc/MU22B3825.pdf> accessed 20 September 2023.

152 Ranjan, *India and Bilateral Investment Treaties* 2019 (n 93) 282.

clauses, as referring to both treaty and contractual disputes.[153] India's JIN with Bangladesh narrows down this provision to only treaty disputes, kicking out contractual claims. The JID to the India-Colombia BIT performs the same function.

Interestingly, the JIN to the India-Mauritius BIT was adopted on 11 July 2022, although this BIT was terminated on 22 March 2017.[154] Thus, unlike India-Bangladesh and India-Colombia BITs that continue to operate, curiously, India adopted a JIN for a terminated BIT with Mauritius. India hasn't done so for any other terminated BITs.[155] Since the BIT already stands terminated, presumably the JIN would be applicable for investments that had already come in by 21 March 2017, until the treaty was not terminated. The JIN to India-Mauritius BIT differs from the ones adopted for the other two BITs. It does not contain the clarification of the kind mentioned before. Instead, it includes a provision inspired by the 2016 Model BIT. Without referring to any specific provision of the India-Mauritius BIT, the JIN states that the "arbitral tribunal constituted under the agreement shall not have the jurisdiction to review the merits of the decision made by a judicial authority of the parties". This provision is like Article 13.5(i) of the 2016 Model BIT.[156] As discussed, it imposes a bar on an ISDS tribunal's jurisdiction. This looks like an amendment to the treaty masquerading as a clarification.

Having briefly looked at India's backlash against ISDS, let's now look at BITs' role in attracting foreign investments.

1.5 Do BITs result in FDI?

Critics of BITs often argue that they do not help attract foreign investment and, thus, are unnecessary. So, what is the empirical evidence on the relationship between Indian BITs and foreign investment inflows to India? Globally, the evidence on this question is mixed. For instance, one study that undertook a meta-analysis of 74 studies concluded that the effect of international investment treaties on FDI inflows is "so small as to be considered as negligible

153 See *Vivendi v Argentina*, Decision on Annulment, 3 July 2022; *SGS v Philippines*, ICSID Case No ARB/02/6, Decision on Objections to Jurisdiction, 29 January 2004, paras 131–35; *Metal-Tech v Uzbekistan*, ICSID Case No ARB/10/3, Award, 4 October 2013, para 378.

154 Government of India, Ministry of Finance and Department of Economic Affairs, 'Bilateral Investment Treaties (BITs)/Agreements' <https://dea.gov.in/bipa?page=2> accessed 20 September 2023.

155 See also Chapter 3.

156 Art. 13.5(a), Bilateral Investment Treaty between the Government of Kyrgyz Republic and the Government of Republic of India (signed on 7 June 2019); art. 13.4(a), Treaty Between the Republic of Belarus and the Republic of India on Investments (entered into force 5 March 2020); art. 13.5(a), Bilateral Investment Agreement Between the India Taipei Association in Taipei and the Taipei Economic and Cultural Center in India (signed on 18 December 2018).

or zero".[157] However, the same study also states one cannot "rule out the possibility that the effect of these agreements is, in fact, positive and that current research methods and measures are insufficiently powerful or precise to identify the underlying genuine effect".[158] Another recent study that surveys the impact of international investment agreements (IIAs) on FDI inflows concludes that "many if not most scholars conclude that IIAs impact FDI flows".[159] It is also essential to bear in mind that not all investment treaties will necessarily have the same impact on FDI inflows. The content of the investment treaty, that is, the substantive and procedural provisions that the treaty contains influences FDI inflows.[160]

Interestingly, in the case of India, there is overwhelming empirical evidence demonstrating a positive relationship between BITs and FDI inflows. One can divide this empirical evidence into two parts. The first set of studies shows that India's signing and ratifying of investment treaties positively influenced FDI flows.[161] Bhasin and Manocha consider the impact of BITs on FDI inflows in India from 2001 to 2012 and conclude that "BITs have contributed to rising FDI inflows by providing protection and commitment to foreign investors contemplating investment in India".[162] The authors also argue that one of the instruments that developing countries like India can use to attract FDI is to negotiate BITs with countries that are prospective investors.[163] Likewise, Jaivir Singh *et al* show that although individual BITs did not positively influence FDI inflows to India, the cumulative effect of BITs significantly impacted FDI inflows.[164] In other words, the study finds that over a period of time, India's BITs containing ISDS protection positively influenced the FDI inflows to India.[165]

Instead of investigating the impact of signed BITs on FDI, the second set of studies examines the influence of BIT terminations on FDI inflows to

157 Josef Brada, Zdenek Drabek and Ikiro Iwasaki, 'Does Investor Protection Increase Foreign Direct Investment? A Meta-Analysis' (2020) 35(1) Journal of Economic Surveys 34–70 <https://onlinelibrary.wiley.com/doi/full/10.1111/joes.12392> accessed 18 September 2023.

158 ibid.

159 Peter Egger, Alan Pirotte and Catherine Titi, 'International Investment Agreements and Foreign Direct Investment: A Survey' (2023) 46(6) The World Economy 1524–65.

160 ibid.

161 Niti Bhasin and Rinku Manocha, 'Do Bilateral Investment Treaties Promote FDI Inflows? Evidence from India' (2016) 41(4) Vikalpa: The Journal for Decision Makers 275–87; Jaivir Singh and others, 'The Impact of Bilateral Investment Treaties on FDI Inflows into India: Some Empirical Results' [2021] Foreign Trade Review <https://doi.org/10.1177%2F00157325211027374> accessed 27 January 2022; R Banga, 'Impact of Government Policies Investment Agreements on FDI Inflows' (2003) Working Paper No 116, Indian Council for Research on International Economic Relations.

162 Bhasin and Manocha (n 161) p. 285.

163 ibid.

164 Jaivir Singh and others (n 161).

165 ibid.

India.[166] Hartmann and Spruk examine 44 unilateral terminations of BITs by India from 2013 to 2019 and their impact on FDI inflows to India.[167] The study finds "a significant reduction in FDI inflows to India in response to BIT terminations by more than 30 percent compared to countries without terminations".[168] Their research also discovers that foreign investors do not necessarily junk India due to BIT terminations but reroute their investments via those countries with whom India continues to have a BIT.[169] This shows foreign investor's importance to BITs while investing in India. It further demonstrates that the rerouting will become increasingly challenging as India continues to get rid of almost all its BITs. Thus, there could be an adverse impact on FDI inflows. Another recent study by Kotyrlo and Kalachyhin finds a significant negative effect on FDI inflows – ranging from -64.2 per cent to -56.3 per cent per quarter on average due to India's action of terminating BITs.[170] The Parliamentary Committee on External Affairs, in its report on India and BITs, said that while it is "aware that BITs are not the sole factor for attracting FDIs into the country", in a developing country like India, "BITs have the potential to attract FDIs" by providing foreign investors a higher degree of confidence.[171] Therefore, one cannot negate the significance of BITs and ISDS for India from the point of view of attracting foreign investment.

Moreover, the moot point is not just about the influence that BITs and ISDS have on foreign investment inflows in India. BITs and ISDS are also significant because they constitute an integral part of the legal infrastructure regulating the global economy. They are essential in the legalization and judicialization of international investment relations. While one may debate and dissent on what should be the contours of this legalization and judicialization, one cannot wish away a critical component of regulating the global economy. A rule-based international order that's fair and transparent will serve everyone well, including India.

1.6 Coming up

So, whether ISDS affronts the sovereignty of nations or indicts their capricious behaviour is a million-dollar question. The answer to this question often

166 Simon Hartmann and Rok Spruk, 'The Impact of Unilateral BIT Terminations on FDI: Quasi-Experimental Evidence from India' (2022) 18 The Review of International Organizations 259–96; Elena Kotyrlo and Hryhorii M Kalachyhin, 'The Effects of India's Bilateral Investment Treaties Termination on Foreign Direct Investment Inflows' [2023] Economics of Transition and Institutional Change <https://onlinelibrary.wiley.com/doi/epdf/10.1111/ecot.12363> accessed 20 September 2023.

167 Hartmann and Spruk (n 166) 260.

168 ibid 292.

169 ibid.

170 Kotyrlo and Kalachyhin (n 166) 15.

171 Committee Report (n 147) 28.

depends on whom this question is posed to. However, this question should be answered based on the facts. It is quite possible that the experience of different countries is not the same on this issue. Thus, ISDS cases against one government could be closer to the Philip Morris pole while for the other toward the Yukos pole. It is also feasible that the ISDS claims against the same country could simultaneously be part of both narratives. Thus, one investor might sue a State to challenge its genuine public health measures that bring down his profits. In contrast, on different facts, another investor might sue the same State because the latter cancelled the former's license without following due process. The discussion in the ensuing chapters examines how the six Indian ISDS cases square up and which narrative they resemble more.

2 ISDS, White Industries, and the Indian judiciary

2.1 Introduction

Generally speaking, foreign investors sue States before ISDS tribunals challenging the actions of their executive or legislature. However, increasingly, one finds States being sued for the actions of their judiciary.[1] This should not come as a surprise because Article 4(1) of the Articles on the Responsibility of States for Internationally Wrongful Acts (ARSIWA) clearly recognizes that "the conduct of any State organ shall be considered an act of that State under international law, whether the organ exercises legislative, executive, judicial or any other functions". Thus, for the purposes of international law, the judiciary is very much part of the State – a fact also corroborated by the Convention on Jurisdictional Immunities.[2] Indeed, it is a well-settled principle in international law that States can be held liable for the actions of their judiciary.[3] This principle has been affirmed by the International Court of Justice[4] and several other international courts, such as the International Tribunal for the Law of the Sea.[5]

Over the last several years, numerous foreign investors have brought ISDS claims against States for the actions of their judiciary, alleging violation of several substantive provisions like fair and equitable treatment (FET),[6] denial of

1 Berk Demirkol, *Judicial Acts and Investment Treaty Arbitration* (CUP 2018).

2 See UN Convention on Jurisdictional Immunities (adopted 2 December 2004, UNGA Resolution A/59/49) article 2(1)(a).

3 James Crawford, *State Responsibility: The General Part* (CUP 2013) 121; Jan Paulsson, *Denial of Justice in International Law* (CUP 2005); Demirkol (n 1) 13–15.

4 See *Difference Relating to Immunity from Legal Process of a Special Rapporteur of the Commission of Human Rights* (Advisory Opinion) [1999] ICJ Rep 62, para 62; *LaGrand Case (Germany v United States of America)* (Judgement) [2001] ICJ Rep 466, paras 50, 52.

5 See *ARA Libertad (Argentina v Ghana)* [2012] ITLOS Case No 20, ITLOS Rep 21.

6 See for example *Jan de Nul and Dredging International NV v Egypt*, ICSID Case No ARB/04/13, Award, 6 November 2008, para 187; *Al-Bahloul v Tajikistan*, SCC Case No 064/2008, Award, 8 June 2010, para 221; *Swisslion v Former Yugoslav Republic of Macedonia*, ICSID Case No ARB/09/16, Award, 6 June 2012, paras 293, 300; *Eli Lily v Canada*, ICSID Case No UNCT/14/2, Award, 16 March 2017; *Renee Rose Levy and Gremcitel SA v Peru*,

DOI: 10.4324/9781003324379-2

justice,[7] and expropriation.[8] An important ground on which foreign investors have challenged the State's judicial conduct is the failure to provide "effective means of asserting claims and enforcing rights" (effective means clause),[9] which is discussed in detail in this chapter. This does not mean that foreign investors have succeeded in all these claims. Indeed, several ISDS tribunals have dismissed investor's allegations and ruled in favour of the State. ISDS tribunals have adopted a deferential attitude while reviewing the judicial conduct of a State.[10] However, the fact remains that in international investment law, just like the larger body of international law, States have been sued for the actions of their judiciary.

The *White Industries v India*[11] award – the first publicly available ISDS award against India – is part of this significant trend of holding the State accountable for the actions of its judiciary. It is exhilarating to note that India's first ISDS award arose, not due to the executive or the legislature exercising their sovereign powers in the public interest that the investor did not like, but due to the (in)actions of the Indian judiciary. This award came when very few in India anticipated that a foreign investor would sue India for a BIT breach, let alone succeeding in it. This award had a gigantic impact on India's BIT programme and India's approach toward ISDS. It sowed the seeds for India's subsequent backlash toward ISDS, as discussed in the introductory chapter. Thus, we focus on this case in this chapter, highlighting three critical aspects. First, in Section 2.2, the chapter discusses the definition of

ICSID Case No ARB/11/17, Award, 9 January 2015; *Stati v Kazakhstan (I)*, SCC Case No 116/2010, Award, 19 December 2013; *Arif v Moldova*, ICSID Case No ARB/11/23, Award, 8 April 2013; *Manchester Securities v Poland*, PCA Case No 2015-18, Award, 7 December 2018; *Krederi Ltd. v Ukraine*, ICSID Case No ARB/14/17, Award, 2 July 2018; *AMF Aircraftleasing Meir (and others) v Czech Republic*, PCA Case No 2017-15, Award, 11 May 2020.

7 See for example *Antoine Abou Lahoud v Democratic Republic of Congo*, ICSID Case No ARB/10/4, Award, 7 February 2014; *Big Sky Energy Corporation v Kazakhstan*, ICSID Case No ARB/17/22, Award, 24 November 2021; *Joshua Dean Nelson v Mexico*, ICSID Case No ICSID Case No UNCT/17/1, Award, 5 June 2020; *Fouad Alghanim v Jordan*, ICSID Case No ARB/13/38, Award, 14 December 2017.

8 *Saipem v Bangladesh*, ICSID Case No ARB/05/7, Award, 30 June 2009; *Sistem v Kyrgyz Republic*, ICSID Case No ARB(AF)/06/1, Award, 9 September 2009; *Vincent J Ryan v Poland*, ICSID Case No ARB(AF)/11/3, Award, 24 November 2015; *Lahoud v DRC* (n 7); *Içkale v Turkmenistan*, ICSID Case No ARB/10/24, Award, 8 March 2016; *Anglia Auto v Czech Republic*, SCC Case No 2014/181, Award, 10 March 2017; *AMF Aircraftleasing Meir v Czech Republic* (n 6).

9 See *Chevron and TexPet v Ecuador (I)*, PCA Case No. 34877, Partial Award on Merits, 30 March 2010; and other cases discussed in the chapter.

10 See Jason Webb Yackee, 'Toward a Minimalist System of International Investment Law' (2009) 32 Suffolk Transnational Law Review 303, 332; Johannes Hendrik Fahner, *Judicial Deference in International Adjudication: A Comparative Analysis* (Bloomsbury 2020) 71–83.

11 *White Industries Australia Limited v The Republic of India*, UNCITRAL, Final Award, 30 November 2011 (hereinafter '*White Industries*').

investment, a crucial jurisdictional issue in this case. Second, in Section 2.3, the chapter focuses on interpreting the most favoured nation (MFN) clause, which the foreign investor successfully used to incorporate a beneficial provision from a third-country BIT. The use of the MFN provision for this purpose has become quite controversial in international investment law. Third, in Section 2.4, the chapter will focus on understanding the scope and ambit of the effective means clause, which ultimately became the reason for India losing this case. After discussing these critical parts, the chapter in Section 2.5 will discuss the interaction between Indian courts and ISDS to demonstrate how a unique interpretation of Indian law has meant that foreign investors do not have access to effective means for asserting claims and enforcing rights when it comes to the enforceability of their ISDS awards in India. Finally, Section 2.6 concludes by emphasizing the closeness of the *White Industries* case with the Yukos narrative.

Before we look at these aspects, here are the brief facts of the case. In 1989, White Industries, an Australian company, signed a contract with an Indian public sector company called Coal India.[12] As per the contract, White was supposed to provide equipment and technical services and help develop a coal mine in the Piparwar area[13] in the Indian State of Jharkhand. Subsequently, a dispute arose between White Industries and Coal India, which was submitted to arbitration operating under the International Chamber of Commerce (ICC) rules. On 27 May 2002, this arbitration tribunal ruled in favour of White Industries.[14] White Industries was entitled to an award of A$4.08 million.

Subsequently, on 6 September 2002, Coal India applied to the High Court of Calcutta to set the commercial award aside under the relevant sections of the Indian Arbitration and Conciliation Act 1996 (set-aside proceedings).[15] Interestingly, White Industries was unaware of this application until early October 2002.[16] On 11 September 2002, White Industries sought to enforce the award in India before the Delhi High Court[17] (enforcement proceedings). Both proceedings experienced substantial delays. Finally, the enforcement proceedings were stayed pending the decision in the set-aside proceedings.[18] The matter eventually went to the Supreme Court of India and remained undecided one way or the other.[19]

With both the enforcement and set-aside proceedings still pending before the Indian courts, White Industries ran out of patience. After more than seven

12 ibid para 3.2.13.
13 ibid paras 3.2.13–3.2.20.
14 ibid.
15 ibid para 3.2.35.
16 ibid.
17 ibid para 3.2.36.
18 ibid para 11.4.4(v).
19 For the full procedural history of this case, see *White Industries* (n 11) 19–24.

years of getting the ICC arbitral award in its favour, White Industries initiated a BIT arbitration against India in 2010[20] under the India-Australia BIT.[21] White Industries claimed, *inter alia*, that the inordinate delay in judicial proceedings amounted to a violation of the FET standard on account of two factors: (1) a denial of justice and (2) a breach of White Industries' legitimate expectation that India would adhere to the New York Convention's standards on enforcement of foreign arbitral awards.[22] Furthermore, White Industries argued that the inaction of the Indian courts had violated the effective means clause.[23] White Industries also accused India of having expropriated its rights under the arbitral award due to the enormous delay on the part of the Indian courts to decide on the enforcement of the ICC award.[24]

The case came before an ad hoc ISDS arbitration tribunal constituted under the UNCITRAL arbitration rules. The tribunal dismissed White Industries' claim of a legitimate expectation about Indian courts not entertaining an application to set aside a foreign award, noting that considering an application to set aside a foreign award was a regular practice in the Indian legal system, one of which White Industries should have been aware.[25] The tribunal also dismissed White Industries' allegation of denial of justice after examining all the factors, including India's assertion that the Indian judiciary was overstretched due to its large population.[26] While the delays were unsatisfactory, they did not meet the high standards required to establish a denial of justice claim.[27] Additionally, the tribunal also rejected White's expropriation claim because the ICC arbitral award had not been "taken" or set aside.[28] Thus, the tribunal dismissed most of White's claims against India. The chapter, therefore, looks closely at issues that went against India in this case.

2.2 White Industries investment

In an investment treaty, the definition of investment plays a decisive role in establishing the scope of applying rights and obligations and establishing an ISDS tribunal's jurisdiction.[29] Only those assets of the foreign investor that

20 See Manu Sanan, 'The White Industries Award – Shades of Grey' (2012) 13(4) Journal of World Investment & Trade 661, 673–74.

21 Agreement Between the Government of Australia and the Government of the Republic of India on the Promotion and Protection of Investments (Austl.-India) (6 February 1999) 2116 UNTS 145 [hereinafter Austl.-India BIT Agreement].

22 See *White Industries* (n 11) paras 91–92.

23 See ibid paras 105–8.

24 See ibid paras 119–21.

25 See ibid paras 94–96.

26 See ibid paras 98–105.

27 See ibid para 105.

28 See ibid para 121.

29 See generally Rudolf Dolzer, Ursula Kriebaum and Christoph Schreuer, *Principles of International Investment Law* (3rd edn, OUP 2022) 82–110; Yannick Radi, *Rules and Practices*

qualify as an investment will be eligible for protection under the BIT. Accordingly, one of the critical questions before the *White Industries* tribunal was whether White made an investment eligible for protection under the India-Australia BIT and whether the tribunal had jurisdiction over White's claim.

India-Australia BIT defines investment following what is known as a broad 'asset-based' definition of investment that lists examples of protected assets such as shares, stocks, contractual rights, direct and indirect investment, intellectual property rights, etc. as part of the definition of investment.[30] Article 1(c) of India-Australia BIT provides:

> *investment means every kind of asset, including intellectual property rights, invested by an investor of one Contracting Party in the territory of the other Contracting Party in accordance with the laws and investment policies of that Contracting Party, and in particular, though not exclusively, includes:*
>
> *(i) moveable and immovable property as well as other rights such as mortgages, liens, or pledges;*
> *(ii) shares, stocks, bonds and debentures and any other form of participation in a company;*
> *(iii) right to money or to any performance having a financial value, contractual or otherwise;*
> *(iv) business concessions and any other rights required to conduct economic activity and having economic value conferred by law or under a contract, including rights to search for, extract and utilise oil and other minerals;*
> *(v) activities associated with investments, such as the organisation and operation of business facilities, the acquisition, exercise and disposition of property rights including intellectual property rights.*

Interestingly, India's arguments before the tribunal were not based on the definition of investment in the BIT. Relying on the writings of Zachry Douglas, India argued that for an asset to qualify as an investment, it must satisfy the legal and economic criteria.[31] The legal criteria, India argued, is that only rights *in rem* qualify for protection under the BIT.[32] Rights *in personam* that are independent of rights *in rem* are not protected investment under the

of International Investment Law and Arbitration (CUP 2020) 387–99; Mavluda Sattorova, 'Defining Investment Under the ICSID Convention and BITs: Of Ordinary Meaning, Telos, and Beyond' (2012) 2(2) Asian Journal of International Law 267, 267–90.

30 See UNCTAD, 'International Investment Agreements and Their Implications for Tax Measures: What Tax Policymakers Need to Know' (2021) 10–12 <https://unctad.org/system/files/official-document/diaepcbinf2021d3_en.pdf> accessed 27 July 2023.

31 ibid para 5.1.2.

32 ibid para 5.1.6.

BIT.[33] Regarding the economic criteria, India relied on the so-called *Salini* test – a test developed by an ICSID tribunal in *Salini v Morocco*[34] – to find the meaning of investment in Article 25(1) of the ICSID Convention.[35] Article 25(1) is part of Chapter II of the ICSID Convention that lays down the rules for an ISDS tribunal to have jurisdiction over a dispute. Article 25(1) provides:

> *The jurisdiction of the Centre shall extend to any legal dispute arising directly out of an investment, between a Contracting State (or any constituent subdivision or agency of a Contracting State designated to the Centre by that State) and a national of another Contracting State, which the parties to the dispute consent in writing to submit to the Centre.*

Thus, for an ISDS tribunal, constituted under ICSID rules, to have jurisdiction over a claim brought by a foreign investor against a State, it must ensure that there is a legal dispute that arises directly out of an investment. The tribunal will not have jurisdiction if the dispute does not directly arise from an investment. However, Article 25(1) does not define the term 'investment'. ICSID tribunals like in *Salini v Morocco* took it upon themselves to supply the normative content to the word 'investment'. The *Salini* tribunal laid down four fundamentals as part of investment: a contribution of money or other assets of economic value by the investor; the investment should be for a certain duration; there should be an element of risk in the investment made; and the investment should contribute to the host State's development.[36] On this basis, India argued that the rights that White Industries enjoyed due to the contract it signed with Coal India for supplying goods and services do not constitute an investment.[37]

However, the *White Industries* tribunal disagreed with India. The tribunal held that Article 1(c) of the India-Australia BIT, which defines investment, does not support India's claims.[38] Article 1(c) expressly includes *in personam* rights such as the right to money or to any performance having a financial value such as contracts.[39] The tribunal held that White Industries' rights under

33 ibid.
34 See *Salini v Morocco*, ICSID Case No ARB/00/4, Decision on Jurisdiction, 23 July 2001.
35 Article 25(1) of the ICSID Convention [575 UNTS 159] provides: "The jurisdiction of the Centre shall extend to any legal dispute arising directly out of an investment, between a Contracting State (or any constituent subdivision or agency of a Contracting State designated to the Centre by that State) and a national of another Contracting State, which the parties to the dispute consent in writing to submit to the Centre".
36 *Salini v Morocco* (n 34) para 52. The approach of the *Salini* tribunal has been criticized by some tribunals such as *Biwater-Gauff v Tanzania*, ICSID Case No ARB/05/22, Award, 24 July 2008, para 312; where it was said that "there is no basis for a rote, or overly strict, application of the five Salini criteria in every case".
37 *White Industries* (n 11) paras 5.1.9–5.1.12
38 *White Industries* (n 11) para 7.3.8.
39 ibid.

the contract with Coal India fall under the definition of investment.[40] The fact that these rights are *in personam*, not *in rem*, is immaterial to determine whether the assets in question qualify as protected investments.

As regards the applicability of the economic criteria provided by the *Salini* test, the tribunal held that this test was developed in the context of ICSID arbitration. Since the current arbitration is non-ICSID, the *Salini* test is not applicable.[41] The *White Industries* tribunal also held that the approach followed by ICSID tribunals to interpret investment is called the 'double-check' method.[42] As part of the 'double-check', also known as the 'double-barrel' method, the tribunal will first examine whether there is an investment under the ICSID convention followed by assessing whether the asset in question falls under the four corners of the BIT's definition of investment.[43] As the *White Industries* tribunal correctly held, this method imposes a higher standard than merely proving that the BIT's definition of investment is satisfied.[44]

Interestingly, after holding this, the tribunal examined whether White's investment satisfied the *Salini* test.[45] The tribunal held that White's investment met the four criteria in *Salini v Morocco*. White's investment in India involved substantial financial and other contributions such as equipment, personnel, training, and know-how.[46] It met the duration requirement since the project was for more than six years.[47] Given the nature of White's investment, it indeed entailed risk,[48] and since it involved increasing the production and mining of coal, it also contributed to India's economic development.[49]

The *White Industries* tribunal can be rightfully criticized for its approach toward the definition of investment in the India-Australia BIT. The tribunal was correct in holding that since the case before it was a non-ICSID arbitration, it wasn't required to apply the *Salini* test. However, inexplicably, the tribunal went on to examine whether White's investment met the *Salini* test.[50]

40 ibid paras 7.4.5–7.4.7.

41 ibid para 7.4.8. *Flemingo Duty-Free v Poland*, UNCITRAL, Award, 12 August 2016, para 298; *Anglia Auto v Czech Republic* (n 8) para 150; *Strabag v Libya*, ICSID Case No ARB(AF)/15/1, Award, 29 June 2020, para 109.

42 *White Industries* (n 11) para 7.4.9.

43 ibid. See also *Phoenix Action, Ltd v The Czech Republic*, ICSID Case No ARB/06/5, Award, April 15 2009, para 74.

44 *White Industries* (n 11) para 7.4.9.

45 ibid para 7.4.10. A recent case seems to have followed this approach of *White Industries*, see *Mercuria Energy Group Limited v Republic of Poland (II)*, SCC Case No 2019/126, Final Award, 29 December 2022, paras 535, 537, 539–40, 546–47.

46 *White Industries* (n 11) para 7.4.13–7.4.14.

47 ibid para 7.4.15.

48 ibid para 7.4.16.

49 ibid para 7.4.18.

50 The *White Industries* tribunal is not the only non-ICSID tribunal that applied the *Salini* test. The following non-ICSID arbitration tribunals have applied the *Salini* test: *Alps Finance and Trade AG v Slovakia*, Award, 5 March 2011, paras 239–46; *MNSS and RCA v Montenegro*,

This way, the tribunal contradicted its stand. Seemingly, the tribunal wanted to bolster its finding that White's made a protected investment. Thus, it showed that even if the *Salini* criteria, part of the double-check test that imposes a strict requirement, were applicable, the asset in question fell under the definition of investment. If indeed this was the tribunal's objective, it should have followed what is known as an 'inherent meaning' approach to investment laid down in *Romak v Uzbekistan*.[51] The *Romak* tribunal held that the term 'investment' in a BIT, irrespective of whether it is an ICSID or a non-ICSID arbitration, has an inherent or an integral meaning that involves three elements: contribution, duration, and risk.[52] These elements are no different from those offered by the *Salini* test. However, methodologically, the inherent or the integral meaning approach is in accordance with the rules of treaty interpretation, where the treaty-interpreter must give ordinary meaning to the words of a treaty.[53] Thus, the *White Industries* tribunal could have held that the ordinary meaning of the term investment will include an examination of aspects like contribution, duration, and risk.

Interestingly, this 'inherent meaning' approach has also caught up with ICSID tribunals. For example, in *Eyre and Montrose v Sri Lanka*,[54] the tribunal held that the term 'investment' has an inherent meaning that includes the three aspects of contribution, certain duration, and economic risk.[55] This 'inherent meaning' approach is also known as the 'objective' approach where the word 'investment' is objectively defined to derive its core economic meaning.[56]

After dealing with White's contractual rights, the tribunal dealt with the issue of whether the ICC arbitral award in its favour constituted an investment under the BIT.

2.2.1 *Arbitral award as an investment*

Since the genesis of White Industries' claim against India was the failure of the Indian judiciary to decide on the ICC arbitral award in its favour, arguably an

---

ICSID Case No ARB(AF)/12/8, Award, 4 May 2016, paras 189–202; *Manchester Securities v Poland* (n 6) paras 369–70.

51 *Romak v Uzbekistan*, PCA Case No 2007-07/AA280, Award, 26 November 2009, para 207.

52 ibid. See also *Spółdzielnia Pracy Muszynianka v Slovak Republic*, PCA Case No 2017-08/AA629, paras 288–89; *Cairn Energy PLC and Cairn UK Holdings Limited v The Republic of India*, PCA Case No 2016-7, Final Award, 21 December 2020, para 706.

53 In this regard also see *Fynerdale Holdings BV v The Czech Republic*, PCA Case No 2018-18, Award, 29 April 2021, paras 539–41, where the tribunal followed the 'objective' approach and concluded that economic development to the host State is also part of the definition of investment.

54 *Raymond Charles Eyre and Montrose Developments (Private) Limited v Democratic Socialist Republic of Sri Lanka*, ICSID Case No ARB/16/25, Award, 5 March 2020.

55 ibid para 293.

56 *Poštová banka, AS and Istrokapital SE v Hellenic Republic*, ICSID Case No ARB/13/8, Award, 9 April 2015, paras 360–71.

important issue before the tribunal was whether the ICC award constituted an investment. As one commentator argues:

> *White's cause of action (in the BIT arbitration) was based on non-enforcement by India of its ICC Award. Hence it was necessary for it to establish that an award in itself constitutes an investment under the BIT. If the ICC Award was not an investment, it was not entitled to any protection under the BIT and nor could any alleged breach relating thereto (by India) be an arbitrable dispute.*[57]

According to this approach, the judiciary's interference with an arbitral award can be challenged before an ISDS tribunal only if it is shown that the award in question is an investment. This is a narrow and incorrect framing of the issue. Such a framing presumes that an arbitral award exists in clinical isolation from the investment made by the foreign investor. It does not look at the investment made holistically. At the same time, the fact is that an arbitral award is inseparable from the original investment made. After all, the reason for an arbitral award is a claim by a foreign investor due to the infringement of the rights she enjoys. When an arbitration tribunal concludes that the investor's rights have indeed been infringed, it issues an award to compensate the investor for the breach. This way, an arbitral award preserves an investor's rights, such as contractual rights that qualify as an investment under the BIT. Thus, an arbitral award is part of an 'entire operation' of an investor.[58] It emanates from an underlying transaction that is a protected investment.[59] If an arbitral award originates from an underlying transaction that is not an investment, things may be different.[60] The *White Industries* tribunal, relying on *Saipem v Bangladesh*,[61] followed this approach and correctly held that the "rights under the [ICC] Award constitute part of White's original investment (i.e., being a crystallisation of its rights under the Contract) and, as such, are subject to such protection as is afforded to investments by the BIT".[62] Other ISDS tribunals have followed a similar approach.[63]

A relatively recent ISDS tribunal that examined the issue of State liability arising due to the inaction of the judiciary to enforce an arbitral award is

57 Sumeet Kachwaha, 'The *White Industries Australia Limited – India* BIT Award: A Critical Assessment' (2013) 29(2) Arbitration International 275, 281.
58 See Loukas A. Mistelis, 'Award as an Investment: The Value of an Arbitral Award or the Cost of Non-Enforcement' (2013) 28(1) ICSID Review, 64–87.
59 *Romak v Uzbekistan* (n 51) para 211.
60 ibid.
61 *Saipem v Bangladesh* (n 8) paras 125–27.
62 *White Industries* (n 11) para 7.6.10.
63 *ATA Construction, Industrial and Trading Company v The Hashemite Kingdom of Jordan*, ICSID Case No ARB/08/2, Award, 18 May 2010, paras 110–14; *Romak v Uzbekistan* (n 51) para 211. For a different view see *GEA v Ukraine*, ICSID Case No ARB/08/16, Award, 31 March 2011, paras 144, 158–64.

Anglia Auto v Czech Republic.[64] In this case, the tribunal held that since it was a non-ICSID arbitration, it was not imperative to inquire into factors like contribution, duration, and risk that have developed in the context of ICSID arbitration.[65] Thus, this dispute falls in the category of those non-ICSID cases mentioned before that have looked at the definition of investment without considering either the *Salini* test or the inherent or objective approach, as discussed before. The *Anglia Auto* tribunal focussed exclusively on the broad asset-based definition of investment in the BIT to determine whether the arbitral award is an investment.[66] The tribunal held:

> *that "investment" under the BIT is defined broadly, covering "every kind of asset belonging to an investor of one Contracting Party in the territory of the other Contracting Party under the law in force of the latter Contracting Party in any sector of economic activity". Under this definition, a final and binding arbitral award granting damages qualifies as an "asset belonging to an investor". This is further confirmed by the non-exhaustive list provided at Article 1(a), which refers, under point (iii), to "claims to money or to any performance under contract having a financial value". In their ordinary meaning, the words "claims to money" encompass a party's right under an award to be paid a sum of money, a right that can be pursued in enforcement proceedings. It follows that the Claimant, who prevailed in the arbitration and who has an entitlement to the damages granted to it by the 1997 Award, has a "claim to money" which it was entitled to pursue before the Czech courts. Likewise, the Claimant may be said to have a "claim to . . . performance under contract having a financial value", by the effect of the 1997 Award which recognized its contractual rights.*[67]

Importantly, the tribunal recognized that an arbitral award is an asset in the hands of the investor. This asset encompasses the investor's right to be paid money, which is recognized as part of the definition of investment in the BIT. The tribunal here came very close to saying that the arbitral award is an investment. Furthermore, the tribunal, on the line of *White Industries* and *Saipem*, held that the arbitral award recognized the contractual rights of the investor.

In sum, one can say that an arbitral award may not constitute an investment in itself.[68] But whether it does or not is of little practical significance.[69] Most ISDS

64 *Anglia Auto v Czech Republic* (n 8).

65 ibid para 150.

66 ibid para 152.

67 ibid.

68 Mistelis (n 58); Varun Mansinghka and Sanjana Srikumar, 'Do Arbitral Awards Constitute Investment' (2017) 5 Indian Journal of Arbitration Law 1.

69 In this regard also important to see *President Allende Foundation, Victor Pey Casado and Coral Pey Grebe v Republic of Chile*, PCA Case No 2017-30, Award, 28 November 2019, paras 308–9, 318–19, 320–22 where the arbitral tribunal dealt with the issue of whether an

tribunals have held that the arbitral award is part of the investor's overall investment and crystalizes or identifies the investor's contractual rights that form part of the protected investment.[70] The real question is whether undue interference with an arbitral award could trigger State liability.[71] The answer is an emphatic "yes".

Having examined how the *White Industries* tribunal navigated through the issue of investment, the chapter now focuses on the MFN provision and how it was used to borrow the effective means clause from the India-Kuwait BIT.

2.3 The MFN issue

The core idea behind the MFN provision is non-discriminatory treatment by ensuring that treaty-signing countries treat each other and their nationals no less favourably than they treat third States and their nationals.[72] Due to an MFN clause in a BIT, the investor will arguably be eligible for such better treatment that the host State provides to foreign investors in BITs with other countries.[73] This is also known as the multilateralizing effect of the MFN provision.[74] International investment law is replete with instances of foreign investors relying on the MFN provision in the primary treaty (that is, the treaty between the host State and the investor's home State) to borrow or incorporate clauses in third-country BITs (that is, treaties between the host State and countries other than the investor's home State) that they consider beneficial or as granting a more favourable treatment in comparison to the primary treaty.[75] Such incorporation could take place in two ways. First, incorporating beneficial procedural provisions such as an ISDS clause from a third-country BIT to overcome a less investor-friendly ISDS provision in the primary treaty.[76] This

ICSID award (as against other arbitral awards) constitute an investment. The tribunal held that an ICSID award does not constitute investment.

70 See also *Gavazzi v Romania*, ICSID Case No ARB/12/25, Award, 21 April 2015, para 120.

71 ibid.

72 Dolzer, Kriebaum and Schreuer (n 29) 264.

73 ibid. For more discussion on the MFN provision see N Jansen Calamita and Ewa Zelazna, 'Most-Favoured-Nation Clauses and the Centrality and Limits of General Principles' in Andrea Gattini, Attila Tanzi and Filippo Fontinelli (eds), *General Principles of Law and International Investment Arbitration* (Brill 2018) 398; Patrick Dumberry, 'The Importation of the FET Standard Through MFN Clauses: An Empirical Study of BITs' (2017) 32(1) ICSID Review 116; Radi (n 29) 119–30.

74 See Stephan W Shill, *The Multilateralization of International Investment Law* (CUP 2009).

75 Radi 2020 (n 29) 125.

76 See Facundo Pérez-Aznar, 'The Use of Most-Favoured-Nation Clauses to Import Substantive Treaty Provisions in International Investment Agreements' (2018) 20(4) Journal of International Economic Law 777, 779. See also the following cases: *Emilio Agustin Maffezini v Kingdom of Spain (Maffezini v Spain)*, ICSID Case No ARB/97/7, Decision on objections to jurisdiction, 25 January 2000; *Hochtief AG v Argentina (Hochtief v Argentina)*, ICSID Case No ARB/07/31, Decision on Jurisdiction, 24 October 2011; *Ansung Housing Co Ltd v People's Republic of China*, ICSID Case No ARB/14/25, Award, 9 March 2017, at paras 136–41; *A11Y v Czech Republic*, ICSID Case No UNCT/15/1, Decision on Jurisdiction,

could take various shapes, such as avoiding pre-conditions to arbitration, present in the primary treaty, like litigating before domestic courts for a certain period before initiating the ISDS process;[77] or invoking other dispute settlement mechanisms like ICSID, not present in the primary treaty;[78] or using the MFN provision to expand the coverage of the ISDS provision;[79] etc.[80] ISDS tribunals have generally allowed the usage of the MFN provision to avoid the pre-conditions to arbitration given in the primary treaty.[81] However, barring a few exceptions,[82] the tribunals have ruled against employing the MFN provision to incorporate beneficial ISDS clauses to create or expand jurisdiction.[83]

Second, incorporating or borrowing a substantive protection provision absent in the primary treaty (say the FET provision) from a third-country BIT (that contains the FET provision), or replacing a substantive protection feature present in the primary treaty with a beneficial one in the third-country BIT (for example, using MFN provision to replace a FET provision ostensibly less friendly to the investor[84] with a more investor-friendly[85] FET).[86] Except for a few examples,[87] an overwhelming number of ISDS tribunals have ruled that the MFN clause can be employed to borrow beneficial substantive protection provisions like the FET provision, full protection and security clause, umbrella clause, etc., from third-country BITs signed by the host State.[88] Often, the

---

9 February 2017; Award, 29 June 2018; *Itisaluna Iraq and others v Iraq*, ICSID Case No ARB/17/10, Award, 3 April 2020.

77 See for example *Hochtief v Argentina* (n 76).

78 See for example *Garanti Koza LLP v Turkmenistan (Garanti Koza v Turkmenistan)*, ICSID Case No ARB/11/20, Decision on the Objection to Jurisdiction for Lack of Consent, 3 July 2013, para 38.

79 See for example *Ivan Peter Busta and James Peter Busta v Czech Republic*, SCC Case No V 2015/014, Final Award, 10 March 2017, paras 163–69.

80 Perez-Aznar (n 76) 779–80.

81 ibid 780–81.

82 See for example *Venezuela US, SRL v Venezuela*, PCA Case No 2013-34, Interim Award on Jurisdiction, 26 July 2016.

83 Perez-Aznar (n 76) 781.

84 A provision that links FET with the customary international law's minimum standard of treatment for aliens, arguably, is less investor-friendly because it has a higher threshold for violation.

85 A provision where FET occurs as a broad and autonomous provision, arguably, is more investor-friendly because it can be interpreted to include several kinds of State conduct within the ambit of the FET.

86 ibid. See also David D Caron and Esmé Shirlow, 'Most-Favored-Nation Treatment: Substantive Protection' in Meg Kinnear and others (eds), *Building International Investment Law: The First 50 Years of ICSID* (Wolters Kluwer 2015) 399–413.

87 See for example *Ickale v Turkmenistan* (n 8) paras 328–29.

88 See for example *Bayindir Insaat Turizm Ticaret Ve Sanayi AS v Islamic Republic of Pakistan (Bayindir v Pakistan)*, ICSID Case No ARB/03/29, Decision on Jurisdiction, 14 November 2005, paras 225–35; *OAO Tatneft v Ukraine (OAO Tatneft v Ukraine)*, UNCITRAL, Award, 29 July 2014, para 365; *Hesham TM Al Warraq v Republic of Indonesia (Warraq v Indonesia)*, UNCITRAL, Final Award, 15 December 2014, paras 551–55, 683; *Mamidoil Jetoil Greek Petroleum Products Societe SA v Republic of Albania (Mamidoil v Albania)*, ICSID Case No ARB/11/24, Award, 30 March 2015, paras 273, 583; *KCI v Gabon*,

actual import of the MFN provision will depend on the precise wording of the provision.[89]

These divergent rulings have triggered fierce debates on the role and scope of the MFN provision in the context of importing substantive protection provisions[90] and ISDS provisions from third-country BITs.[91] Commentators have argued that letting foreign investors employ the MFN clause to borrow beneficial provisions from third-country BITs could lead to disruptive treaty shopping.[92] On the other hand, some authors defend the multilateralizing effect of the MFN provision.[93] The argument is that based on the language of the MFN provision, it is possible to interpret it in a manner that allows the investor to benefit from favourable substantive protection features present in third-country BITs.[94]

Coming back to the *White Industries* case, the MFN provision in Article 4(2) of the India-Australia BIT (the primary BIT under which the dispute arose) is as follows:

> *A Contracting Party shall at all times treat investments in its own territory on a basis no less favourable than that accorded to investments or investors of any third country.*

The MFN provision is evidently couched in broad terms with limited exceptions given in Article 4(4):

> *This Article shall not require a Contracting Party to extend to investments any treatment, preference or privilege resulting from:*
>
> *(a) any customs union, economic union, free trade area or regional economic integration agreement to which the Contracting Party belongs; or*
> *(b) the provisions of a double taxation agreement with a third country; or*
> *(c) any legislation relating wholly or mainly to taxation.*

UNCITRAL, Award, 23 December 2016, paras 168–70; *Micula v Romania (II)*, ICSID Case No ARB/14/29, Award, 5 March 2020; *Consutel v Algeria*, PCA Case No 2017-33, Final Award, 3 February 2020.

89 See for example *Muhammet Çap and Sehil v Turkmenistan*, ICSID Case No ARB/12/6, Award, 4 May 2021, paras 789–90.

90 See Simon Batifort and J Benton Heath, 'The New Debate on the Interpretation of MFN Clauses in Investment Treaties: Putting the Brakes on Multilateralization' (2018) 111(4) American Journal of International Law 873, 873–913. See also Stephan W Schill, 'MFN Clauses as Bilateral Commitments to Multilateralism: A Reply to Simon Batifort and J. Benton Heath' (2018) 111(4) American Journal of International Law 914, 914–35.

91 See Yannick Radi (n 29) 125.

92 Yannick Radi, 'The Application of the Most-Favoured-Nation Clause to the Dispute Settlement Provisions of Bilateral Investment Treaties: Domesticating the "Trojan Horse"' (2007) 18(4) European Journal of International Law 757–74. See also Jorun Baumgartner, *Treaty Shopping in International Investment Law* (OUP 2016).

93 Schill (n 90).

94 ibid.

Thus, the exceptions to the MFN provision are restricted to benefits or privileges that extend from an economic agreement like a customs union or a free trade area; or preferences that emerge from an international double taxation agreement or domestic legislation related to taxation.[95] There is no mention of the MFN provision not being applicable to substantive provisions or dispute settlement provisions in BITs signed by the host State with a third country.

Article 4(2) uses words like "at all times", which signify its wide import. Relying on the broad language of the MFN provision, the *White Industries* tribunal permitted the incorporation of the effective means clause.[96] The tribunal held that contrary to the assertion that using Article 4(2) to incorporate the effective means clause would subvert the carefully negotiated balance of the India-Australia BIT, such incorporation would help accomplish the objective of the MFN.[97] Interestingly, the tribunal seemed inclined to accept the proposition that the MFN provision should not be used to obtain the benefits of a dispute resolution clause present in a third-country BIT.[98] However, the tribunal held that the extension of the MFN provision to substantive protection features, like the effective means clause, is legitimate.

The *White Industries* ruling falls in the category of those cases where the investor successfully used the MFN provision to incorporate a substantive protection feature missing in the primary treaty. Since the *White Industries* case, there are examples of ISDS tribunals allowing the incorporation of the effective means clause through the MFN provision. For example, in *Tatneft v Ukraine*[99] the effective means clause in the Energy Charter Treaty was imported relying on the MFN provision in the Russia-Ukraine BIT.[100] In *Gramercy v Peru,*[101] the investor contended that the MFN provision in Article 10.4 of the United States-Peru Free Trade Agreement (FTA) allows the importation of the effective means clause in the Italy-Peru BIT.[102]

The tribunal, interestingly, left this issue open-ended, perhaps because it believed that the effective means clause articulates the denial of justice standard – a point discussed later in the chapter.[103] In other words, seemingly, the tribunal believed that since the effective means clause does not offer any extra layer of protection to the foreign investor, it would be of no practical significance even if it were imported into the US-Peru FTA. Yet, the tribunal

95 For a detailed discussion on the MFN provision including its history and origin see Stephan W Schill, *Multilateralization of International Investment Law* (CUP 2009).
96 *White Industries* (n 11) paras 11.2.1–11.2.9.
97 ibid para 11.2.1–11.2.4.
98 ibid para 11.2.2–11.2.3.
99 *OJSC "Tatneft" v Ukraine*, UNCITRAL, Award, 29 July 2014.
100 ibid para 358.
101 *Gramercy v Peru*, ICSID Case No UNCT/18/2, Final Award, 6 December 2022.
102 ibid paras 720–22.
103 ibid paras 1226–30.

concluded that Peru did not breach the effective means clause.[104] Perhaps the tribunal's net conclusion can be summarized as follows. The MFN clause cannot be used to import the effective means clause (perhaps this argument is not applicable to other substantive protection features), and even if it was brought into the primary BIT, the State didn't breach the standard.

After ruling that the MFN provision could incorporate the effective means clause, the *White Industries* tribunal examined the latter's meaning. Thus, we focus on comprehending the effective means clause with a focus on the doctrinal issues involved and its application by the *White Industries* tribunal.

2.4 The 'effective means' clause

The effective means clause, whereby the host State undertakes the obligation to provide effective means of asserting claims and enforcing rights to foreign investors with respect to their investments, is not a commonly found provision in BITs.[105] The effective means clause obligates countries to create an efficacious, workable, and operative system of legislations, courts, institutions, and other authorities that investors can access to enforce their rights and to defend their claims following due process. One of the few investment treaties that contain this provision is Article 10(12) of the Energy Charter Treaty (ECT), which provides as follows:

> *Each Contracting Party shall ensure that its domestic law provides effective means for the assertion of claims and the enforcement of rights with respect to investments, investment agreements and investment authorizations.*

Another formulation of the effective means clause can be found in Article II (7) of the US-Ecuador BIT, which provides as follows:

> *Each Party shall provide effective means of asserting claims and enforcing rights with respect to investment, investment agreements, and investment authorizations.*[106]

Not many ISDS tribunals have dealt with the effective means clause and its content.[107] Typically, this clause has been invoked by foreign investors in cases

104 ibid para 1229.

105 Demirkol (n 1) 39–40. See also Dolzer, Kriebaum and Schreuer (n 29) 286–89.

106 See also Article II(6) of US-Jamaica BIT; Article 3(5) of Kuwait-Croatia BIT.

107 *Chevron v Ecuador* (n 9) Partial Award on the Merits, 30 March 2010; *AMTO v Ukraine*, SCC Case No 080/2005, Final Award, 26 March 2008; *Petrobart v Kyrgyz Republic*, SCC Case No 126/2003, Arbitral Award, 29 March 2005; *Duke Energy v Ecuador*, ICSID Case No ARB/04/19, Award, 18 August 2008; *Charanne v Spain*, SCC Case No V 062/2012, Award, 21 January 2016; *Mercuria v Poland (II)* (n 45) Final Award, 29 December 2022.

involving judicial function.[108] However, in a recent case, *Mercurio Energy v Poland*, the tribunal held that the effective means clause also applies to non-adjudicatory proceedings, such as in matters before administrative authorities.[109]

An important issue in interpreting the effective means clause is its scope. The tribunal in *AMTO v Ukraine*, where it was interpreting Article 10(12) of the ECT, held that the effective means clause requires that the host State should have a legislation that recognizes and allows for the enforcement of the contractual rights of the investor.[110] Furthermore, procedural rules should allow for the effective implementation of the legislation before domestic courts.[111] Accordingly, foreign investors' access to courts is also an important part of the effective means clause.[112]

2.4.1 The threshold question

The *AMTO* tribunal recognized the difficulty in determining the criteria to evaluate 'effectiveness' in the 'effective means' clause. It explained the 'effective' part in the following manner:

> *The difficulty is to identify the criteria by which to assess the effectiveness of the legislation and rules called into question under Article 10(12) ECT. Bearing in mind the context and the object and purpose of the ECT, the Tribunal considers that "effective" is a systematic, comparative, progressive and practical standard. It is systematic in that the State must provide an effective framework or system for the enforcement of rights, but does not offer guarantees in individual cases. Individual failures might be evidence of systematic inadequacies, but are not themselves a breach of Article 10(12). It is comparative in that compliance with international standards indicates that imperfections in the law might result from the complexities of the subject matter rather than the inadequacies of the legislation. It is progressive in the sense that legislation ages and needs to be modernized and adapted from time to time, and results might not be immediate. Where a State is taking the appropriate steps to identify and address deficiencies in its legislation – in other words improvement is in progress – then the progress should be recognized in assessing effectiveness. Finally, it is a practical standard in that some areas of law, or the application of legislation in certain circumstances, raise particular difficulties which should not be ignored in assessing effectiveness.*[113]

108 Demirkol (n 1) 40.
109 *Mercuria v Poland (II)* (n 45) para 761. Compare this with *Apotex v USA (III)*, ICSID Case No ARB(AF)/12/1, Award, 25 August 2014, para 9.70.
110 *AMTO v Ukraine* (n 107) para 87.
111 ibid.
112 See *Gramercy v Peru* (n 101) para 1217.
113 *AMTO v Ukraine* (n 107) para 88. See also Mavluda Sattarova, 'Denial of Justice Disguised? Investment Arbitration and the Protection of Investors from Judicial Misconduct' (2012) 61(1) International and Comparative Law Quarterly 223, 239–40.

Thus, the tribunal said that the determination of means being 'effective' will depend on whether the means are systematic (that is, whether there is an effective framework for the enforcement of rights), comparative (that is, one may have to account for complexities while judging compliance with international standards), progressive (that is, whether there are constant improvements in the law), and practical (that is, whether difficulties arising in the implementation of the law are taken into account). The focus on the 'systematic' nature of the means, as the *AMTO* tribunal identified, means the host State creating an overall or a generally effective system for the enforcement of rights. In other words, this requirement does not mandate ensuring effectiveness in each individual case.[114] As long as the host State provides an overall effective system for enforcing rights, individual instances of failure are inconsequential.

In *Chevron v Ecuador (I)*, where the tribunal had to interpret Article II (7) of the US-Ecuador BIT, Ecuador, relying on the test laid down by the *AMTO* tribunal, argued that the effective means standard is only concerned with "system attributes" and not a review of investor treatment in individual cases.[115] However, the tribunal disagreed with Ecuador. It laid down a different threshold for violation, which includes not just the overall system of laws and institutions but also how this system operates and functions in individual cases.[116] In other words, while effective means of "asserting rights" will require the presence of an overall system of laws and institutions where claims can be made, the effectiveness of "enforcing rights" will require judging the efficacy of administering one's rights in individual cases.[117]

The threshold provided by the *Chevron* tribunal is the correct one.[118] If a State fails to provide an overall system of laws and procedures to investors to assert their claims, it will undoubtedly not act according to the effective means clause. Assuming the host State provides such a mechanism, that is not dispositive of the State complying with the effective means obligation. In other words, merely having an overall system of laws and procedures that enables individual investors to assert their claims will be of limited value if the system does not deliver, is too arduous to work, or does not provide a viable opportunity to the investor. Not holding the State accountable in individual cases, despite unwarranted and unfounded delays, will allow States to get away by creating an overall system of laws and procedures that are not functional on the ground. Therefore, if an individual investor faces inordinate or undue delay in judicial proceedings or gratuitous interferences by the executive in enforcing her rights, the State would have failed the obligation of providing

114 *AMTO v Ukraine* (n 107) para 88. Also see Demirkol (n 1) 41–42. See also Sattarova (n 113).
115 *Chevron v Ecuador (I)* (n 9) para 245.
116 ibid paras 246–47.
117 ibid para 247.
118 For a criticism of this approach see Campbell McLachlan, Laurence Shore and Matthew Weiniger, *International Investment Arbitration: Substantive Principles* (2nd edn, OUP 2017) para 7.127.

effective means to the investor despite the presence of an overall mechanism of asserting claims. In short, the effective means is to assert claims and enforce rights, which will merit an individual examination.

In adjudicating whether the State has acted in accordance with the effective means clause, the ISDS tribunals have followed a deferential standard of review.[119] That is, a measure of deference is given to the domestic courts and the host State's judicial system, and the ISDS tribunal does not act as a court of appeal.[120] The *Mercuria* tribunal called this standard of review a "high level of deference".[121] The ISDS tribunal will not undertake a *de novo* review.[122] Furthermore, the effective means clause does not obligate the host State to organize its judiciary or judicial system in a particular fashion.[123] Thus, the host States have ample regulatory leeway to design their judicial systems and laws as per their priorities as long as it is effective for the investor to assert claims and enforce rights in the real sense of the term.

2.4.2 Independent treaty standard

Another important issue in the discourse on the effective means clause is whether it is an independent treaty standard or whether it is part of the larger normative framework of denial of justice and the FET provision. Here again, we find a split between the ISDS tribunals. Some tribunals have held that the effective means clause formulates the denial of justice standard.[124] Put differently, the effective means clause is a specific articulation of the denial of justice standard and forms part of the FET provision.[125] Specifically, the tribunal in *Gramercy v Peru* held that the effective means clause does not create an additional layer of investor protection beyond the customary international law minimum standard of treatment of aliens.[126]

On the other hand, some ISDS tribunals regard the effective means standard as an independent treaty standard.[127] A prominent example is the *Chevron* tribunal, which held that the effective means clause in the US-Ecuador BIT is an independent treaty standard because it does not specifically refer to denial of justice, or customary international law.[128] In other words, the effective

119 ibid; *Mercuria v Poland (II)* (n 45) para 771.
120 *Chevron v Ecuador (I)* (n 9) para 247; *Mercuria v Poland (II)* (n 45) para 771.
121 *Mercuria v Poland (II)* (n 45) para 771.
122 *Chevron v Ecuador (I)* (n 9) para 247.
123 *Charanne v Spain* (n 107) para 470, 472.
124 *Gramercy v Peru* (n 101) para 1228; *Duke Energy v Ecuador* (n 107) para 391.
125 *Tatneft v Ukraine* (n 99) para 441. See Demirkol (n 1) 44. See also Sattarova (n 113) who calls this as a disguised form of denial of justice.
126 *Gramercy v Peru* (n 101) para 1228.
127 *Chevron v Ecuador (I)* (n 9) para 242.
128 ibid.

means clause is a *lex specialis* provision (the law governing a specific subject matter) and does not restate the law on denial of justice.[129]

The tribunal in *Mercuria v Poland (II)* made a clear exposition of this holding:

> *the Tribunal considers that the effective means standard under the ECT is formulated as a separate obligation of the host state and must be treated as such. Neither the fact that some other international investment treaties do not contain such separate standard, nor the fact that some other legal standards, such as the denial of justice or fair and equitable treatment, may be interpreted to create some overlap in investment protection is sufficient to override the clear language of the ECT. Any other interpretation would, in the Tribunal's view, undermine the effet utile of Article 10(12) of the ECT.*[130]

Thus, the tribunal, like in *Chevron v Ecuador (I)*, paid close attention to the language of the treaty that clearly lays down the effective means standard as an independent standard, not linked to the denial of justice clause or the FET provision. When a treaty provides an independent standard, not connected to any other substantive standard, there is a robust argument that the said standard should be interpreted autonomously. This is even though such a standard may be read as part of some other provision in other treaties. For instance, as several ISDS tribunals have held, a FET provision appearing as an autonomous standard, not linked to customary international law, in a BIT should be treated as such[131] even though, arguably, the FET provision reflects customary international law's minimum standard of treatment of aliens. Interpreting the effective means clause as part of the denial of justice or FET clauses will render it redundant.[132] This will violate a fundamental doctrine of treaty interpretation, *effet utile* or the principle of effectiveness, which requires that the clauses of a treaty should be interpreted in a manner that does not make them superfluous or rob them of their significance.[133] If the countries intended to include the

129 ibid. For a criticism of the Chevron tribunal's approach see McLachlan, Shore and Weiniger (n 118) para 7.126; Jessica Wirth, '"Effective Means" Means? The Legacy of Chevron v Ecuador' (2013) 52(1) Columbia Journal of Transnational Law 326, 349–52.

130 *Mercuria v Poland (II)* (n 45) para 758.

131 See *Vivendi v Argentina*, ICSID Case No ARB/97/3, Award, 20 August 2007, paras 7.4.5 to 7.4.7; *CC/Devas v India*, PCA Case No 2013-9, para 457. See also Andrew Newcombe and Lluís Paradell, *Law and Practice of Investment Treaties: Standards of Treatment* (Wolters Kluwer 2009) 255.

132 See also *AMF Aircraftleasing Meir v Czech Republic* (n 6) para 708.

133 See *Case Concerning Application of the International Convention on the Elimination of All Forms of Racial Discrimination (Georgia v Russia)*, Preliminary Objections, 2011 ICJ Reports 70, para 134; Steven R Ratner, 'International Law Rules on Treaty Interpretation' in Christopher McCrudden (ed), *The Law and Practice of the Northern Ireland Protocol* (CUP 2022) 84.

effective means clause as a mere restatement of the denial of justice standard or the FET clause, they would have said so in the text. However, because the treaty provides an effective means clause, over and above the denial of justice and the FET provisions, it has its own significance and meaning.

Since the effective means clause has its autonomous existence as an independent treaty standard, tribunals have held that it imposes a distinct and potentially less demanding test than what would be required to prove a violation of the denial of justice.[134] In other words, the threshold to prove that a State has breached the effective means clause is lower than showing a denial of justice, which requires egregious conduct on the part of the State that shocks or surprises a sense of judicial propriety.[135]

This approach has been criticized as being either controversial or lacking precision.[136] Thus, it is argued that the line segregating the threshold for a breach of effective means clause and denial of justice may often get blurred.[137] For example, suppose a tribunal concludes that a State has breached the effective means clause. In that case, the implication will be that no further effective means are available to the investor to assert claims and enforce rights. Why will this situation not qualify as denial of justice?[138] While precisely articulating the difference between the two is undoubtedly important, the real variance may depend on the case's facts. For instance, an inordinate delay in judicial proceedings might lead to a breach of the effective means but, on its own, will not be sufficient to show a denial of justice, which will require outstandingly bad or shocking conduct on the part of the host State. This outrageous conduct might require proof of the investor being denied access to courts,[139] serious defects in the adjudicative process,[140] or irrational and abusive outcomes.[141] In other words, while a case of denial of justice will mean a breach of the effective means clause, *vice-versa* might not always be accurate.

Having understood the doctrinal issues involved in interpreting the effective means clause, the chapter now focuses on examining how the *White Industries* tribunal interpreted and applied this clause.

2.4.3 White Industry's interpretation of the effective means clause

The tribunal in *White Industries v India* relied extensively on *Chevron v Ecuador (I)* to lay down the effective means clause.[142] Thus, the *White Industries*

134 *Chevron v Ecuador (I)* (n 9) para 244.
135 ibid; Demirkol (n 1) 44.
136 Demirkol (n 1) 46–47.
137 ibid.
138 ibid.
139 See *Siemens v Argentina*, ICSID Case No ARB/02/8, Award, 6 February 2007, para 308.
140 *Loewen v United States*, ICSID Case No ARB(AF)/98/3, Award, 26 June 2003, para 54.
141 See *Siag v Egypt*, ICSID Case No ARB/05/15, Award, 1 June 2009, paras 451–55.
142 *White Industries* (n 11) paras 11.3.2–11.3.3.

tribunal endorsed the threshold laid down in *Chevron v Ecuador (I)* that effectiveness not only means having a system of laws and institutions but also that the system should work effectively in a particular case.[143] The *White Industries* tribunal also certified the independent and autonomous standard of the effective means clause and that proving its breach mandates a less demanding test compared to what a denial of justice claim will require.[144] Another noteworthy aspect highlighted in *White Industries v India* is the relationship between the effective means clause and the exhaustion of local remedies.[145] The tribunal held:

> *a claimant alleging a breach of the [effective means] standard does not need to prove that it has exhausted local remedies. A claimant must, however, adequately utilise the means available to it to assert claims and enforce rights. It will be up to the host State to prove that local remedies are available and the claimant to show that those remedies were ineffective or futile.*[146]

In other words, a claim for the breach of the effective means clause can be made even when the investor has not exhausted local remedies. The onus is on the investor to prove why pursuing the remedies is ineffective or pointless.

The *White Industries* tribunal then applied the effective means clause to the facts at hand, that is, it applied the effective means clause to the enforcement proceedings (White's application to the Delhi High Court to enforce the ICC award, that is, to enforce its right) and the set-aside proceedings (White was asserting its claim before the Calcutta High Court that it lacked the jurisdiction to entertain Coal India's application to set aside the ICC award).

After a conscientious deliberation of the procedural history regarding the enforcement proceedings,[147] the tribunal held that White did not show that India failed to provide effective means to enforce its rights under the ICC award.[148] The procedural history showed that despite delays, White had the opportunity to defend itself. It also had the prospect to appeal against the decision of the Delhi High Court, which stayed White's enforcement petition *sine die* since the set-aside proceedings continued before the Calcutta High Court. The Delhi High Court did so to avoid a situation of conflicting decisions.[149] However, White exercised the option of not appealing this decision.[150]

143 ibid para 11.3.2 (b).
144 ibid para 11.3.2 (a).
145 ibid para 11.3.2 (g).
146 ibid.
147 ibid paras 11.4.4 to 11.4.15.
148 ibid para 11.4.15.
149 ibid para 11.4.4 (v).
150 ibid para 11.4.4 (w).

In other words, White Industries did not exhaust all options before it in the enforcement proceedings.[151]

On the other hand, on the issue of set-aside proceedings, the tribunal held:

> *In these circumstances, and even though we have decided that the nine years of proceedings in the set aside application do not amount to a denial of justice, the Tribunal has no difficulty in concluding the Indian judicial system's inability to deal with White's jurisdictional claim in over nine years, and the Supreme Court's inability to hear White's jurisdictional appeal for over five years amounts to undue delay and constitutes a breach of India's voluntarily assumed obligation of providing White with "effective means" of asserting claims and enforcing rights.*[152]

The tribunal held that the inordinate delay that White's set-aside proceedings faced did not constitute a denial of justice. As discussed before, the tribunal applied a higher threshold to show a denial of justice, which will require more than undue or inordinate delay in court proceedings.[153] However, the incomprehensible failure of the Indian judiciary, including the Supreme Court of India to decide on the set-aside proceedings for nine long years, constituted a failure on the part of India to accord effective means of asserting claims to White Industries pursuant to Article 4(2) of the India-Australia BIT that incorporated Article 4(5) of the India-Kuwait BIT.

A few Indian lawyers have criticized the *White Industries* tribunal's approach. A significant criticism is that the *White* tribunal misapplied the effective means standard because it ignored the following words given in Article 4(5) of the India-Kuwait BIT, "in accordance with its applicable laws and regulations".[154] In other words, Article 4(5), as mentioned earlier, requires the host State to provide effective means to the investor in accordance with its domestic laws. Thus, the argument is that the effective means standard is subject to the domestic laws of the host State.[155] Thus, the argument goes that the meaning of the effective means standard must be found within the four corners of

151 ibid paras 11.4.4–11.4.5. Also see, L Yves Fortier, 'Investor-State Tribunals and National Courts: A Harmony of Spheres?' in David Caron and others (eds), *Practising Virtue: Inside International Arbitration* (OUP 2015) 306.

152 *White Industries* (n 11) para 11.4.19.

153 One commentator, disagreeing with the tribunal, argues that the judicial delays the investor faced including at the hands of the Supreme Court of India were not apparently reasonable even in the denial of justice framework. See Berk Demirkol, 'Enforcement of International Commercial Arbitration Agreements and Awards in Investment Treaty Arbitration' (2015) 30(1) ICSID Review 56, 71.

154 Fali S Nariman, 'Investment Arbitration under the Spotlight – What Next for Asia' (2014) Herbert Smith Freehills – SMU Arbitration Lecture Series <https://ink.library.smu.edu.sg/hsmith_lect/3/> accessed 27 July 2023; Kachwaha (n 57) 287.

155 Nariman (n 154); Kachwaha (n 57) 287.

Indian law.[156] One commentator argued that reference to domestic laws in Article 4(5) mandated the tribunal to apply Indian law.[157] In Indian law, no right or cause of action exists for any litigant to claim damages because of the delay in hearing a case, notwithstanding how painfully prolonged the delay is.[158] Therefore, the argument is that inordinate delay in the court proceedings couldn't have been the grounds for finding India in breach of the effective means clause.

This argument is flawed. While it is true that the *White Industries* tribunal should have given meaning to the words "in accordance with its applicable laws and regulations", these words cannot be interpreted to mean that the content of the effective means clause is hostage to the domestic laws of the host State. Such an interpretation will render the effective means clause, an international treaty standard, superfluous. It will allow a host State to conveniently hide behind the cloak of domestic law to avoid accountability under international law. International law does not support such a proposition. Article 27 of the Vienna Convention on Law of Treaties states that a country "may not invoke the provisions of its internal law as justification for its failure to perform a treaty".[159] In this context, the effective means standard is a treaty obligation that cannot be frustrated by reliance on domestic laws.

So, what meaning can one give to the words "in accordance with its applicable laws and regulations" in Article 4(5) of the India-Kuwait BIT? It is not uncommon for BITs to refer to the country's domestic laws. For instance, the definition of investment in several investment treaties refers to the host State's domestic laws. For instance, as already pointed out before, the definition of investment in India-Australia BIT states that investment "means every kind of asset, including intellectual property rights, invested by an investor of one Contracting Party in the territory of the other Contracting Party in accordance with the laws and investment policies of that Contracting Party". Does the reference to the domestic laws of the host State suggest that the meaning of investment is determined by reference to the municipal laws of the country admitting the investment? Several ISDS tribunals have held that this is not the case.[160] Reference to domestic laws does not concern the meaning of investment but only the legality of investment.[161] Thus, it is to be used as a reference point to determine whether the investment in the host State has been made lawfully.

In the same vein, reference to domestic laws in Article 4(5) means that the ISDS tribunal must give deference to the host State to decide on the layout

156 Kachwaha (n 57) 287.
157 Nariman (n 154).
158 ibid.
159 Vienna Convention on the Law of Treaties (United Nations [UN]) 1155 UNTS 331.
160 See for example, *Salini v Morocco* (n 34); *Convial Callao v Peru*, ICSID Case No ARB/10/2, Final Award, 21 May 2013, paras 382–90.
161 Dolzer, Kriebaum and Schreuer (n 29) 108.

and design of its domestic laws and institutions to provide investors with effective means to assert claims and enforce rights. Put differently, as ISDS tribunals have emphasized, the host State is not required to organize its domestic laws and institutions in a particular way to achieve its obligation of providing effective means. The reference to the host State's domestic laws in Article 4(5) performs this function. The reference to domestic laws in Article 4(5) does not mean relegating the meaning of a treaty standard, like effective means, to what the host State has defined in its domestic laws. Such an approach will result in incoherent and inconsistent meanings of a common treaty term across different BITs based on the meaning given in the host State's domestic laws.

Another criticism levelled against the *White Industries* tribunal is that it ignored the following words in Article 4(5) that follow the effective means standard:

> *and ensure to investors of the other Contracting State, the right of access to its courts of justice, administrative tribunals and agencies, and all other bodies exercising adjudicatory authority, and the right to employ persons of their choice, for the purpose of the assertion of claims and the enforcement of rights with respect to their investments.*[162]

The argument is that if the effective means clause is read with the aforementioned part, it would be clear that the focus of Article 4(5) is on judicial access.[163] In other words, the argument seems to be that as long as the foreign investor has access to the national courts and the judicial processes, the host State has complied with Article 4(5). But this is a wrong argument to make. Indeed, the *White Industries* tribunal did not consider a part of Article 4(5) mentioned earlier while interpreting the effective means standard. However, the outcome would not have been different even if it did. This is because the focus of Article 4(5) is not limited to judicial access. The critical part of Article 4(5) is that judicial access should be effective for the investor to assert claims and enforce rights. Thus, Article 4(5) has two parts as clearly denoted by the conjunction 'and'. These parts are effective means 'and' the right to judicial access. Before the *White Industries* tribunal, the issue was not whether the investor had access to courts [the second part of Article 4(5)]. But whether the access was effective [the first part of Article 4(5)].

After an exhaustive examination of three facets of the *White Industries* award, the chapter now focuses on how Indian courts have dealt with ISDS. This discussion aims to show that the Indian judiciary has interpreted the Arbitration and Conciliation (A&C) Act[164] in a manner that does not provide effective means to foreign investors to assert their claims and enforce

162 Kachwaha (n 57) 287–88.
163 ibid.
164 The Arbitration and Conciliation Act 1997 (Act No 26 of 1996).

their rights in connection to enforcement of ISDS awards. The A&C Act is the primary legislation in India governing arbitration, including international commercial arbitration (ICA).[165] It regulates all facets related to arbitrations in India and outside India such as enforcement and setting aside the arbitral awards, the nature of judicial interference allowed in arbitration, etc. While Part I of the Act deals with arbitrations, including ICA, seated in India,[166] Part II governs issues related to the recognition and enforcement of foreign arbitral awards[167] under the New York Convention 1958 (NYC).[168]

2.5 Indian courts and ISDS: failure to meet the effective means clause

Domestic courts have quickly emerged as significant actors in international investment law.[169] There could be several interaction points between domestic courts and ISDS, such as using domestic courts to exhaust local remedies before approaching an ISDS tribunal.[170] Our discussion focuses on the intervention domestic courts make in ISDS arbitration through various means, such as issuing anti-arbitration injunctions. Typically, at the executive's request, this will take the shape of a domestic court of the host State, issuing an injunction to the foreign investor forbidding the pursuance of ISDS arbitration.[171] In

165 See, Indu Malhotra, *OP Malhotra on law and Practice of Arbitration and Conciliation* (Thomson Reuters 2014); RS Bachawat, *Law of Arbitration and Conciliation* (LexisNexis 2010). See also the discussion in Chapter 3 on the A&C Act.

166 See, Arbitration and Conciliation Act 1996, Part I, ss 1–43.

167 See, Arbitration and Conciliation Act 1996, Part II, ss 44–60; the Part II also deals with the enforcement of the awards rendered in the States which are parties to the Convention on the Execution of Foreign Arbitral Awards 1927.

168 Convention on the Recognition and Enforcement of Foreign Arbitral Awards (adopted 10 June 1958, entered into force 7 June 1959) ('NYC 1958').

169 For instance, see, Hanno Wehland, 'Domestic Courts and Investment Treaty Tribunals: The Effect of Local Recourse Against Administrative Measures on the Breach of Investment Protection Standards' (2019) 36(2) Journal of International Arbitration 207–29; A Sarvanan and SR Subramanian, 'Role of Domestic Courts in Investor-State Dispute Settlement Process: The Case of South Asian BITs' (2017) 20(2) International Arbitration Law Review 42–54. See also Gabrielle Kaufmann-Kohler and Michele Potestà, 'The Interplay Between Investor-State Arbitration and Domestic Courts in the Existing IIA Framework' in *European Yearbook of International Economic Law: Investor-State Dispute Settlement and National Courts* (Springer 2020) <https://link.springer.com/chapter/10.1007/978-3-030-44164-7_3> accessed 27 July 2023.

170 See Christoph Schreuer, 'Interaction of International Tribunals and Domestic Courts in Investment Law' in Arthur W Rovine (ed), *Contemporary Issues in International Arbitration and Mediation: The Fordham Papers* (Brill Nijhoff 2010) 71–94; Jacomijn J van Haersolte-Van Hof and Anne K Hoffmann, 'The Relationship Between International Tribunals and Domestic Courts' in Peter Muchlinski, Federico Ortino and Christoph Schreuer (eds), *The Oxford Handbook of International Investment Law* (OUP 2008).

171 See for example *SGS Société Générale de Surveillance SA v Islamic Republic of Pakistan*, ICSID Case No ARB/01/13.

India, all three instances of domestic court's interaction with ISDS arose due to the Indian government approaching the Indian courts with a request to refrain foreign investors from pursuing ISDS under different BITs.[172] These three cases are *Port of Kolkata v LDA*,[173] *India v Vodafone*,[174] and *India v Khaitan*.[175] The Calcutta High Court decided the first case whereas the Delhi High Court handled the other two. In all these cases, requests for an anti-arbitration injunction were made under the A&C Act. Although the A&C Act does not explicitly talk about ISDS, the presumption is that both commercial and treaty arbitration fall under its ambit.

The *Port of Kolkata v LDA* case arose from a French company, Louis Dreyfus Armaturs SAS (LDA), bringing an ISDS claim against India under the India-French BIT.[176] As mentioned in the introductory chapter, this is one of the ISDS claims that India won. In 2009, LDA invested in an Indian company, Haldia Bulk Terminals Private Limited (HBT). The Kolkata Port Trust – a public sector entity involved in the porting business – awarded a contract to HBT. Subsequently, in 2012, a dispute arose between HBT and Kolkata Port Trust, which was submitted to contractual arbitration. Simultaneously, in 2013, LDA initiated an ISDS claim against India, making the Kolkata Port Trust one of the parties.[177] This prompted the Kolkata Port Trust to approach the Calcutta High Court requesting an anti-arbitration injunction under the A&C Act to refrain LDA from proceeding against it under the India-France BIT.[178] The Calcutta High Court, presuming the applicability of the A&C Act to investment treaty arbitration, issued an anti-arbitration injunction under Section 45 of the Act.[179]

However, a different approach was followed in the other two cases mentioned earlier that were decided by the Delhi High Court. In *India v Vodafone* and *India v Khaitan*, the Delhi High Court, while deciding whether to issue an anti-arbitration injunction to restrain foreign investors from continuing with ISDS, held that the A&C Act does not apply to investment treaty arbitration.[180] The *India v Vodafone* case arose in connection with Vodafone's

172 See also Prabhash Ranjan and Pushkar Anand, 'Indian Courts and Bilateral Investment Treaty Arbitration' (2020) 4(2) Indian Law Review 199–220.

173 *The Board of Trustees of the Port of Kolkata v Louis Dreyfus Armatures* [2014] GA 1997 of 2014 and CS No 220 of 2014 (Calcutta HC).

174 *Union of India v Vodafone Group Plc United Kingdom & Anr* [2018] CS(OS) 383/2017 & IA No 9460/2017 (Delhi HC).

175 *Union of India v Khaitan Holdings (Mauritius) Limited & Ors.* [2019] CS (OS) 46/2019, I.As. 1235/2019 & 1238/2019 (Delhi HC).

176 *Louis Dreyfus Armateurs SAS (France) v The Republic of India*, PCA Case No 2014-26, Award, 11 September 2018.

177 ibid para 270.

178 ibid para 271.

179 *Port of Kolkata v LDA* (n 173).

180 *India v Vodafone* (n 174) para 90; *India v Khaitan* (n 175) para 36.

ISDS claim against India for imposing taxes retroactively.[181] The *India v Khaitan* case is related to a 2013 ISDS claim brought by Khaitan,[182] a Mauritian company, due to the cancellation of the second-generation telecom licenses owing to a Supreme Court of India decision.[183] It is interesting to note that this ISDS claim also occurred due to the judiciary's actions. The Indian Supreme Court in the *Centre for Public Interest Litigation v Union of India*[184] cancelled the allocation of second-generation telecom licenses because it was arbitrary without examining India's obligations under BITs. However, since the *Khaitan Holdings v. India* case is still pending and most documents are not in the public domain, the book doesn't focus on this dispute in detail.

Circling back to the Delhi High Court's decision in the *Vodafone* and *Khaitan* cases, the court reasoned that Part II of the A&C Act would be applicable in these two instances (both arbitrations are seated outside India), only if the legal relationship between the parties is commercial in nature. India signed the New York Convention with an important reservation, which limits the Convention's application "only to differences arising out of legal relationships, whether contractual or not, which are considered as commercial under the national law of the State making such declaration".[185] Interestingly, the A&C Act incorporates this aspect but does not define the term 'commercial'. This gives scope for judicial discretion.

The Delhi High Court, in both cases, held that there is a fundamental difference between ISDS and commercial arbitration disputes because the 'cause of action' in the former is not commercial in nature but based on a country's obligations under the BIT.[186] In other words, unlike commercial arbitrations rooted in private contracts, ISDS has its basis in public international law.[187] Thus, according to the court, given the international law foundations of ISDS, it cannot be treated as based on a legal relationship that is commercial. On this basis, the court concluded that ISDS disputes are not commercial in nature and, therefore, the A&C Act does not apply to investment treaty arbitration. The court's reasoning that ISDS is not commercial is specious. The court muddled the critical distinction between the cause of action, on the one hand, and the legal relationship being commercial between the parties, on the other hand.[188] An ISDS claim indeed arises due to an alleged violation of an

181 Vodafone's ISDS claim is discussed in detail in Chapter 4.
182 *Khaitan Holdings (Mauritius) Limited v Republic of India* <https://pca-cpa.org/en/cases/206/> accessed 27 July 2023. The case is pending, though a decision on jurisdiction was rendered in September 2021. This decision is not available in public domain.
183 *Centre for Public Interest Litigation v Union of India* (2012) 3 SCC 1.
184 See *Centre for Public Interest Litigation* (n 183).
185 See Arbitration and Conciliation Act 1996, s 44.
186 *India v Vodafone* (n 174) para 91.
187 ibid. *India v Khaitan* (n 175) para 36.
188 Ranjan and Anand (n 172).

investment treaty by the host State. However, this does not change the legal relationship between the host State and the investor, which is commercial in nature. The Delhi High Court interpreted the term 'commercial' in Section 44 of the A&C Act in a restrictive manner and thus reached an erroneous conclusion.[189] Interestingly, the Indian Model BIT recognizes that ISDS claims arise out of a commercial relationship. Specifically, Article 27.5 of the Model BIT provides: "A claim that is submitted to arbitration under this Article shall be considered to arise out of a commercial relationship or transaction for purposes of Article I of the New York Convention".[190]

Be that as it may, the Delhi High Court's rulings about the non-applicability of the A&C Act to investment treaty arbitration gives rise to troubling questions about the enforcement of ISDS awards in India.[191] The enforcement of non-ICSID ISDS awards globally is achieved through NYC.[192] However, in India, since the legislation that implements the NYC, the A&C Act, is not applicable to ISDS awards, it leaves the foreign investor high and dry. The only option for a foreign investor desirous of enforcing an ISDS award in India will be to approach the Indian courts for enforcement under Order XXI of India's general Civil Procedure Code 1908.[193] In such a situation, since the Indian courts will not be restrained by the limits that the A&C Act imposes on them while intervening with arbitration, it will give the Indian courts vast powers, leading to enormous delays in the enforcement process.[194] It will become near impossible for ISDS awards to be enforced for all practical terms.

189 See Samarth Khanna, 'Is the New York Convention Applicable for the Enforcement of Investment Awards in India' (*The American Review of International Arbitration Blog*, 21 November 2021) <https://aria.law.columbia.edu/is-the-new-york-convention-applicable-for-the-enforcement-of-investment-arbitration-awards-in-india/> accessed 27 July 2023.

190 See art 27.5, Treaty Between the Republic of Belarus and the Republic of India on Investments (entered into force 5 March 2020); art 26.5, Bilateral Investment Agreement Between the India Taipei Association in Taipei and the Taipei Economic and Cultural Center in India (signed on 18 December 2018); art 27.5, Bilateral Investment Treaty between the Government of Kyrgyz Republic and the Government of Republic of India (signed on 7 June 2019).

191 See generally on enforcement of BIT awards in India, Prabhash Ranjan and Deepak Raju, 'The Enigma of Enforceability of Investment Treaty Arbitration Awards in India' (2011) 6 Asian Journal of Comparative Law 1–33; Satish Bhushan, 'BIT Arbitration in India: Exploring Applicability of the 1996 Act and Enforcement of Resultant Arbitral Awards' (2011) 4(2) Contemporary Asia Arbitration Journal 273–304.

192 Schreuer (n 170) 71–94.

193 See, *Bharti Televentures Ltd v DSS Enterprise Private Ltd and Ors* [2005] IA Nos 9735, 923, and 9925/03 in CS(OS) No 1769/2003 (Delhi HC) para 5.

194 In respect of the recognition and enforcement of the foreign arbitral awards the Delhi High Court in the case of *Cruz City 1 Mauritius Holdings v Unitech Limited* [2017] EXP132/2014 & EA(OS) Nos. 316/2015, 1058/2015 & 151/2016 & 670/2016, held that an enforcement court is not bound by the findings of the set aside court exercising the supervisory jurisdiction. The principle of *res judicata* is not applicable since, according to the court the subject matter of the set-aside proceedings and the enforcement proceedings are different. See paras 23–24, 44.

When all this is seen from the perspective of the effective means clause, the Delhi High Court's interpretation has resulted in a situation where the investor is denied effective means of asserting claims and enforcing rights in matters related to the enforceability of ISDS awards. For India to come out of this situation, the Supreme Court should clarify the law on this, which can only happen if such a case comes up before it. The other option is to amend the A&C Act either to define 'commercial' as including investment treaty arbitration or to add a provision explicitly stating that the Act applies to ISDS as well. But sadly, the Indian executive and the parliament have done precious little on this issue.

2.6 Conclusion

If White Industries had not faced such judicial delays in Indian courts to enforce its legal rights, this case would not have arisen. While apologists for the Indian judiciary may try to rationalize a delay of nine years to decide on the enforcement of an ICA award, the fact remains that the *White Industries* case was the Yukos moment for India's judicial system. It was judicial slackness that brought this ISDS claim to India's door. This claim did not arise because India adopted a regulatory measure to safeguard public health or the environment or to protect some other critical sovereign objective. Indian judiciary is overburdened with meagre judicial resources. While much lip service is paid to this problem, very little actual reform has happened. For instance, India's judge-to-population ratio is a miserable 21 per million people.[195] This has improved marginally from 14.7 in 2002.[196] But it is not just the overburdened judiciary that is the problem. The judicial mindset is equally disconcerting.

The Law Commission of India (LCI) in its 246th report in 2014 recognized this problem.[197] The LCI observed that judicial interference in arbitration proceedings leads to significant delays in the arbitration process, eventually

195 PTI, 'India Has India Has 21 Judges Per Million Population: Govt' (*The Economic Times*, 2 February 2023) <https://economictimes.indiatimes.com/news/india/india-has-21-judges-per-million-population-govt/articleshow/97559581.cms?utm_source=contentofinterest&utm_medium=text&utm_campaign=cppst; https://economictimes.indiatimes.com/news/india/india-has-21-judges-per-million-population-govt/articleshow/97559581.cms?from=mdr>.

196 Increasing Strength of Judges, Ministry of Law and Justice (10 December 2002) <https://archive.pib.gov.in/archive/releases98/lyr2002/rdec2002/10122002/r101220022.html>.

197 Government of India, Law Commission of India, 'Amendments to the Arbitration and Conciliation Act 1996' (Report No 246, August 2014) 15 <http://lawcommissionofindia.nic.in/reports/report246.pdf> accessed 24 February 2018. The commission was entrusted with the task of reviewing the provisions of the Arbitration and Conciliation Act of 1996.

negating the benefits of arbitration. The LCI offered two reasons for such delays.

> *First, the [Indian] judicial system is over-burdened with work and is not sufficiently efficient to dispose cases, especially commercial cases, with the speed and dispatch that is required. Second, the bar for judicial intervention (despite the existence of section 5 of the [Arbitration and Conciliation] Act) has been consistently set at a low threshold by the Indian judiciary, which translates into many more admissions of cases in Court which arise out of or are related to the Act.*[198]

The LCI report then went on to make recommendations for amending the A&C Act to ensure that international commercial arbitral awards involving foreign parties are dealt with expeditiously by the Indian courts.[199] As the report shows, the outcome of the *White Industries* case weighed heavily on LCI's minds in making the preceding recommendation.[200] The LCI report observed that the *White Industries* case "serves as a reminder to the Government to urgently implement reforms to the judicial system in order to avoid substantial potential liabilities that might accrue from the delays presently inherent in the system".[201] Thus, it is evident that there is recognition of the fact that the Indian courts erred in the *White Industries* case. However, will this recognition ensure no repeat of a Yukos moment in the future? It does not look like seeing the decisions rendered by the Delhi High Court in the *Vodafone* and *Khaitan* cases. The central government should ask the Supreme Court to clarify the law on this point or amend the law to bring ISDS under the A&C Act explicitly. Otherwise, due to judicial slackness, more ISDS claims might land on India's door.

Unfortunately, India drew the wrong lesson from the *White Industries* case. Instead of working toward fixing the problem of substantial judicial backlogs and excessive judicial interference in the arbitration process, which was the root cause of this claim, India concluded that the real villain of the piece was the MFN clause. Thus, the argument goes that India lost the case because White Industries indulged in disruptive treaty shopping. But this is not entirely true. While using the MFN provision to expand the jurisdiction of an ISDS tribunal or to create missing jurisdiction is indeed problematic, the same cannot be said when a foreign investor uses MFN to import a beneficial substantive provision from a third-country BIT. Indeed, this is precisely the function of the MFN provision.

Accordingly, India's 2016 Model BIT and its investment treaties with Belarus, Taiwan, Kyrgyzstan, and Brazil do not contain the MFN clause. There is a

198 ibid 15–16.

199 ibid 16.

200 ibid. Also important to note that the Arbitration and Conciliation Act 1996 was amended.

201 ibid.

solid argument for circumscribing the arguably wide import of the MFN provision through meticulous treaty drafting to ensure it does not apply to ISDS. However, doing away with the MFN provision is a classic case of throwing the baby out with the bathwater. The conspicuous absence of an MFN provision sends a disconcerting signal to the foreign investor that the host State is not promising non-discriminatory treatment – a fundamental principle of not just international investment law but also international economic law.

3 The unending spectrum saga

3.1 Introduction

One of the most intriguing sagas in India's ISDS story is the twin cases brought against India due to the cancellation of a contract for leasing electromagnetic spectrum. The tale started in 2005 when the marketing arm of the Indian Space Research Organisation (ISRO), Antrix, signed a contract with Devas, an Indian multimedia services provider.[1] Since then, this story has been a roller coaster ride of ISDS awards, extensive use of public power, including amendments in domestic law and international treaties, allegations of fraud and corruption, and multiple court rulings and decisions, adding significantly to the already complicated legal labyrinth.

The Antrix-Devas contract was signed when India was at the cusp of an information technology and communication revolution. As per this agreement, Antrix – a State-owned commercial corporation – leased to Devas, for 12 years, the portion of the electromagnetic spectrum found at 2500–2690 megahertz (MHz), also known as S-band, on two satellites that were to be launched by ISRO.[2] The total amount of S-band capacity leased to Devas was 70 MHz[3] to let Devas provide multimedia services to mobile users across India.[4] Two parts comprised this 70MHz: the broadcast satellite services (BSS) part of 60 MHz, and the mobile satellite services (MSS) part of 10MHz.

Once Antrix and Devas signed the contract, several foreign investors were interested in investing in the project. These included the three Mauritian

1 See *CC/Devas (Mauritius) Ltd, Devas Employees Mauritius Private Limited, and Telcom Devas Mauritius Limited v Republic of India*, PCA Case No 2013-9, Award on Jurisdiction and Merits, 25 July 2016 (hereinafter '*CC/Devas v India*').

2 *Deutsche Telekom AG v The Republic of India, PCA Case No 2014–10*, Interim Award, 13 December 2017, para 59. (hereinafter '*DT v India*').

3 ibid. See also Prabhash Ranjan, 'Devas v Antrix: Lessons for India in Navigating Bilateral Investment Treaty Disputes' (2022) ORF Issue Brief No 537, Observer Research Foundation <https://www.orfonline.org/research/devas-v-antrix/> accessed 20 August 2023.

4 *CC/Devas v India* (n 1).

DOI: 10.4324/9781003324379-3

investors who brought the CC/Devas claim,[5] and Deutsche Telekom, a German investor and one of world's leading telecommunication companies, who brought the other ISDS claim. In 2006 and 2007, Mauritian investors made a combined investment of about US$30 million.[6] Likewise, in 2008 and 2009, Deutsche Telekom made an equity investment in Devas of US$75 million and US$22.5 million, respectively.[7] Indian governmental bodies like the Foreign Investment Promotion Board approved these foreign investments.[8]

Soon, Devas also secured the licenses and necessary government approvals to deliver internet services throughout India.[9] As per the agreement between Devas and Antrix, the satellites were to be launched by June 2009. However, Antrix failed to meet the deadline but promised that the launch would happen by the end of 2009 or early 2010.[10] Notwithstanding these delays, the claimants continued meeting their financial obligations and other requirements, like injecting fresh capital into the project.[11]

Two other developments took place simultaneously. First, from 2005 to 2007, several public officials, including senior military officers, recommended reserving the S-band spectrum for military and strategic purposes.[12] Second, allegations of corruption against Indian space officials about leasing the S-band to Devas started surfacing in the media.[13]

The government constituted a committee to investigate the alleged wrongdoings in the deal. This committee submitted its report in 2010 and found the Devas system technically sound. Yet, it recommended revisiting the agreement considering the limitations on the availability of the spectrum for essential future demands.[14] It is critical to underline that this committee recommended revisiting or reviewing the agreement, not annulling it.

Meanwhile, allegations of corruption in the deal continued to appear in the media.[15] Next, on 30 June 2010, the Indian Department of Space recommended the annulment of the Antrix-Devas agreement, which the Indian Space Commission accepted on 2 July 2010.[16] This decision to annul the

5 These three Mauritius investors are: CC/Devas (Mauritius) Ltd. ("CC/Devas"), Devas Employees Mauritius Private Limited ("DEMPL"), and Telcom Devas Mauritius Limited ("Telcom Devas").
6 *CC/Devas v India* (n 1) paras 107–8.
7 *DT v India* (n 2) paras 69–70.
8 *CC/Devas v India* (n 1) para 200; *DT v India* (n 2) para 178.
9 *CC/Devas v India* (n 1) para 109.
10 ibid para 110.
11 ibid para 111.
12 *DT v India* (n 2) para 72.
13 ibid paras 71, 76.
14 ibid para 77.
15 ibid para 78.
16 ibid para 82; *CC/Devas v India* (n 1) para 468.

contract was made public by the Indian government on 8 February 2011[17] – more than seven months after the government decided to rescind the contract. Finally, on 17 February 2011, the Cabinet Committee on Security[18] (CCS) cancelled the Antrix-Devas agreement.[19] The reason offered was as follows:

> *taking note of the fact that Government policies with regard to allocation of the spectrum have undergone a change in the last few years and there has been an increased demand for allocation of spectrum for national needs, including for the needs of defence, para-military forces, railways, and other public utility services as well as for societal needs, and having regard to the needs of the country's strategic requirements, the Government will not be able to provide orbit slot in S-band to Antrix for commercial activities, including for those which are the subject matter of existing contractual obligations for S-band. In light of this policy of not providing orbit slot in S-Band to Antrix for commercial activities, the 'Agreement for the lease of space segment capacity on ISRO/Antrix S-Band spacecraft by Devas Multimedia Pvt. Ltd.' entered into between Antrix Corporation and Devas Multimedia Pvt. Ltd. on 28th January 2005 shall be annulled forthwith.*[20]

On 25 February 2011, Antrix notified Devas about the annulment of the contract due to a force majeure event.[21] Following the repeal of the agreement, Devas commenced arbitration proceedings, as per the contract, under the International Chamber of Commerce (ICC) against Antrix, alleging that the sudden repudiation of the contract by Antrix had breached Devas's rights.[22] The ICC tribunal ruled in favour of Devas, ordering Antrix to pay US$562.5 million as damages for the wrongful repudiation of the contract.[23] In late 2020, a US district court dismissed all of Antrix's claims and upheld the ICC award, ruling in favour of Devas.[24] Antrix also requested Indian courts to set aside the ICC arbitral award under Section 34 of the Arbitration and

17 *CC/Devas v India* (n 1) para 142; *DT v India* (n 2) para 86.

18 CCS is a select Cabinet committee that, among other matters, deals with all defence-related issues and comprises of the Prime Minister, the Minister of Home Affairs, the Minister of External Affairs, the Minister of Finance, and the Minister of Defence of the Indian government.

19 Press Information Bureau, Government of India, 'CCS Decides to Annul Antrix-Devas Deal' (February 2011) <https://pib.gov.in/newsite/PrintRelease.aspx?relid=69856> accessed 12 July 2023.

20 ibid.

21 *DT v India* (n 2) para 92.

22 *Devas Multimedia Private Limited v Antrix Corporation Limited*, ICC Case No 18051/CYK, Final Award, 14 September 2015.

23 ibid.

24 *Devas Multimedia Private Ltd v Antrix Corporation Limited*, C18–1360 TSZ (WD Wash, 4 November 2020).

Conciliation (A&C) Act.[25] Under the A&C Act, the courts can set aside an arbitral award on specific grounds, including public policy. This matter was eventually decided by the Delhi High Court, as is discussed later in the chapter.

In this chapter, we discuss the two BIT claims in Section 3.2. Here, the focus is on interpreting critical treaty provisions like the essential security interest, necessary as the nexus requirement and the FET provision, in light of the arbitral case law. Section 3.3 of the chapter examines the journey after issuing the ISDS awards against India. The emphasis here is India's corruption and fraud argument against Devas and how responsive courts have been to this charge. Next, in section 3.4, the chapter deals with Devas's second ISDS claim against India. Finally, section 3.5 concludes by drawing up the Yukos dimensions of this persistent spectrum saga.

3.2 BIT claims

3.2.1 The defence of essential security interest

In the ISDS claims brought against India by *CC/Devas* and *DT*, India invoked the essential security interest (ESI) defence. India argued that it repudiated the contract with Devas because its national security was at stake. This position is reflected in India's press release, as previously noted. India said that one of the key reasons for taking back the spectrum was its need for "defence" and "para-military forces". However, it is essential to note that apart from military needs, the press release also mentioned other reasons for taking back the spectrum, including the requirements of the railways, public utilities, and other societal needs. Nonetheless, both tribunals prioritized determining the extent to which national security reasons guided India's decision.

It is important to remember that unlike the General Agreement on Tariffs and Trade (GATT), which mentions general and security exceptions in separate provisions,[26] BITs, especially of the first-generation variety, often combine security exceptions with other general exceptions. For instance, Article 11(3) of the India-Mauritius BIT provides as follows:

> *The provisions of this Agreement shall not in any way limit the right of either Contracting Party to apply prohibitions or restrictions of any kind or take any other action which is directed to the protection of its essential security interests, or to the protection of public health or the prevention of diseases in pests and animals or plants.*

25 The Arbitration and Conciliation Act 1996 is the primary legislation in India dealing with arbitration, including international commercial arbitration (ICA).

26 See Articles XX and XXI of GATT. While Article XX contains the general exception clause covering public health, conservation of exhaustible natural resources, etc., Article XXI contains the security exceptions.

Thus, the aforementioned provision combines protecting ESIs with other non-security public policy objectives, including safeguarding public health and preventing diseases in animals and plants. Likewise, Article 12 of the India-Germany BIT provides as follows:

> *Nothing in this Agreement shall prevent either Contracting Party from applying prohibitions or restrictions to the extent necessary for the protection of its essential security interests or for the prevention of diseases and pests in animals or plants.*

In this provision, the protection of ESI exists along with other non-security objectives like safeguarding animal and plant health. In the international investment law literature, provisions like Articles 11(3) and 12 of the India-Mauritius and India-Germany BITs, respectively are known as non-precluded measures (NPM) provisions. An NPM provision in a BIT is a clause that does not preclude host States from adopting measures for the protection of public policy concerns like health, environment, etc., that may otherwise violate the treaty.[27] NPM provisions bestow regulatory latitude to countries to deviate from the substantive obligations in circumstances that warrant adopting public policies that prefer non-investment policy goals over investment protection. As Caroline Henckels argues, these NPM provisions perform a different function than carve-outs and reservations in investment treaties.[28] While carve-outs and exceptions isolate specific sectors or explicit policy areas (like taxation or issuance of compulsory licenses) from the scope of an investment treaty, NPMs aim to protect broad policy space for States to adopt measures for permissible objectives like health, environment, security, etc.[29]

Affirmative defence or permission

A critical issue regarding the interpretation of NPM provisions is whether they constitute affirmative defences or permissions.[30] Reading NPM provisions as affirmative defences implies that it provides policy space to the host State to adopt measures for attaining non-investment objectives that would otherwise

27 For general discussion on NPM provisions, see Dilini Pathirana and Mark McLaughlin, 'Non-Precluded Measures Clauses: Regimes, Trends and Practice' in International Investment Law and Arbitration' in Julien Chaisse, Leila Choukroune and Sufian Jusoh (eds), *Handbook of International Investment Law and Policy* (Springer 2020).

28 Caroline Henckels, 'Should Investment Treaties Contain Public Policy Exceptions?' (2018) 59 Boston College Law Review 2825, 2827–28.

29 ibid.

30 ibid; Wolfgang Alschner and Kun Hui, 'Missing in Action: General Public Policy Exceptions in Investment Treaties' in Lisa Sachs, Jesse Coleman and Lise Johnson (eds), *Yearbook on International Investment Law and Policy* (OUP 2018).

breach substantive BIT obligations.[31] Consequently, if a country's regulatory measure breaches BIT provisions like the FET standard, it may be excused if it falls within the scope of the NPM provision.[32] Some ISDS tribunals have viewed NPMs as affirmative defences.[33]

On the other hand, construing NPMs as permissions means carving out specific policy objectives mentioned in the NPM provision from the scope of the BIT.[34] As a result, the State can enact regulatory measures to pursue permissible policy areas. NPMs, as permissions, restrict the scope of the substantive BIT obligations.[35] If a host State enacts a measure following the NPM provision, the substantive BIT obligations do not apply to such a measure. For instance, the *Continental Casualty v Argentina* tribunal held that if a State regulatory measure falls under the NPM provision, such action would be outside the treaty's scope.[36]

The salience of this issue arises in the current context due to the *CC/Devas* and *DT* tribunals taking up the case of ESI before discussing whether India breached its BIT obligations like the FET and expropriation. The tribunal in *DT v India* cited the Annulment Committee decision in *CMS v Argentina* to hold that the substantive treaty provisions do not apply if the ESI clause applies.[37] Thus, it recognized the conception of the NPM provision as permission and not an affirmative defence. The *CC/Devas v India* tribunal too recognized the NPM provision as a permission, not an affirmative defence. It held that if a State properly invokes the national security exception, the treaty's provisions shall not apply to such a measure. Thus, the tribunal cannot hold it liable for paying compensation.[38]

Essential security interest

Let us understand how the two ISDS tribunals interpreted ESI in the NPM provisions in India's BITs with Mauritius and Germany. India-Mauritius and India-Germany BITs list ESI as a key permissible objective – a regulatory goal specifically listed in the NPM provision, granting countries the permission to

31 See Amelia Keene, 'The Incorporation and Interpretation of WTO-Style Environmental Exceptions in International Investment Agreements' (2017) 18 The Journal of World Investment & Trade 62.

32 See Jurgen Kurtz, *The WTO and International Investment Law: Converging Systems* (CUP 2015) 217–18.

33 See *CMS Gas Transmission Co v Argentine Republic*, ICSID Case No ARB/01/08, Decision on Annulment, 25 September 2007, para 129; *Bear Creek Mining Corporation v Republic of Peru*, ICSID Case No ARB/14/21, Award, 30 November 2017, para 475.

34 Henckels (n 28).

35 ibid 2832–34.

36 ibid paras 164, 168. See also *Copper Mesa Mining Corp v Republic of Ecuador*, PCA No 2012-2, Award, 15 March 2016, para 6.58.

37 *DT v India* (n 2) para 227.

38 *CC/Devas v India* (n 1) para 293.

pursue and achieve it actively. The tribunal in *CC/Devas v India* held that the words 'security interest' are qualified by 'essential'.[39] In other words, the State's action should not be directed at protecting any 'security interests' or ordinary 'security interests' but only those that are 'essential' or vitally important.[40]

Likewise, The *DT* tribunal qualified ESI's meaning by laying down its two critical elements, elucidating its natural meaning. First, the State's interests to be protected should be concerned with security and not public or other societal interests.[41] The tribunal placed interests under the ESI clause at a higher pedestal than other public interests because adopting a measure to protect ESI would imply the non-application of the treaty obligations to that measure.[42] On the other hand, when the State acts to protect non-security public interests, the situation is quite different. For example, if the State expropriates foreign investment for a public interest, the obligation to pay compensation would remain. Second, the security interests should be 'essential', that is, the interests at stake should relate to the core of State security.[43] In other words, the threshold to invoke the ESI clause is higher.

Notably, both these tribunals restricted the meaning or scope of ESI to pure security-related threats, such as military dangers like war, armed attack, or terrorism. Under this narrow definition, the *CC/Devas* tribunal held that India's decision to take back the spectrum for defence and para-military purposes was to protect ESI.[44] Although the tribunal rightly held that the ESI clause in Article 11(3) is not self-judging,[45] it accorded a wide degree of deference to India.[46] The tribunal held that it would not sit in judgement over national security matters since they relate to the existential core of the State.[47] Adhering to a broad extent of deference, the tribunal restrained itself from examining whether the military's needs for the spectrum were indispensable or

39 ibid para 234.

40 ibid para 235. This interpretation of ESI is not different from what other ISDS tribunals have held like *CMS v Argentina* (n 33) Award, 12 May 2005, para 361. (hereinafter '*CMS v Argentina*').

41 *DT v India* (n 2) para 236.

42 ibid.

43 ibid.

44 *CC/Devas v India* (n 1) para 354.

45 ibid para 219.

46 ibid paras 244–45, 354. Compare this with the approach of a few Argentine tribunals that did not provide deference to the State on the issue of *CMS v Argentina* (n 33) Award, 12 May 2005 para 374; *Enron Creditors Recovery Corporation (Formerly Enron Corporation) and Ponderosa Assets, LP v Argentine Republic*, ICSID Case No ARB/01/3, Award, 22 May 2007, para 332 (hereinafter '*Enron v Argentina*); *Sempra Energy International v Argentine Republic*, ICSID Case No ARB/02/16, Award, 28 September 2007, para 388 (hereinafter '*Sempra v Argentina*').

47 ibid para 245.

essential.[48] It accepted India's assertion that a part of the spectrum taken back was indeed for military and defence needs.

Nonetheless, the *CC/Devas* tribunal held that taking back the spectrum for other social objectives including the so-called strategic requirements did not qualify as a measure to protect ESI.[49] The *DT* tribunal also held that the spectrum needs of the armed forces and the paramilitary would be eligible as ESI.[50] Simultaneously, the tribunal determined that the spectrum requirement for societal needs such as train tracking and tele-education did not qualify as ESI.[51] According to the tribunal, reading these social objectives as part of the ESI clause will distort its natural meaning.[52]

Before these two cases, many tribunals dealing with claims brought by American investors against Argentina, under the US-Argentina BIT, interpreted the ESI clause.[53] As also mentioned in the introductory chapter, American investors brought these claims, challenging Argentina's regulatory measures aimed at tackling a severe financial and economic crisis.[54] Argentina invoked the ESI clause arguing that its severe economic crisis was an issue of national security. The Argentine tribunals agreed with Argentina and held that a non-military crisis like an economic one, in principle, can qualify as ESI.[55] For instance, the *LG&E v Argentina* tribunal held that a severe financial crisis leading to an entire economy being under siege, resulting in unprecedented challenges for the people is the same as a military invasion.[56] However, the Argentine tribunals

48 Ridhi Kabra, 'Return of the Inconsistent Application of the 'Essential Security Interest' Clause in Investment Treaty Arbitration: CC/Devas v India and Deutsche Telekom v India' (2019) 34(3) ICSID Review 723–53, 732. For a general discussion on deference and ESI in the context of ISDS see William W Burke-White and Andreas von Staden, 'Investment Protection in Extraordinary Times: The Interpretation and Application of Non-Precluded Measures Provisions in Bilateral Investment Treaties'(2008) 48(2) Virginia Journal of International Law 307–410.

49 *CC/Devas v India* (n 1) paras 354, 356.

50 *DT v India* (n 2) paras 281, 284. Although the tribunal's final finding on this issue was based on the interpretation of 'necessary', the nexus requirement.

51 ibid.

52 ibid.

53 Article XI of the US-Argentina BIT, which, contains the national security exception, provides as follows: "This Treaty shall not preclude the application by either Party of measures necessary for the maintenance of public order, the fulfilment of its obligations with respect to the maintenance or restoration of international peace or security, or the Protection of its own essential security interests".

54 For more on the Argentine crisis and the ISDS claims see José E Alvarez and Kathryn Khamsi, 'The Argentine Crisis and Foreign Investors' in Karl P Sauvant (ed), *Yearbook on International Investment Law and Policy* (OUP 2009) 379–478.

55 See *CMS v Argentina* (n 41); *Enron v Argentina* (n 47); *Sempra v Argentina* (n 47); LG&E Energy Corp, *LG&E Capital Corp and LG&E International Inc v Argentine Republic*, ICSID Case No ARB/02/1, Decision on Liability, 3 October 2016 (hereinafter '*LG&E v Argentina*'); *Continental Casualty Company v Argentine Republic*, ICSID Case No ARB/03/9, Award, 5 September 2008 (hereinafter '*Continental Casualty v Argentina*').

56 *LG&E v Argentina* (n 55) para 238.

differed on the high threshold for an economic crisis to qualify as an ESI. While some tribunals required that for the economic crisis to qualify as ESI, it should be so severe to lead to the 'total collapse' of the State,[57] others held that a threshold lower than 'total collapse' such as one where an economic crisis relentlessly undermines the economic, social, and political life and throws it out of gear, would be sufficient to qualify as ESI.[58]

Since the *CC/Devas* and *DT* tribunals restricted the meaning of ESI to pure security-related threats, their approach differs from the Argentine tribunals. This aspect makes the decisions of these two tribunals noteworthy. The *CC/Devas* and *DT* tribunals did not examine whether a non-military crisis of sufficient gravity would constitute an ESI because this was not an issue before them.[59]

Next, we discuss the nexus requirement, which played an essential role in the findings of the *CC/Devas* and *DT* tribunals concerning the NPM provision.

Nexus requirement

The nexus requirement is the connection between the adopted regulatory measure and the policy objective the measure seeks to accomplish. The degree of connection between the regulatory measure and the policy objective will depend on the text of the NPM provision. For instance, Article 11(3) of the India-Mauritius BIT states that the country's regulatory measures should be *directed to* achieving ESI. Here, 'directed to' is the nexus requirement. In contrast, Article 12 of the India-Germany BIT states that the regulatory measure adopted by the host State should be *necessary* to protect ESI. So, the nexus requirement here is 'necessary'. Since the meaning of 'necessary' differs from 'directed to', the degree of connection between the regulatory measure and the ESI will also vary between the two treaties. As the *DT* tribunal held, 'necessary', as a nexus requirement, implies a more stringent nexus between the regulatory measure adopted (cancellation of the contract) and the objective pursued (protection of ESI) when compared to 'directed to'.[60] In other words, a regulatory measure may be 'directed to' achieving a public policy objective. But this, on its own, will not make the measure 'necessary'. On the other

57 *CMS v Argentina* (n 41) para 355.

58 See *Continental Casualty v Argentina* (n 55) paras 179–81. See also Irene M Ten Cate, 'The Costs of Consistency: Precedent in Investment Treaty Arbitration' (2013) 51 Columbia Journal of Transnational Law 418, 429; Peter Tomka, 'Defenses Based on Necessity Under Customary International Law and on Emergency Clauses in Bilateral Investment Treaties' in Meg Kinnear and others (eds), *Building International Investment Law: The First 50 Years of ICSID* (Kluwer Law International 2015) 485.

59 Kabra (n 48) 736.

60 See *Deutsche Telekom* (n 2) para 288; *CC/Devas v India* (n 1) paras 230–43. See also Prabhash Ranjan, 'Non-Precluded Measures in Indian International Investment Agreements and India's Regulatory Power as a Host Nation' (2012) 2 (1) Asian Journal of International Law 21–58.

hand, if a measure is 'necessary' to achieve a public policy objective, it will be 'directed to' or 'directed at' achieving that objective.[61]

DIRECTED TO

One reason the *CC/Devas v India* case is significant is that, for the first time, it involved the interpretation of a nexus requirement other than 'necessary' in an NPM provision for pursuing ESI. So far, the Argentine cases – claims brought by American investors against Argentina under the US-Argentina BIT – have interpreted the NPM provision containing 'necessary' as the nexus requirement. The critical inquiry in all these cases was determining the point at which it can be established that the State's measures are 'necessary' for safeguarding ESI. Amongst these tribunals, *CMS*, *Enron*, and *Sempra* interpreted 'necessary' in the NPM provision based on the customary international law defence[62] given in Article 25 of the International Law Commission's Articles on Responsibility of States for Internationally Wrongful Acts (ARSIWA).[63] The necessity defence given in Article 25 that precludes wrongfulness can be invoked under very stringent conditions including when the measure adopted is the "only way" to safeguard an essential interest of the State.[64] On the other hand, the *Continental Casualty v Argentina* tribunal interpreted 'necessary' in the same NPM provision using a much less stringent approach known as the *least restrictive alternative measure* (LRM) test.[65] The *Continental Casualty v Argentina* tribunal laid down a two-prong LRM test to determine whether a measure is 'necessary'. First, it examined whether the measure contributed materially to the realization of the regulatory objective.[66] Second, it checked if alternative measures were reasonably available to the State that made an equivalent contribution to the regulatory objective and were less conflicting with international obligations.[67] The second step of this two-tiered test is LRM *strictō sēnsū*.

The pursuit of different approaches by the Argentine tribunal to interpret the same treaty term, 'necessary', has created uneven and contradictory

61 For interpretation of 'directed to' see Burke-White and von Staden (n 49) 342; Amit Sinha, 'Non-Precluded Measures Provisions in Bilateral Investment Treaties of South Asian Countries' (2017) 7 Asian Journal of International Law 227, 261.

62 See Jürgen Kurtz, 'Adjudging the Exceptional at International Investment Law: Security, Public Order and Financial Crisis' (2010) 59(2) The International and Comparative Law Quarterly 325–71.

63 James Crawford, *Articles on Responsibility of States for Internationally Wrongful Acts* (Cambridge University Press 2002).

64 ibid.

65 This is discussed later in the chapter. Different versions of the LRM test have been applied by international courts and tribunals. For instance, look at the jurisprudence of the World Trade Organization in cases like *Brazil-Measures Affecting Imports of Retreaded Tyres*, WT/DS332/AB/R (WTO AB 17 December 2007).

66 *Continental Casualty v Argentina* (n 55) paras 196, 198.

67 ibid para 198.

jurisprudence on this issue. Taking all these cases together, we get two approaches to determine the meaning of 'necessary' – one based on Article 25 of ARSIWA and the other less stringent one based on the LRM test.

Taking a clue from these disputes, the claimant in *CC/Devas v India* argued that the ESI exception could only be triggered when the measures adopted by the State are 'necessary' to safeguard a country's national security.[68] The tribunal did not agree. It held that the word 'necessary' is absent in Article 11(3) of the India-Mauritius BIT and thus, this NPM provision varies from the one the Argentine tribunals interpreted.[69] The tribunal said that when non-'necessary' nexus requirements like 'directed to' are given in the NPM provision, the host State is not required to demonstrate the necessity of the measure, that is, it is not required to show that the adopted measure was the only available option for safeguarding ESI.[70] In other words, even if alternative measures or options were available to the State, the measure adopted may be 'directed to' achieving ESI. Hence, if the adopted measure is connected to or is related to accomplishing ESI, it will satisfy the nexus requirement of 'directed to'. While this surely shows that the connection between the measure and the objective has to be less severe, it does not answer how less severe it should be.

The standard the *CC/Devas* tribunal ultimately applied was a lax one.[71] One of the claimants' arguments was that India did not offer a definite reason to reacquire the spectrum, which raised doubts about India's assertion that it needed the spectrum for defence purposes. As noted, India offered multiple or a mix of reasons for annulling the contract. By a majority, the tribunal held that this, on its own, did not prove that the measure was not 'directed to' the protection of ESI because it is not unusual in public administration that various reasons, including political ones, influence a government's decision.[72] In other words, just because India gave multiple reasons to reacquire the spectrum, it does not mean that the action to take back the spectrum was not 'directed to' protecting ESI. The tribunal did not pay much credence to the fact that although the spectrum was taken back allegedly for military needs, it was not given to the military for several years.[73] By majority, the tribunal concluded that 60 per cent of the S-band spectrum allocated could serve India's ESI.[74] The tribunal's reasoning shows that a tenuous link between the measure and the ESI was sufficient to prove that the said measure was 'directed to' protect the nation's security interest. The tribunal was highly deferential to India on this issue. In the same breadth, the tribunal held that taking back the remaining 40 per cent of the spectrum for other social purposes was not

68 *CC/Devas v India* (n 1) para 237.
69 ibid paras 238–39.
70 ibid para 243.
71 Kabra (n 48) 751.
72 *CC/Devas v India* (n 1) paras 329–30.
73 ibid paras 335, 372.
74 ibid para 372.

'directed to' protecting ESI. Thus, for this part, the substantive treaty provisions will apply.[75]

However, one arbitrator dissented.[76] As pointed out earlier, while the Cabinet Committee on Security decided to take back the spectrum allegedly for defence needs, the government did not allocate the spectrum to the military for several years. This was due to protracted debates and competing demands for the reacquired spectrum by different Indian government departments.[77] The Department of Telecom wished to use the reacquired spectrum for terrestrial and commercial purposes. On the other hand, the Department of Space wanted to utilize it for societal purposes. Finally, in 2015, after almost four years of reacquiring the spectrum, it was given to the military.[78]

This showed that there was no clarity of purpose in reacquiring the spectrum. If the government took back the spectrum for military purposes, that is, for the protection of ESI, one would have expected its instant allocation to the military. The needs of the military and the paramilitary appeared to be an excuse for what was essentially a political decision. Thus, the dissenting arbitrator held that the decision to take back the spectrum was not 'directed to' the protection of ESI.[79] In other words, the dissenting arbitrator required a stronger connection between the measure adopted and the regulatory objective (ESI) to pass muster under the 'directed to' requirement.

NECESSARY

One of the most controversial issues in international investment law scholarship has been the interpretation of 'necessary' in the NPM provision. As mentioned, the Argentine tribunals used different approaches to interpret 'necessary'. Some used the customary international law necessity defence given in Article 25 of the ARSIWA articles, while some used the LRM test. Tribunals adopt these different approaches because of a lack of definition of 'necessary' as a nexus requirement in most NPM provisions. India's recent investment treaties, based on the 2016 Model BIT, are an exception to this aspect. They indicate the meaning of 'necessary' in the NPM provision. For instance, Article 32 of the India-Belarus BIT provides:

> *in considering whether a measure is necessary, the tribunal shall take into account whether there was no least restrictive alternative measure reasonably available to a Party.*

75 ibid.

76 *CC/Devas (Mauritius) Ltd, Devas Employees Mauritius Private Limited and Telecom Devas Mauritius Limited v India*, UNCITRAL, PCA Case No 2013-9, Dissenting Opinion of David R. Haigh QC, para 3.

77 *CC/Devas v India* (n 1) para 335.

78 *DT v India* (n 2) para 276.

79 ibid paras 94–98.

A similar formulation for the determination of 'necessary' is given in India-Taiwan,[80] India-Kyrgyzstan,[81] and India-Brazil[82] BITs.[83] Thus, India's new investment treaty practice reveals adopting the LRM test to interpret 'necessary' in the NPM provision. This represents a significant development in the new and emerging investment treaty practice aimed at preserving the host State's right to regulate in the public interest.[84]

However, Article 12 of the India-Germany BIT, under which Deutsche Telekom brought the claim, does not define 'necessary'. Before the *DT* tribunal, the question was whether to interpret 'necessary' by relying on Article 25 of the ARSIWA articles or employing the LRM test. To answer this question, the *DT* tribunal first explained that the ESI clause in Article 12 substantially differs from the necessity defence in Article 25 of the ARSIWA.[85] As rightly held by the *DT* tribunal, this difference arises because the treaty-based ESI clause containing the treaty-based defence of necessity is subject to different conditions and serves a separate purpose compared to the customary law-based defence of necessity enshrined in Article 25 of the ARSIWA.[86] The customary international law-based necessity defence is subject to very stringent conditions, including the requirement that the measure adopted should be the only way to address an essential interest or the State must not have contributed to the situation of necessity.[87] These conditions are stricter than those in Article 12 of the India-Germany BIT.[88] Moreover, if a State's action falls under the treaty defence of necessity, it means that the State has not breached its international law obligations, including those contained in the BIT. Thus, the question of precluding wrongfulness under Article 25 of the ARSIWA does not arise.[89]

After clarifying that it will not use a strict standard of review, the *DT* tribunal laid down a two-prong test to interpret 'necessary'. First, for a measure to be 'necessary', it must be 'principally targeted' to protect the ESI; second, the measure should be objectively required to achieve the essential security goal, considering if there were alternative measures, reasonably available and least in conflict or more compliant with international legal obligations (LRM

80 See footnote 2 of India-Taiwan BIT 2002.
81 See footnote 6 of India-Kyrgyzstan BIT 2019.
82 See footnote 4 of India-Brazil BIT 2020.
83 For a detailed discussion on this see Prabhash Ranjan, '"Necessary" in Non-Precluded Measures Provisions in Bilateral Investment Treaties: The Indian Contribution' (2020) 67(3) Netherlands International Law Review 473–501.
84 ibid.
85 *Deutsche Telekom v Republic of India* (n 2) para 228.
86 ibid.
87 ibid para 229.
88 ibid.
89 See also *CMS Gas Transmission Co v The Republic of Argentina* (2007) (Annulment Proceedings) (ICISD Case No ARB/01/8) paras 129–31; *Sempra Energy International v The Argentine Republic* (2010) (Annulment Proceedings) (ICSID Case No ARB/02/16) para 200.

strictō sēnsū).[90] This two-tiered test is a version of the LRM approach discussed before. While the second step of this two-tiered test is the same as the one that the *Continental Casualty v Argentina* tribunal advocated,[91] the first step is different. As against the *Continental Casualty* tribunal's requirement that the adopted measure make a material contribution to the avowed objective, the *DT* tribunal only requires the measure to be 'principally targeted', that is, the measure should have the potential of contributing to the realization of the regulatory objective. As Kabra argues, the determination of whether the measure has the potential to contribute to accomplishing ESI is not the same as an actual contribution.[92] If the onus on the State were to show its measures have the potential to contribute to the protection of ESI rather than proving an actual or a real contribution, it would grant the State greater regulatory freedom. Policymaking is fraught with risks. It often involves making decisions amidst several variables and uncertainties. Thus, it is quite possible that the State, in good faith, might contemplate a measure believing it has the potential to contribute. Still, it may not make any material contribution. If a host State is chastised because it did not adopt a foolproof measure that decisively contributed to the objective, it will inflict a high restriction on the State's right to regulate.

Applying this theoretical understanding of 'necessary' to the facts, the *DT* tribunal concluded that India's measure was not 'necessary' to protect its ESI.[93] Three critical factors weighed heavily on the mind of the *DT* tribunal in reaching this decision. First, the fact that India referred to various needs, ranging from military to non-military, as the reason to take back the spectrum, which showed the absence of a clear purpose justifying the action.[94] Second, as the dissenting arbitrator in the *CC/Devas* case held, the fact that there were protracted debates between different branches of the Indian government on the use of the S-band spectrum after reacquiring it to safeguard national security also reveals a lack of clarity on its usage.[95] If the spectrum was needed for defence purposes, it should have been immediately assigned or allocated to the military. But, as already pointed out, the military got the spectrum in 2015, and that too the MSS part of the spectrum, that is only 10 MHz out of the 70 MHz that was reacquired.[96] Third, despite the shortage of the S-band spectrum for defence needs, which prompted the cancellation of the contract with Devas, the Department of Telecommunication of the Indian government was allowed to retain 40 MHz of the S-band spectrum for commercial purposes in 2015.[97] This means that a large part of the spectrum taken back was

90 *DT v India* (n 2) para 239.
91 *Continental Casualty v Argentina* (n 56) paras 196, 198.
92 Kabra (n 48) 723.
93 *DT v India* (n 2) paras 286, 291.
94 ibid para 286.
95 ibid para 288.
96 ibid para 276.
97 ibid para 290.

put for commercial use, not for safeguarding ESI, the avowed objective. These factors collectively elucidate that national security was a camouflage to support a politically motivated decision to cancel the contract due to the government getting cold feet over corruption allegations.[98]

In sum, the *DT* tribunal held that India's measure was not necessary to protect ESI, and thus, the substantive provisions of the BIT applied to the measure. Likewise, the *CC/Devas* tribunal held that the substantive provisions of the India-Mauritius BIT were applicable to the reacquisition of that part of the spectrum that was not for ESI. Next, we discuss the allegations that the reacquisition of the spectrum breached India's FET obligations under both treaties.

3.2.2 Violation of FET – India's smoke and mirrors approach

As mentioned earlier, foreign investors in both cases accused India of violating the FET provision. The FET provision in Article 4(1) of the India-Mauritius BIT provides as follows:

> *Investments and returns of investors of either Contracting Party shall at all times be accorded fair and equitable treatment in the territory of the other Contracting Party.*

Similarly, Article 3(2) of the India-Germany BIT includes the FET provision and states the following:

> *Each Contracting Party shall accord to investments as well as to investors in respect of such investments at all times fair and equitable treatment and full protection and security in its territory.*

Neither of the two treaties defines the FET provision. In both cases, India contended that the FET provision reflects the international minimum standard (IMS) of treatment under customary international law.[99] However, both tribunals disagreed because, textually, the two treaties do not link the FET provision to the IMS.[100] Therefore, FET provision cannot be restricted to the IMS standard. The tribunals gave an objective and autonomous interpretation of the FET standard. The *CC/Devas* tribunal held that a core component of the FET provision is the investor's legitimate expectations that the host State will deal with them in good faith.[101] Relying on other ISDS

98 For example, see Editorial, 'Behind the S-Band Spectrum Scandal' (*The Hindu*, 10 February 2011) <https://www.thehindu.com/opinion/editorial/Behind-the-S-band-spectrum-scandal/article13614709.ece> accessed 14 July 2023.
99 See *DT v India* (n 2) para 310; *CC/Devas v India* (n 1) paras 452–53.
100 *CC/Devas v India* (n 1) para 457; *DT v India* (n 2) para 331.
101 *CC/Devas v India* (n 1) paras 463–65.

tribunals like *Tecmed v Mexico*[102] and *Sempra v Argentina*,[103] the tribunal defined the good faith principle as a requirement of treating foreign investment in a manner that does not affect the basic expectations that the investor took into account at the time of making the investment.[104] While the *CC/Devas* tribunal can be legitimately criticized for invoking the subjective notions of investors' "basic expectations" into the calculus of determining good faith, its application of the principle to the facts exhibits a nuanced approach, as the chapter will explore in greater detail. In any case, quite a few ISDS tribunals have held that as part of the FET provision, the host State is required to act in good faith.[105] The tribunal in *Frontier Petroleum v Czech Republic* held that terminating an agreement with a foreign investor for reasons other than those advanced by the government is an example of the State not acting in good faith.[106] It is also important to note that a few tribunals like *Crystallex v Venezuela*[107] have held such practices as part of the State's arbitrary behaviour.[108]

The *DT* tribunal did not indulge in a detailed doctrinal exposition of the FET standard. Based on an objective and autonomous interpretation and relying on past ISDS decisions, the tribunal held that the FET standard includes protection of legitimate expectations, protection from arbitrary, unreasonable, and disproportionate State conduct that lacks good faith, and principles of transparency and due process.[109]

Both tribunals concluded that India's conduct breached the FET provision. After carefully analysing all the facts, the *CC/Devas* tribunal found that India decided to annul the contract with Devas on 2 July 2010. However, the claimants were not informed about this decision immediately. The claimants learned about the termination of the agreement on 8 February 2011 when the government publicly announced the decision. In other words, for more than seven months, the claimants were "completely left in the dark" about the space commission's decision and the alleged growing needs of the military about the spectrum.[110] The foreign investors were completely unaware of any impending developments within the government that could severely jeopardize their

102 *Técnicas Medioambientales Tecmed, SA v Mexico*, ICSID Case No ARB (AF)/00/2, Award, 29 May 2003, para 154.
103 *Sempra v Argentina* (n 47) para 298.
104 *CC/Devas v India* (n 1) para 467.
105 *Frontier Petroleum v Czech Republic*, Final Award, 12 November 2010, para 300 (hereinafter '*Frontier Petroleum v Czech Republic*'); *Saluka v Czech Republic*, Partial Award, 17 March 2006, para 307. See also Ursula Kriebaum, Christoph Schreuer and Rudolf Dolzer, *Principles of International Investment Law* (3rd edn, OUP 2022) 228.
106 *Frontier Petroleum v Czech Republic* (n 108) para 307.
107 *Crystallex International Corporation v Bolivarian Republic of Venezuela*, ICSID Case No ARB(AF)/11/2, Award, 4 April 2016.
108 ibid para 578.
109 *DT v India* (n 2) para 336.
110 *CC/Devas v India* (n 1) para 468.

investment.[111] In these seven months, the officials of Devas and DT met various Indian government officials, including the national security advisor who reports directly to the Prime Minister.[112] However, the officials did not share this decision with the Devas and DT officials, at any of these meetings.[113]

On the contrary, as the *DT* tribunal held, India positively misled foreign investors by assuring them that the project was on track.[114] The tribunal rejected India's argument that since this matter involved security issues, it was not shared with the investor.[115] India was not required to share classified or sensitive national security information with investors. But, it could have at least indicated to the investor that a portion of the spectrum was needed by the military, which would have alerted the investors about the changing situation.[116]

Moreover, India's decision to annul the agreement was arbitrary and unjustified because "it was manifestly not based on facts, but on conclusory allegations, and was the product of a flawed process".[117] As discussed, India offered the growing military and defence needs for the S-band spectrum as the reason to terminate the contract. However, India's cabinet secretary, in a note to the Prime Minister, gave the following reason for annulment: "since the agreement has now had to be cancelled on account of reasons related to non-transparency and one-sided skew in risk-sharing arrangements, ISRO/DoS [Department of Space] are left with a satellite . . . which has no immediate commercial application".[118] As discussed, India did not cite these reasons for cancelling the contract. Thus, it is pretty evident that the substantial reason to cancel the agreement was something else, not the expanding needs of the military and the paramilitary. The reasons professed were a smokescreen for the real reason: fear of another political scandal breaking out due to alleged wrongdoings in the deal. At that time, the central government was battling several such corruption allegations.[119] It wanted to avoid another controversy and thought exiting the deal would be a face-saver. The *CC/Devas* tribunal recognized that India repudiated the contract due to fear of a political

111 ibid. Also see *DT v India* (n 2) para 388.
112 *CC/Devas v India* (n 1) para 468.
113 ibid.
114 *DT v India* (n 2) para 376.
115 ibid para 377.
116 ibid.
117 ibid para 363.
118 ibid para 357. The Cabinet Secretary, Mr. KM Chandrashekhar, in his recommendation (also known as the Chandrashekhar note) submitted that investigations be launched into the possible violations of the Foreign Exchange Management Act or FEMA and the Prevention of Money Laundering Act by Devas – see *Deutsche Telekom AG v The Republic of India* [2023] SGHC(I) 7, para 35.
119 See 'UPA Report Card: Nine Years, Nine Scams' *India Today* <https://www.indiatoday.in/india/photo/upa-govt-9-years-9-scams-sonia-manmohan-369868-2013-05-22/1> accessed 14 July 2023.

scandal.[120] If the real purpose of cancelling the contract was suspicion of corruption, India should have offered this as the reason. In sum, India terminated the contract for reasons other than those professed, which points to the arbitrariness of the decision.

The developments after the annulment of the contract corroborate this point. Since the spectrum was denied to Devas for the purported mounting military needs, it should have been allocated to the military immediately after the annulment. However, as previously highlighted, the Indian government kept discussing how to use the spectrum for four years.[121] Moreover, as established by the *DT* tribunal, India did not make any attempt to initiate a dialogue with the investors to reconcile the alleged increase in military requirements.[122]

Based on these facts, both tribunals held that India violated the FET obligation. Specifically, the *CC/Devas* tribunal held that India's conduct constitutes a clear breach of the simple good faith required under international law and the FET provision of the India-Mauritius BIT.[123] The tribunal's ultimate finding of violation of good faith wasn't based on the "basic expectations" of the foreign investor but on lack of transparency and arbitrariness. The tribunal found India liable for this wrongful behaviour and held that it must compensate the claimants for damages suffered from 2 July 2010 to 17 February 2011 – the date of the CCS decision.[124] Accordingly, in its award on quantum delivered in 2020, the tribunal ordered India to pay US$160 million plus accrued interest as damages to *CC/Devas*.[125]

The *DT* tribunal particularly concluded that India's conduct demonstrates a "wilful disregard of due process of law", which shocks or at least surprises a sense of judicial propriety, resulting in a violation of the FET standard.[126] In its final award issued on 27 May 2020, the *DT* tribunal ordered India to pay the investor damages of US$132 million.[127]

Both CC/Devas and DT also alleged that the cancellation of the contract amounted to an indirect expropriation of their investment. The subsequent section discusses what the tribunals said on the issue of expropriation of foreign investment.

120 ibid para 322.
121 ibid paras 274–76.
122 ibid para 376.
123 *CC/Devas v India* (n 1) para 470.
124 ibid para 470.
125 *CC/Devas (Mauritius) Ltd, Devas Employees Mauritius Private Limited, and Telcom Devas Mauritius Limited v Republic of India*, PCA Case No 2013-9, Award on Quantum, 13 October 2020.
126 *DT v India* (n 2) para 389.
127 *Deutsche Telekom AG v The Republic of India*, PCA Case No 2014-10, Final Award, 27 May 2020.

3.2.3 Expropriation

The *CC/Devas* tribunal undertook a curious examination of whether India's regulatory measure amounted to expropriation. To understand this point better, let us look at the relevant part of the expropriation provision given in Article 6(1) of the India-Mauritius BIT. The first sentence of Article 6(1) provides as follows:

> *Investments of investors of either Contracting Party in the territory of the other Contracting Party shall not be nationalised, expropriated or subjected to measures having effects equivalent to nationalisation or expropriation except for public purposes, under due process of law, on a non-discriminatory basis and against fair and equitable compensation.*

The host State is not precluded from expropriating foreign investment as long as it is lawful. To determine whether a host State has breached the expropriation provision in the BIT will involve two analytical steps.[128] First, the tribunal must determine whether an expropriation has taken place. In other words, if the allegation is of indirect expropriation, the tribunal should find out whether the regulatory measure has resulted in a substantial deprivation of foreign investment.[129] If the answer to the first question is no, the conclusion will be that the State has not engaged in expropriation. However, if the answer is in the affirmative, the second step will be to determine whether expropriation is lawful.[130] This would include examining whether the State has expropriated the investment for a public purpose, following due process of law, on a non-discriminatory basis and against fair and equitable compensation. If the host State expropriates investment satisfying all these requirements cumulatively, it will be a lawful conduct, and thus not a breach of the BIT.

Interestingly, the *CC/Devas* tribunal, instead of following this two-step analytical test, simply presumed that the expropriation provision covered India's reacquisition of 40 per cent of the S-band spectrum.[131] As already discussed, the tribunal held that 60 per cent of the reacquired spectrum was for the protection of ESI. For the remaining 40 per cent, the tribunal held "by majority" that since it was "allocated for other public interest purposes", it was "subject to the expropriation conditions under Article 6 of the Treaty".[132] Thus, the

128 Jürgen Kurtz, 'Building Legitimacy Through Interpretation' in Zachary Douglas and others (eds), *The Foundations of International Investment Law: Bringing Theory into Practice* (OUP 2010) 290–91.

129 List here a few latest ISDS cases that have used substantial deprivation test to determine indirect expropriation.

130 Kurtz (n 128) 290–91.

131 *CC/Devas v India* (n 1) para 373.

132 ibid para 373.

tribunal's reasoning seems to be that since 40 per cent of the S-band spectrum was taken for public purposes instead of security purposes, it falls under the ambit of the expropriation provision in Article 6.

As noted, under Article 6, the State can adopt regulatory measures for public purposes even if such an action leads to the expropriation of foreign investment. However, under Article 6, whether measures qualify as public purposes becomes relevant only when it is first established that expropriation has occurred. In other words, the threshold for examining whether the State's regulatory measures are for public purposes is the expropriation of foreign investment. Just because a State's measure is for public purpose does not mean that it automatically falls under the expropriation provision. In fact, governmental measures adopted for accomplishing public purposes that do not result in a substantial deprivation of foreign investment shall not come under the purview of Article 6. Accordingly, the *CC/Devas* tribunal's reasoning is specious. Without answering the fundamental question of whether India's decision to take back 40 per cent of the spectrum led to substantial deprivation of foreign investment, it examined if India's measure ticked all the boxes for the expropriation to be lawful.[133] The tribunal concluded that since India did not compensate the investor, it violated the expropriation provision of the India-Mauritius BIT.[134]

The *DT* tribunal, for judicial economy, dispensed with the requirement of determining whether India's regulatory measure amounted to expropriation.[135] Since the tribunal had already found India's conduct to be in breach of the FET provision, an adverse finding on expropriation would not have made any difference.

India has not complied with these awards. India has vigorously pursued a strategy aimed at challenging the ISDS awards at their seats of arbitration to get them set aside. The chapter now turns its focus to discussing these aspects.

3.3 The journey after the awards

The developments that have taken place after the issuance of these two ISDS awards against India and the ICC award against Antrix have been quite riveting. The discussion here is in three parts. First, the chapter deals with the 'fraud' argument that resulted in the winding up of Devas. Second, the chapter examines whether foreign courts have given credence to India's argument of fraud to set aside the ISDS awards. Third, the chapter looks at the amendment to the Arbitration and Conciliation Act (A&C) that directly impacted the enforcement of Devas's ICC award against Antrix.

133 ibid paras 412–22.
134 ibid paras 422, 425.
135 *DT v India* (n 2) para 416.

3.3.1 The 'fraud' argument

When the Devas-Antrix deal was inked, the United Progressive Alliance (UPA) – a centre-left political coalition headed by the Indian National Congress – India's oldest political party – ruled India. As pointed out before, several corruption allegations were made against the UPA government, including allocating the S-band spectrum to Devas.[136] In power since 2004, the UPA government was voted out in May 2014. A new government, the National Democratic Alliance (NDA) – a right-wing conservative alliance headed by the Bhartiya Janata Party (BJP) – came to power in May 2014 on an anti-corruption plank. Holding the UPA government accountable for its alleged corruption deals occupied a salient position on the agenda of the NDA regime. Thus, the new government sharpened its attack on the Devas-Antrix deal since it believed it was mired in corruption. As soon as the new government came into office, the Central Bureau of Investigation (CBI) – India's national crime-investigating agency – launched a criminal investigation into this case. In, 2015 the CBI filed a first information report (FIR) for criminal conspiracy and cheating.[137] The CBI alleged that the Devas-Antrix deal resulted in a wrongful gain of 578 crore rupees (approximately US$73 million) to Devas Multimedia.[138] In 2016, the CBI filed a chargesheet against several ISRO and Devas officials.[139] CBI accused these officials of committing various offences under the Indian Penal Code, such as cheating and violating multiple provisions of the Prevention of Corruption Act of 1998.[140] In early 2017, the Enforcement Directorate (ED) – a domestic law enforcement agency in India mandated to fight economic offences – seized nearly 80 crore rupees (approximately US$10 million) of Devas under the Prevention of Money Laundering Act.[141] The CBI filed a supplementary chargesheet against ISRO and Devas officials in 2019 to bolster its criminal investigation.[142]

136 Reuters Staff, 'India Govt Hit by Two New Telecom Scandals-Reports' *Reuters* (8 February 2011) <https://www.reuters.com/article/india-telecoms-scandal-idUSSGE71702F20110208> accessed 14 July 2023.

137 Neeraj Chauhan, 'Antrix-Devas Deal: CBI Registers Case Against Senior Officials' *Times of India* (19 March 2015) <https://timesofindia.indiatimes.com/india/antrix-devas-deal-cbi-registers-case-against-senior-officials/articleshow/46610844.cms> accessed 14 July 2023.

138 ibid.

139 PTI, 'CBI Files Chargesheet in Antrix-Devas Deal, Names Ex-ISRO Chief Madhavan Nair' *The Deccan Herald* (11 August 2016) <https://www.deccanherald.com/content/563784/cbi-files-chargesheet-antrix-devas.html> accessed 14 July 2023.

140 ibid.

141 IANS, 'ED Attaches Rs 80 Crore of Devas in Antrix Deal' *The Business Standard* (28 February 2017) <https://www.business-standard.com/article/news-ians/ed-attaches-rs-80-crore-of-devas-in-antrix-deal-117022801000_1.html> accessed 14 July 2023. The Prevention of Money Laundering Act in India is a legislation aimed at fighting against the crime of legalizing the income or profits derived from an illegal source.

142 *Devas Multimedia (P) Ltd v Antrix Corporation Ltd* (2023) 1 SCC 216, para 15.

In light of the initiation of the criminal investigation for fraud and corruption, India in October 2016, after the *CC/Devas* tribunal had issued the award on jurisdiction and merits, requested the tribunal to stay its proceedings till the time the Indian courts decided on the fraud and corruption allegations contained in the CBI chargesheet.[143] India argued that if Indian courts were to uphold the fraud and corruption charges, it would make the Devas-Antrix contract void *ab initio* under Indian law.[144] This, in turn, will mean that the investment made in India was not in accordance with Indian laws and regulations. Consequently, treaty protection will not be available for such an investment.[145]

The *CC/Devas* tribunal dismissed India's contention, holding it has "exclusive subject matter jurisdiction" on the issues brought before it under the India-Mauritius BIT.[146] The fact that there are legal issues before Indian courts does not affect the tribunal's determinations.[147] Thus, the tribunal went on to adjudicate the case of the quantum of compensation and delivered an award in 2020, as already pointed out.

India raised the same objection before the *DT* tribunal.[148] The *DT* tribunal also declined India's contention because it was not timely.[149] Notably, the tribunal also held that even if India's assertion were timely, it would have rejected it on merits.[150] According to the tribunal, India did not substantiate its corruption claim, which was not yet proven in a court of law. The tribunal also held that none of India's corruption or fraud claims was related to DT. In other words, India could not substantiate how DT's investment in India, made through the acquisition of shares in Devas, would have been contrary to Indian law.[151]

Winding up of Devas

Although India failed before international forums in invoking the corruption and fraud argument to stay arbitral proceedings, this contention was successfully raised before Indian courts. The difference is that the issue of corruption before the Indian judicial authorities was not raised in connection with the ICC or the two BIT arbitral proceedings. But they were introduced to show

143 *CC/Devas (Mauritius) Ltd, Devas Employees Mauritius Private Limited, and Telcom Devas Mauritius Limited v Republic of India*, PCA Case No 2013-9, Procedural Order No 7 (Concerning the Respondent's Request for Suspension of the Proceedings, 21 December 2016).
144 ibid para 6.
145 ibid.
146 ibid para 15.
147 ibid.
148 *DT v India* (n 2) para 115.
149 ibid paras 117–18.
150 ibid para 119.
151 ibid.

that the incorporation of Devas was for fraudulent purposes, warranting its winding up. In early 2021, Antrix, after obtaining approval from the Ministry of Corporate Affairs, petitioned the National Company Law Tribunal (NCLT) to wind up Devas under Section 271(c) of the Companies Act.[152] Section 271(c) of the Companies Act provides as follows:

> *A company may . . . be wound up by a tribunal if on an application made by the Registrar or any other person authorised by the Central Government by notification under this Act, the Tribunal is of the opinion that the affairs of the company have been conducted in a fraudulent manner or the company was formed for fraudulent and unlawful purpose or the persons concerned in the formation or management of its affairs have been guilty of fraud, misfeasance or misconduct in connection therewith and that it is proper that the company be wound up.*

Stated differently, Section 271(c) allows for the winding up of a company in three conditions related to fraudulent practices. First, if the company has conducted its affairs fraudulently. Second, if the creation of the company was to accomplish or further fraudulent and unlawful purposes. Third, if the persons related to the formation of the company or responsible for the management of the company have been found guilty of fraud, misfeasance, or misconduct.

The NCLT agreed with the petitioners.[153] The NCLT was highly deferential to the petitioner and, therefore, the Indian government in this case. Based on the facts presented to the NCLT by the petitioner, it held that since Devas was incorporated on 17 December 2004 and obtained the contract on 28 January 2005, within a timeframe of less than 45 days, it raises doubts about the competence of Devas to sign such a deal.[154] The tribunal also said that Devas lacked the technical expertise to fulfill a contract of this nature.[155] It is unclear how these facts, on their own, show that Devas's incorporation was for fraudulent reasons. It is quite possible that a company may not have the technical ability at the time of its incorporation, but it may develop competence along the way. Arguably, the investment of DT – one of the world's leading telecommunications companies with an impeccable record – in Devas was for building technical capability. Astonishingly, the NCLT said that Devas initiated an ICC arbitration against Antrix because the latter annulled the contract is also an example of the former continuing its fraudulent activities.[156] Regardless,

152 ibid para 3.14.
153 *Devas Employees Mauritius (P) Ltd v Antrix Corporation Ltd* [2021] SCC Online NCLT 484.
154 ibid.
155 ibid.
156 ibid.

the NCLT finally concluded that the establishment of Devas was indeed for deceitful motives and unlawful objectives and, thus, ordered its liquidation.[157]

The National Company Law Appellate Tribunal (NCLAT) upheld the NCLT order.[158] The Supreme Court of India, in turn, upheld the NCLAT order, in January 2022.[159] The Supreme Court allowed the winding up of Devas under Section 271(c) of the Companies Act. In this context, it is essential to mention that the criminal charge of collusion or conspiracy between Devas and some officials of Antrix that allegedly caused a wrongful gain to Devas has not yet been proven in an Indian court.[160] It is unclear what 'standard of proof' the Supreme Court followed to reach this conclusion. Like the NLCT and NCLAT, the apex court's approach was deferential to Antrix and the Indian government.[161]

Devas argued before the Supreme Court that Antrix's winding up petition, backed by the Indian government, was motivated by the latter's intention to deprive the former of the benefits accruing under the ICC and the two BIT awards.[162] However, the Supreme Court refused this contention, holding that,

> *if as a matter of fact, fraud as projected by Antrix, stands established, the motive behind the victim of fraud, coming up with a petition for winding up, is of no relevance. If the seeds of the commercial relationship between Antrix and Devas were a product of fraud perpetrated by Devas, every part of the plant that grew out of those seeds, such as the Agreement, the disputes, arbitral awards etc., are all infected with the poison of fraud. A product of fraud is in conflict with the public policy of any country including India.*

Although the enforcement of the ICC or the two BIT awards was not a matter before the court, it indicated that the arbitral awards were also affected by what the court called "poison of fraud" and thus violated public policy. This was an unblemished direction to any court in India to disallow the enforcement of these awards if such a matter came before them.

For this reason, it didn't come as a surprise when the Delhi High Court, in August 2022, agreed to set aside the ICC award in favour of Devas, holding

157 ibid.

158 Ayushi Kar, 'NCLAT Upholds Order to Wind Up Devas Multimedia' *Business Line* (9 September 2021) <https://www.thehindubusinessline.com/companies/nclat-upholds-order-to-wind-up-devas-multimedia/article36366124.ece> accessed 14 July 2023. See also *Devas Multimedia (P) Ltd v Antrix Corporation Ltd* (n 153) 448.

159 *Devas v Antrix* (n 145).

160 Avi Singh, 'India's Response in Antrix-Devas Fiasco Has Landed It in a Mess' *The Quint* (28 January 2022) <https://www.thequint.com/opinion/indias-response-in-antrix-devas-fiasco-has-landed-it-in-a-mess#read-more> accessed 14 July 2023.

161 ibid.

162 ibid.

that the award suffered from patent illegalities and fraud.[163] The court held that the award was against the public policy of India and was liable to be set aside under Section 34 of the A&C Act.[164] The Division Bench of the Delhi High Court upheld this decision.[165]

3.3.2 Foreign courts and the fraud argument

Since India hasn't complied with the ISDS awards, Devas and DT have been making several efforts to enforce their awards in multiple jurisdictions like the Netherlands,[166] Canada,[167] the United States,[168] and Singapore.[169] India, on its part, armed with the 2022 Supreme Court judgement that upheld the winding up of Devas due to its creation being for fraudulent purposes, has been trying to defend itself in these proceedings. However, foreign courts have not been sympathetic to India's assertion. For instance, the Dutch Supreme Court dismissed India's bid to set aside the *CC/Devas v India* award.[170] Likewise, the Higher Regional Court of Berlin, while hearing India's argument on the issue of fraud during the enforcement proceeding of the DT award, held that India failed to provide any evidence of involvement of DT in any fraudulent activity.[171] India could not show a direct connection between fraud allegations against Devas and DT's action. The court recalled that DT acquired shares in

163 *Antrix Corporation Ltd v Devas Multimedia (P) Ltd* [2022] SCC Online Del 2622.

164 ibid.

165 *Devas Employees Mauritius (P) Ltd v Antrix Corporation Ltd* [2023] SCC Online Del 1608.

166 Ayushi Kar, 'Devas-Antrix Dispute: Netherlands Top Court Refuses to Overturn $111.3 Million Award Against India' *Business Line* (6 February 2023) <https://www.thehindubusinessline.com/info-tech/devas-antrix-dispute-netherlands-top-court-refuses-to-overturn-1113-award-against-india/article66478312.ece> accessed 16 July 2023.

167 Prabhash Ranjan, 'A Big Blow to India: Canadian Court's Decision in Antrix-Devas Matter Shows the Issue Is Far from Resolved' *Indian Express* (11 February 2023) <https://indianexpress.com/article/opinion/columns/a-big-blow-to-india-canadian-courts-decision-in-antrix-devas-matter-shows-the-issue-is-far-from-resolved-8437667/> accessed 16 July 2023. See also PTI, 'Canada Court Allows Devas Shareholders to Continue Seizure of 50% of Air India's Funds' *The Wire* (10 January 2022) <https://thewire.in/business/canada-court-allows-devas-shareholders-to-continue-seizure-of-50-of-air-indias-funds> accessed 16 July 2023.

168 Ayushi Kar, 'Devas Multimedia Wins Award of $87,457 Against Antrix in US Court' *Business Line* (17 August 2022) <https://www.thehindubusinessline.com/info-tech/devas-multimedia-wins-award-of-875-thousand-against-antrix-in-us-courts/article65779837.ece> accessed 16 July 2023.

169 Jack Ballantyne, 'Singapore Court Denies India's Fraud Challenge' (*Global Arbitration Review*, 12 May 2023) <https://globalarbitrationreview.com/article/singapore-court-denies-indias-fraud-challenge>.

170 *Republic of India v CC/Devas*, High Council of the Netherlands (3 February 2023) <https://www.italaw.com/sites/default/files/case-documents/italaw171245.pdf> accessed 20 July 2023.

171 *Republic of India v Deutsche Telekom*, Judgment of the Higher Regional Court of Berlin 12 Sch 7/21 (26 January 2023) <https://jusmundi.com/en/document/decision/

Devas's investment as per the Indian law.[172] Referring to the decision of the Indian Supreme Court in the Devas case, the German court held that there were no concrete facts regarding any fraudulent activity of DT in the Supreme Court judgement.[173] Thus, according to the court, linking DT to the Supreme Court's judgement on Devas wasn't apposite.[174]

India's 'fraud' arguments met the same fate in the Singapore International Commercial Court (SICC) during DT's enforcement proceedings in January 2023.[175] India challenged DT's enforcement proceedings, arguing that the latter's investment fell outside the scope of Article 9 of the BIT that the former signed with Germany.[176] Article 9 of the India-Germany BIT – the investment treaty DT used to sue India – contains the ISDS clause.[177] As per Article 9, an investor can bring a claim against a State only if she has made an "investment" in the host State's territory. An "investment", as per Article 1(b) of the India-Germany BIT, should be made following the host State's laws.[178] That is, if an investment is made in breach of the host State's laws it will not be eligible for treaty protection. Of the multiple reasons India offered to challenge the enforcement of the award, one pertained to DT having made an "illegal" investment in India.[179] India's illegality argument sprung from the Supreme Court judgement that upheld the decision of Devas's incorporation for fraudulent purposes. India argued that when DT invested in Devas in 2008 it conducted due diligence and that this due diligence should have alerted it about Devas's fraud.[180] Yet, DT continued with the investment, which makes it

en-deutsche-telekom-ag-v-the-republic-of-india-judgment-of-the-higher-regional-court-of-berlin-thursday-26th-january-2023> accessed 21 July 2023.

172 ibid para 32.

173 ibid para 39.

174 ibid.

175 *Deutsche Telekom AG v The Republic of India* [2023] SGHC(I) 7 (hereinafter *DT v India, SICC*).

176 ibid para 42.

177 Article 9 (1) of the India-Germany BIT provides as follows: "Any dispute between an investor of one Contracting Party and the other Contracting Party in connection with an investment in the territory of the other Contracting Parry shall, as far as possible, be settled amicably through negotiations between the parties to the dispute. The party intending to resolve such dispute through negotiations shall give notice to the other of its intentions". Article 9 (2) states: "If the dispute cannot be thus resolved as provided in paragraph l of this Article within six months from the date of notice given thereunder, then the dispute may be referred to conciliation in accordance with the United Nations Commission on International Trade Law Rules on Conciliation, 1980, if both parties agree. If either party does not agree to conciliation or if conciliation fails, either party may refer such dispute to arbitration in accordance with the United Nations Commission on International Trade Law Rules on Arbitration, 1976".

178 Article 1(b) of India-Germany BIT states: " 'Investment' means every kind of asset invested in accordance with the national laws of the Contracting Party where the investment is made".

179 *DT v India, SICC* (n 175) para 47.

180 ibid para 48.

either complicit or tainted in the perpetration of fraud.[181] However, the SICC disagreed with India. The court held that even if one were to proceed on the assumption that Devas was engaged in fraudulent misrepresentation, DT couldn't have known about it despite conducting due diligence.[182] If India, as a sovereign nation and despite having all the investigative and regulatory agencies at its disposal, could not detect Devas's fraud, it is foolhardy to expect DT to have accomplished this task.[183] Thus, the court held that India could not prove that DT's investment in India was unlawful.

Likewise, India challenged the DT award in the Swiss courts based on the Supreme Court's 2022 judgement. However, the Swiss Federal Supreme Court, too, rejected India's contention in a judgement dated 8 March 2023.[184]

3.3 Amendment of the A&C Act

Another vital issue in the Devas-Antrix context is the amendment to the A&C Act in 2021.[185] This amendment was preceded by an ordinance brought in 2020 to amend the A&C Act.[186] As highlighted earlier and in Chapter 2, the A&C Act is the primary legislation in India dealing with domestic and foreign arbitration.[187] The A&C Act is divided into two parts – Part I applies to all arbitrations including ICAs seated in India,[188] and Part II deals with recognizing and enforcing foreign arbitral awards[189] under the New York Convention 1958 (NYC).[190] Part I of the A&C Act contains provisions governing each aspect of arbitration in India, such as arbitration agreement, arbitral

181 ibid.
182 ibid para 75.
183 ibid.
184 *Deutsche Telekom AG v The Republic of India*, PCA Case No 2014-10, Decision of the Swiss Federal Tribunal 4A_184/2022 (8 March 2023) <https://jusmundi.com/en/document/decision/en-deutsche-telekom-ag-v-the-republic-of-india-decision-of-the-swiss-federal-tribunal-4a-184-2022-wednesday-8th-march-2023#decision_47713>.
185 The Arbitration and Conciliation (Amendment) Bill (2021) <https://prsindia.org/files/bills_acts/bills_parliament/2021/Arbitration%20and%20Conciliation%20(Amendment)%20Bill,%202021.pdf>.
186 The Arbitration and Conciliation (Amendment) Ordinance (2020) <https://prsindia.org/billtrack/the-arbitration-and-conciliation-amendment-ordinance-2020#:~:text=The%20Arbitration%20and%20Conciliation%20(Amendment)%20Ordinance%2C%202020%20was%20promulgated,law%20for%20conducting%20conciliation%20proceedings>.
187 See, Indu Malhotra, *OP Malhotra on law and Practice of Arbitration and Conciliation* (Thomson Reuters 2014); RS Bachawat, *Law of Arbitration and Conciliation* (LexisNexis 2010).
188 See, Arbitration and Conciliation Act (n 25) pt I, ss 1–43.
189 See, ibid pt II, ss 44–60; Part II also deals with the enforcement of the awards rendered in the States which are parties to the Convention on the Execution of Foreign Arbitral Awards, 1927.
190 Convention on the Recognition and Enforcement of Foreign Arbitral Awards (adopted 10 June 1958, entered into force 7 June 1959) ('NYC 1958').

procedure, instances where courts can intervene, awards and their enforcement, etc.[191] Under Section 36 of the A&C Act,[192] an arbitral award rendered in India is enforceable following the provisions of the Civil Procedure Code in the same manner as if it were a decree of a court.

However, the A&C Act also contains provisions for setting aside the arbitral award in certain conditions.[193] Section 36(3) allows a court to stay the operation of an arbitral award for reasons that it deems fit, which are to be recorded in writing. The 2021 amendment has added a proviso as follows:

> *where the Court is satisfied that a Prima facie case is made out that, – (a) the arbitration agreement or contract which is the basis of the award; or (b) the making of the award, was induced or effected by fraud or corruption, it shall stay the award unconditionally pending disposal of the challenge under section 34 to the award.*
>
> *Explanation – For the removal of doubts, it is hereby clarified that the above proviso shall apply to all court cases arising out of or in relation to arbitral proceedings, irrespective of whether the arbitral or court proceedings were commenced prior to or after the commencement of the Arbitration and Conciliation (Amendment) Act, 2015 (3 of 2016).*

So, the new amendment states that if a *prima facie* case is made of fraud or corruption, not just in the making of the arbitral award, but even the arbitration agreement or the contract, which is the basis of the award, the award shall be stayed unconditionally pending the disposal of the challenge made to the award under Section 34. In other words, if a *prima facie* case is established that a contract, signed between two or more entities, is affected by fraud or corruption, any arbitral award arising out of that contract shall be stayed unconditionally.

The preceding explanation gives Section 36(3) a retrospective effect in those cases where the court or arbitral proceedings have already begun, irrespective of whether they started before or after the 2015 amendment. One object and reason for bringing in the 2021 amendment is "to address the issue of corrupt practices in securing contracts or arbitral awards".[194] Thus, the amendment aims to "ensure that all the stakeholder parties get an opportunity to seek an unconditional stay of enforcement of arbitral awards, where the underlying arbitration agreement or contract or making of the arbitral award is

191 See, Arbitration and Conciliation Act (n 25) ss 35–36.

192 Section 36(1) of the ACA 1996 – "*Enforcement – (1) Where the time for making an application to set aside the arbitral award under section 34 has expired, then, subject to the provisions of sub-section (2), such award shall be enforced in accordance with the provisions of the Code of Civil Procedure, 1908 (5 of 1908), in the same manner as if it were a decree of the court*".

193 See Section 34 of the A&C Act 1996.

194 The Arbitration and Conciliation (Amendment) Bill 2021 (n 185).

induced by fraud or corruption".[195] The 2021 amendment has been criticized as a retrogressive one that nullifies the reforms introduced in the A&C Act by the 2015 amendment aimed at reducing judicial interference in arbitration.[196] It is unclear why this was brought about.

The Indian arbitration regime has been notoriously famous for what is called 'automatic stay jurisprudence', that is, the moment an arbitral award is challenged under Section 34 of the A&C Act, it becomes inexecutable.[197] The courts have no discretion to issue any interlocutory order *vis-à-vis* the award in question, barring deciding whether the request to set aside is correct.[198] This created a regime where parties would eventually end up challenging every arbitral award in courts, thus inordinately delaying its enforcement and increasing opportunities for judicial interference.

The 2015 amendment corrected this anomaly by inserting a proviso in Section 36 of the A&C Act, which provides as follows:

> *Provided that the Court shall, while considering the application for grant of stay in the case of an arbitral award for payment of money, have due regard to the provisions for grant of stay of a money decree under the provisions of the Code of Civil Procedure, 1908 (5 of 1908).*

The 2021 amendment has undone this reform because, as discussed, it has inserted a new provision that allows a party (against whom the arbitral award has been issued) to get an "automatic" and "unconditional" stay alleging grounds of "fraud" or "corruption", that are not valid grounds to stay a decree under the Civil Procedure Code.[199]

There are two reasons why this amendment assumes importance in the context of the Devas-Antrix case. First, this amendment focuses explicitly on arbitral awards and contracts influenced by "fraud or corruption". As the chapter has discussed, 'fraud' and 'corruption' have been the constant theme in India's narrative against Devas. Second, the 2021 amendment is retroactive. In other words, it will also apply to past 'fraud' or 'corruption' cases. This clearly brings the Devas-Antrix case within the ambit of the amendment. India's former Attorney General said that the timing of this amendment is "very suspicious"

195 ibid.

196 Ashish Dholakia, Ketan Gaur and Kaustub Narendran, 'India's Arbitration and Conciliation (Amendment) Act 2021: A Wolf in Sheep's Clothing?' (*Kluwer Arbitration Blog*, 23 May 2021) <https://arbitrationblog.kluwerarbitration.com/2021/05/23/indias-arbitration-and-conciliation-amendment-act-2021-a-wolf-in-sheeps-clothing> accessed 14 July 2023.

197 *National Aluminium Co Ltd v Pressteel & Fabrication (P) Ltd* (2004) 1 SCC 540, para 10.

198 ibid. See also Gracious Timothy, 'The Conundrum Underlying Section 26 of the Arbitration Amendment Act 2015: Prospective or Retrospective?' (2016) 5 Indian Journal of Arbitration Law.

199 Dholakia and others (n 196).

because it has come at a time when the Delhi High Court was going to start the hearings in the Devas ICC arbitral award proceedings.[200] One commentator argues that the A&C Act was amended to frustrate the Devas-Antrix ICC award in favour of Devas.[201]

Arguably, the 2021 amendment to the A&C Act and the Devas-Antrix case being heard simultaneously is just a coincidence. But it is quite an uncanny coincidence. Irrespective of whether this amendment was made keeping the Devas-Antrix ICC award in mind, it would have considerably impacted the enforcement of the ICC award in favour of Devas. In other words, since India's argument throughout has been that there was corruption in the Devas-Antrix deal, any arbitral award coming out from this contract will also be tainted with the same transgression. This amendment is tantalizingly reminiscent of the retroactive amendment to the Income Tax Act discussed in Chapter 4. Just like the tax law was amended retroactively, keeping one particular dispute and investor in mind, the A&C Act was debatably altered, bearing in mind a specific case and investor.

3.4 Devas's second BIT arbitration

After the Supreme Court decision upholding the winding up of Devas on the ground that it was created to further fraudulent objectives, Devas issued a fresh notice of arbitration to India under the India-Mauritius BIT.[202] As already pointed out, India unilaterally terminated the India-Mauritius BIT on 22 March 2017. However, as per Article 13(3) of the BIT, in case of unilateral termination, the investment made before the denunciation of the treaty will continue to enjoy treaty protection for the next ten years.

Devas claims that India has breached Article 6 of the India-Mauritius BIT, which imposes an obligation on the State not to expropriate foreign investment unlawfully.[203] Specifically, according to Devas:

> *India has breached this provision by unlawfully expropriating or subjecting to measures having effects equivalent to expropriation through India's liquidation of Devas and its takeover by the Liquidator, an Indian government employee and agent of the state. These actions ultimately destroyed the*

200 Payaswini Upadhyay, 'A Change to the Arbitration Law Whose Purpose Is Unclear' (24 November 2020) <https://www.bqprime.com/law-and-policy/a-change-to-the-arbitration-law-whose-purpose-is-unclear> accessed 13 July 2023.

201 Singh (n 160).

202 *CC/Devas v Republic of India*, Notice of Arbitration (2 February 2022) <https://jusmundi.com/en/document/other/en-cc-devas-mauritius-ltd-telcom-devas-mauritius-limited-and-devas-employees-mauritius-private-limited-v-republic-of-india-notice-of-arbitration-wednesday-2nd-february-2022> accessed 11 July 2023 (hereinafter *CC/Devas v India (II)*).

203 ibid para 101.

> *value of Claimants' investments, as the Liquidator has refused to pursue enforcement of the ICC Award, which is currently Devas's largest asset.*[204]

This case resurrects the ghost of the *White Industries* case, discussed in Chapter 2, which also arose due to the failure of India to decide on the enforcement of an ICC award in favour of the investor.[205] It is critical to recall that just months after Devas's second notice of arbitration, the Delhi High Court set aside the ICC award in favour of Devas.[206] Thus, now this case has gone beyond the *White Industries* case because the ICC award has been set aside. But, as we discussed in Chapter 2, the actions of the Indian judiciary are integral to this new ISDS claim. Devas also alleges a breach of the FET provision due to India launching multiple legal proceedings against the investor for harassment.[207]

Interestingly, just a few months after Devas's second ISDS notice, India and Mauritius adopted a joint interpretative statement (JIS) to the India-Mauritius BIT.[208] Although none of India's first-generation BITs – those signed in the 1990s and 2000s – talk of the possibility of adopting a JIS, India has gone down this path on a few occasions. As also pointed out in Chapter 1, this is the third instance of India and its treaty partner country adopting a JIS for their BIT. The other two examples are JIS adopted for India-Bangladesh and India-Colombia BITs. However, the critical difference is that the India-Mauritius BIT stands unilaterally terminated, unlike the India-Bangladesh and India-Colombia investment treaties. It is unusual to have a JIS for a terminated treaty. India has terminated more than 70 BITs, but a JIS has been adopted only for the investment treaty with Mauritius. There is no information that India has done this for other terminated BITs or plans to do so. Therefore, this appears to be specific to the BIT with Mauritius. This raises the question of whether Devas's second ISDS claim motivated India to convince Mauritius to adopt this JIS.

This question is even more pertinent because the JIS states that parties acknowledge that

> *the protection under this agreement shall not be extended to investors or investments that have, concluded or pending, judicial or administrative proceedings against them at any stage, where fraud, money laundering,*

204 ibid.

205 Prabhash Ranjan and Harisankar K Sathyapalan, 'The Devas Saga: Another Twist and the Ghost of a Past BIT Case' (8 February 2022) <https://www.bqprime.com/opinion/the-devas-saga-another-twist-and-the-ghost-of-a-past-bit-case> accessed 14 July 2023.

206 *Antrix Corporation Ltd v Devas Multimedia* (n 166).

207 ibid paras 103–6.

208 Joint Interpretative Statement to the Agreement Between the Government of the Republic of India and the Government of the Republic of Mauritius (signed on 4 September 1998) (hereinafter *JIS to India-Mauritius BIT*).

> ***round-tipping or corruption or similar illegal mechanism have been alleged or being investigated into.***[209]

The following issues are relevant here. First, generally, the purpose of a JIS is to clarify or elucidate the meaning of provisions not defined in the original treaty. However, no provision related to corruption or fraud in the original India-Mauritius BIT exists. Thus, to include a clarification or a statement on a point or an issue not covered by the original treaty is uncommon. Second, since this JIS came into existence just a few months after Devas's second ISDS claim, it is apparent that the JIS's reference to fraud and corruption is motivated by the legal and judicial proceedings against Devas. Third, the JIS does not mention that the India-Mauritius BIT was unilaterally terminated in March 2017. Fourth, will the JIS apply to disputes brought after its adoption, or will it have a retroactive effect? In other words, will the JIS apply to ISDS disputes initiated before its adoption, such as Devas's second arbitration? The JIS is silent on this point. A JIS should not have a retroactive effect, or else it will not respect the principle of 'equality of arms' by ensuring a fair balance between the opportunities available to both the investor and the host State, to defend their positions in arbitration. Since the host State is a party to the dispute, it would be disingenuous to allow the host State to abuse its position as a party to the treaty to change the treaty once a claim has been brought or initiated by serving a notice.[210] Fifth, the fraud or corruption charge in the JIS to deny jurisdiction to an ISDS tribunal is of far-reaching import. A foreign investor doesn't need to be convicted of corruption. An allegation of corruption is sufficient.

As pointed out in Chapter 1, another key feature of the JIS is that it bars an ISDS tribunal review the 'merits' of a case decided by the host State's domestic court. The word 'merits' is not defined. Arguably, such a provision cripples the ability of an ISDS tribunal. In the *Devas v India (II)* case, it is plausible that India may use this provision to argue that the ISDS tribunal cannot examine the decisions of the Indian courts, including the apex court's decisions, because that would amount to reviewing the 'merits' of the case. On the other hand, the ISDS tribunal cannot deal with Devas's chief claim of expropriation related to the liquidation of the company and the commercial arbitral award without examining the decisions of the Indian courts. It will be interesting to see how the ISDS tribunal in this case will interpret the word 'merits' in the India-Mauritius JIS.

Additional critical development in this case has been India obtaining an anti-arbitration injunction at the Mauritius Supreme Court enjoining Devas

209 ibid. On the issue of corruption also see Prabhash Ranjan, 'Corruption and Investment Treaty Arbitration in India' in Nobumichi Teramura and Luke Nottage (eds), *Corruption and Illegality in Asian Investment Arbitration* (Springer 2024 [forthcoming]).

210 See also Catharine Titi, 'The Timing of Treaty Party Interpretations' (*EJIL: Talk!*, 18 August 2020) <https://www.ejiltalk.org/the-timing-of-treaty-party-interpretations/> accessed 14 July 2023.

from pursuing its second ISDS claim.[211] Approaching a national court to stop a foreign investor from pursuing an ISDS claim is tantamount to interfering with the treaty-based arbitration process. Once the State has consented to ISDS in the treaty, then to use other means not to honour this commitment is not apt. This is not the first time India has done something like this. As mentioned in Chapter 2, the central government of India approached the Delhi High Court to stop Vodafone from pursuing an ISDS claim.[212]

The tribunal in *CC/Devas v India (II)*, in an interim award on provisional measures issued on 10 March 2023 held that the anti-arbitration injunction obtained by India undermined the integrity of the arbitration process.[213] The tribunal ordered India to refrain from taking any action that would chip away at the arbitration process's procedural integrity or interfere with the tribunal's mandate to adjudicate in the case.[214]

3.5 Conclusion

The relentless Devas saga has undoubtedly been the most extended set of ISDS claims against India. The story that started in 2005 continues unabated till this day. In the last 18 years or so, the spectrum soap opera has witnessed several twists and turns and is replete with innumerable Yukos moments. Suppose India suspected incongruities, corruption, and fraud in the deal. In that case, the Devas-Antrix contract should have been rescinded, stating so rather than hiding behind the cloak of national security and spectrum use for societal objectives. India did not cover itself in glory by annulling a contract for reasons other than those professed. Even this cancellation and the re-acquisition of the S-band spectrum wasn't followed by due process and complete clarity regarding the purpose. The termination of the contract was a bolt from the blue for the investors. They were left in the dark.

After India lost both BIT awards and Antrix lost the ICC commercial arbitration claim brought by Devas, no stone was left unturned in deploying all procedural tactics not to comply and to set aside these awards. Thus, India went around challenging the enforcement of these awards in multiple jurisdictions

211 *Republic of India v CC/Devas*, Supreme Court of Mauritius (12 January 2023) <https://jusmundi.com/en/document/pdf/decision/en-cc-devas-mauritius-ltd-telcom-devas-mauritius-limited-and-devas-employees-mauritius-private-limited-v-republic-of-india-order-of-the-supreme-court-of-mauritius-thursday-12th-january-2023> accessed 1 August 2023.

212 See Prabhash Ranjan, *India and Bilateral Investment Treaties: Refusal, Acceptance, Backlash* (OUP 2019) 250–51.

213 Lisa Bohmer, 'Tribunal in CC/Devas v India (2) Issues Interim Award on Provisional Measures, as India Seeks to Halt the Arbitration Through Mauritian Courts' (*IA Reporter*, 19 May 2023) <https://www.iareporter.com/articles/tribunal-in-cc-devas-v-india-2-issues-interim-award-on-provisional-measures-as-india-seeks-to-halt-the-arbitration-through-mauritian-courts/> accessed 25 July 2023.

214 ibid.

on the grounds of fraud and corruption but couldn't succeed much. The A&C Act was also amended retroactively to create new procedural bottlenecks in the enforcement of the ICC award in India. When Devas launched the second ISDS claim, India adopted a JIS with Mauritius for the unilaterally denounced India-Mauritius BIT, denying jurisdiction to the ISDS tribunal on a broad allegation of corruption or fraud. The timing of this JIS indicates that this was done keeping Devas's second ISDS claim in mind. The JIS looks like a desperate attempt to wriggle out of the consent given in the India-Mauritius BIT. Despite having conferred consent for arbitration in the India-Mauritius BIT, India obtained an anti-arbitration injunction to meddle in the treaty-based arbitration process. The ISDS tribunal rightly chastised India for this.

The purpose here is not to defend Devas or anyone else for his or her alleged involvement in corruption or fraud. If India genuinely believed in wrongdoings in the deal, it should have re-acquired the S-band spectrum on those grounds. It should have contested the ISDS claims, arguing before the tribunals that the foreign investors were not eligible for treaty protection because they did not invest in India following India's laws. This would have been a bona fide exercise of regulatory power. Instead, India's approach in this saga has been of a respondent unclear of its strategy that hasn't hesitated from using the public power to tilt things in its favour in the ongoing litigation.

4 The retroactive tax misadventure

4.1 Introduction

Frederick the Great, the king of Prussia, famously said, "No government can exist without taxation. This money must necessarily be levied on the people; and the grand art consists of levying so as not to oppress".[1] The power to impose a tax on domestic citizens and aliens,[2] such as foreign investors, has long been recognized as an intrinsic element of the State's sovereignty[3] and an indispensable part of the State's police powers.[4] Police powers are understood as "the exercise of the sovereign right of a government to promote order, safety, security, health, morals and general welfare within constitutional limits and is an essential attribute of government".[5] Thus, in accordance with their police powers, governments impose taxes for many reasons, such as to raise revenue to finance their developmental obligations, regulate economic activities in their territories, manage fiscal challenges, perform public and welfare functions toward their people, etc.

Governments draw the power to impose taxes from their national constitutions. For instance, Article 265 of the Indian Constitution states, "no tax shall be levied or collected except by the authority of law". The same constitutions, at the same time, also lay down the confines in which the power to impose taxes should be exercised.[6] Thus, Article 265 outlaws taxation without a law.

1 Frederick, the Great cited in Brandon Dupont, *The History of Economic Ideas* (Routledge 2017) 126.
2 AR Albrecht, 'The Taxation of Aliens Under International Law' (1952) 29 British Yearbook of International Law 145.
3 P Dietsch, 'Rethinking Sovereignty in International Fiscal Policy' (2011) 37(5) Review of International Studies 2107.
4 A Newcombe and L Paradell, *Law and Practice of Investment Treaties* (Kluwer 2009) 358.
5 ibid; C Titi, *The Right to Regulate in International Investment Law* (Nomos and Hart Publishing 2014) 281. For more on the police powers doctrine, see Jorge E Viñuales, 'Sovereignty in Foreign Investment Law' in Zachary Douglas and others (eds), *The Foundations of International Investment Law: Bringing Theory into Practice* (OUP 2014) 317–62.
6 See Ruth Mason, 'Federalism and the Taxing Power' (2011) 99 California Law Review 975, 977–79, 985.

DOI: 10.4324/9781003324379-4

Likewise, the taxes imposed should not be confiscatory or abusive.[7] The power to levy taxes should not be exercised in an oppressive, vexatious, arbitrary, or discriminatory manner. If taxes are confiscatory, unjust, or collected employing oppressive means, it will trigger resentment and, thus, disputes. National courts have the power to review the actions of tax authorities to see whether the power to tax has been exercised in accordance with the law.[8]

Put another way, the State's power to impose taxes is not unlimited and has its boundaries. This is true not just for national legal systems but also under international law. The debate on the increasing interface between taxation and international investment law, which has attracted considerable attention,[9] needs to be viewed from this standpoint. In international investment law, one line of argument is that since the right to impose taxes is so inextricably linked to a State's sovereignty, ISDS tribunals should not adjudicate tax-related claims of foreign investors. As we will discuss later, India, for example, argued in the *Cairn Energy* case that taxation disputes are not arbitrable as a matter of public policy.[10] India's arguments suggest that since taxation matters are part of the country's fiscal sovereignty, they are outside the scope of an investment treaty claim.[11]

The other way of looking at the State's power to impose taxes is that it is like any other sovereign regulatory measure. As William Park argues, there is no particular reason to put tax-related regulatory measures on a higher pedestal in comparison to other sovereign measures like the administration of justice or protection of the environment, which routinely gives rise to ISDS claims.[12] The very *raison d'etre* of investment treaties is to shield a foreign investor from State excesses arising from unbridled use of governmental power amounting to undue interferences in investor's rights. Hence, if a tax measure excessively intrudes into an investor's treaty-protected rights, such sovereign action will fall under the purview of the investment treaty unless stated otherwise. Moreover, a country's consent to protect foreign investment under an investment

7 See *McCulloch v Maryland* [1819] 17 US 316, 431.

8 See generally Thomas Cooley, 'Remedies of Illegal Taxation' (1881) 29(1) The American Law Register 1–16. Article 265 of the Indian Constitution states "no tax shall be levied or collected except by the authority of law".

9 Cornel Marian, *The State's Power to Tax in the Investment Arbitration of Energy Disputes: Outer Limits and the Energy Charter Treaty* (Kluwer Law International 2020); William W Park, 'Tax and Arbitration' (2020) 36 Arbitration International 166–97; V Vasudev, 'Interactions Between Taxation Measures and International Investment Agreements' in J Chaisse and others (eds), *Handbook of International Investment Law and Policy* (Springer 2019); Mathew Davie, 'Taxation-Based Investment Treaty Claims' (2015) 6(1) Journal of International Dispute Settlement 202; Julien Chaisse, 'International Investment Law and Taxation: From Coexistence to Cooperation' (2016) E15 Task Force on Investment Policy.

10 *Cairn Energy PLC and Cairn UK Holdings Limited v Republic of India*, PCA Case No 2016-7, Award, 21 December 2020, paras 774–78, 792 (hereinafter '*Cairn Energy*').

11 ibid paras 774, 778.

12 Park (n 9) 172–73.

treaty also flows from the same source of State sovereignty that gives that country the power to impose taxes.[13] It is also critical to remember that ISDS tribunals address tax-related investment disputes, that is, claims brought by foreign investors alleging that a taxation measure breaches one of the substantive protection rights under the investment treaty.[14] Such disputes should be differentiated from tax disputes proper, that is, claims arising from taxing a specific transaction or due to the quantum of tax levied.[15]

The real challenge is where to draw a line distinguishing the legitimate exercise of the State's sovereign right to tax and the abuse of the power to tax. The scholarly community and the ISDS tribunals have grappled with this question. Before we look at the approach of the ISDS tribunals, it will be worthwhile to briefly sketch the overall global context of taxation and ISDS claims by looking at some numbers and critical facts.

According to UNCTAD, from 1987 till the end of 2021, the total number of publicly owned ISDS claims brought by foreign investors stood at 1190.[16] Of these 1190 ISDS claims, 165 were brought by foreign investors challenging tax-related measures of host States.[17] In other words, almost 14 per cent of the total ISDS claims pertain to tax-related measures. Another interesting fact is that out of these 165 ISDS claims, as many as 162 have been brought between 2000 to 2021.[18] UNCTAD classifies these cases as tax-related because taxation was a major issue in these disputes. Moreover, tax here is defined broadly, given the debate surrounding the scope of the term in ISDS cases.[19]

It is not just the number of tax-related ISDS claims that is noteworthy, but also the scope of the claims. Foreign investors have challenged a wide array of tax measures before ISDS tribunals, including increases in windfall profits taxes and royalties,[20] denial of value-added tax credits,[21] initiation of tax investigations and extensive tax assessments,[22] revocation of subsidies or

13 Błażej Kuźniacki and Stef van Weeghel, 'Cairn Energy: When Retroactive Taxation Not Justified by Prevention of Tax Avoidance' (2023) 39(1) Arbitration International 125–54, 130.

14 *Cairn Energy* (n 10) para 793.

15 ibid.

16 UNCTAD, 'Facts on Investor-State Arbitrations in 2021: With a Special Focus on Tax-Related ISDS Cases' (2022) IIA Issues Note, Issue 1 <https://unctad.org/system/files/official-document/diaepcbinf2022d4_en.pdf> accessed 1 July 2023.

17 ibid.

18 ibid.

19 ibid.

20 For example, see *Burlington Resources, Inc v Republic of Ecuador*, ICSID Case No ARB/08/5, Decision on Liability, 14 December 2014.

21 For example, see *EnCana Corporation v Republic of Ecuador*, LCIA Case No UN3481, Award, 3 February 2006.

22 For example, see *Yukos Universal Limited (Isle of Man) v The Russian Federation*, PCA Case No 2005-04/AA227, Final Award, 18 July 2014.

exemption given for taxation,[23] and alterations made to feed-in-tariffs to produce renewable energy.[24] While challenging these taxation measures, foreign investors have alleged that the State violated several substantive protections in investment treaties, including national treatment,[25] full protection and security,[26] expropriation,[27] fair and equitable treatment (FET),[28] umbrella clauses,[29] etc. This does not mean that the investors have succeeded in all these claims. For instance, as Sonia Rolland argues, foreign investors haven't been successful in most claims where they challenged taxation measures constituting indirect expropriation.[30] This is because establishing indirect expropriation requires satisfying the very high threshold of substantial deprivation of the investment's value.[31] Nonetheless, these numbers and the fact that extensive range of State fiscal measures have been contested before ISDS tribunals make the interface between taxation and international investment law enthralling.

To set the broader context, the chapter in Section 4.2 sketches out the larger debate on the country's sovereign right to tax and its limits. Next, Section 4.3, which constitutes the bulk of the chapter, focuses on India's retroactive tax story, figuring out how it started, evolved, and culminated. Here the focus will be on the *Cairn Energy* tribunal award and how it dealt with India's retroactive tax measure. Section 4.4 concludes.

4.2 Limits on sovereignty

Let's circle back to the issue of ISDS tribunals' approach to tax-related investment claims. It will be pertinent to state upfront that international investment law is replete with examples of ISDS tribunals recognizing the fundamental principle that imposing taxes is the cornerstone of a States's sovereignty.

23 *Ioan Micula, Viorel Micula and others v Romania (I)*, ICSID Case No ARB/05/20, Final Award, 11 December 2013.

24 *Charanne and Construction Investments v Spain*, SCC Case No V 062/2012, Final Award, 21 January 2016.

25 For example, see *Marvin Feldman v Mexico*, ICSID Case No ARB(AF)/99/1, Award, 16 December 2002.

26 For example, see *Occidental Exploration and Production Company v Republic of Ecuador (I)*, LCIA Case No UN3467, Final Award, 1 July 2004.

27 For example, see *Link-Trading Joint Stock Company v Moldova*, UNCITRAL, Final Award, 18 April 2002.

28 For example, see *Glencore International AG and CI Prodeco SA v Republic of Colombia (I)*, ICSID Case No ARB/16/6; *Jan Oostergetel and Theodora Laurentius v The Slovak Republic*, UNCITRAL, Final Award, 23 April 2012.

29 For example, see *Enron Creditors Recovery Corporation (Formerly Enron Corporation) and Ponderosa, LP v Argentina*, ICSID Case No ARB/01/3, Award, 22 May 2007.

30 Sonia Rolland, 'The Impact of Trade and Investment Treaties on Fiscal Resources and Taxation in Developing Countries' (2020) 21(1) Chicago Journal of International Law 48, 65–66.

31 ibid.

For instance, in *Eiser v Spain*,[32] foreign investors challenged a tax imposed by Spain on energy producers and the repealing of feed-in-tariffs under the Energy Charter Treaty (ECT). The tribunal held that the power to tax is a core sovereign authority of the State that should not be questioned lightly.[33]

Likewise, in *El Paso v Argentina*,[34] the investors challenged several facets of Argentinian tax measures as breaching the United States-Argentina BIT. The tribunal held that a country's tax policy is a matter pertaining to that country's sovereign power.[35] Thus, the tribunal recognized that a country has a sovereign right to develop tax measures at any time as per its priorities.[36] Not just this, the tribunal also observed that there is a presumption of validity; that is, there is an assumption that a country's taxation laws are consistent with that country's international law obligations.[37] Accordingly, the burden of proof is on the investor to prove the invalidity of a nation's tax measures *vis-a-vis* that country's investment treaty obligations.

The presumption of validity in favour of a country's taxation measures was also laid down in *Renta 4 v Russia*.[38] The tribunal, while adjudicating whether taxation measures amount to expropriation, held that the assumption is that imposing taxes is a bona fide exercise of a country's public powers unless there is contrary evidence to demonstrate that these measures constitute a 'taking', that is, amount to the expropriation of foreign investment.[39]

Notwithstanding the State's sovereign right to impose taxes and the presumption that the taxes imposed by the State are valid or consistent with international law obligations, the tribunals have also identified certain limits on the State's right to impose taxes. For instance, in *Encana v Ecuador*,[40] the foreign investor in the petroleum sector alleged that Ecuador's decision to issue interpretative rulings retroactively excluding petroleum companies from refunds of value-added taxes amounted to an expropriation of their investment.[41] While upholding the State's sovereign right to impose taxes,[42] the tribunal said

32 *Eiser Infrastructure Limited and Energía Solar Luxembourg SÀRL v Kingdom of Spain*, ICSID Case No ARB/13/36, Award, 4 May 2017.
33 ibid para 270.
34 *El Paso Energy International Company v Argentine Republic*, ICSID Case No ARB/03/15, Award, 31 October 2011.
35 ibid para 290.
36 ibid.
37 ibid.
38 *Quasar de Valores SICAV SA, Orgor de Valores SICAV SA, GBI 9000 SICAV SA and ALOS 34 SL v The Russian Federation*, SCC Case No 24/2007, Award, 20 July 2012, para 181.
39 ibid.
40 *EnCana Corporation v Republic of Ecuador*, LCIA Case No UN3481, Award, 3 February 2006.
41 See also *RosInvest Co UK Ltd v the Russian Federation*, SCC Case No V079/2005, Award, 12 September 2010; *Tza Yap Shum v PeruTza Yap Shum v Republic of Peru*, ICSID Case No ARB/07/6, Award, 7 June 2011.
42 *Encana v Ecuador* (n 40) para 173.

that tax measures that are extraordinary, punitive in amount, or arbitrary in incidence will result in foreign investment's expropriation.[43] Likewise, in another case involving Ecuador, *Burlington v Ecuador*,[44] the tribunal identified the following limits on the State's taxation powers in customary international law: the tax should not be discriminatory or confiscatory.[45]

In another case, *Glencore v Colombia*,[46] the tribunal recognized that while Colombia, a sovereign nation, can tax any asset located in its territory or any payment originating in its land, this right is not unlimited.[47] The tribunal held that the restitution awarded to the investor has to be tax-neutral, that is, Colombia cannot tax the restitution awarded under the investment treaty.[48]

After this brief doctrinal exposition of a country's sovereign right to impose taxes and the limits that BITs impose on this right, let us now focus on India's taxation measures.

4.3 India's tax misadventure

Considering the overall global context delineated before, we will try to understand the treatment of India's retroactive taxation measures by ISDS tribunals. India's imposition of retroactive taxes has triggered four ISDS claims. Of these four claims, Vodafone, a telecom company, initiated two claims under the India-Netherlands BIT[49] (*Vodafone I*) and the India-UK BIT (*Vodafone II*).[50] Cairn Energy, a company in the energy sector, initiated a claim, *Cairn Energy v India*.[51] Vedanta, a mining and quarrying company, has also initiated a claim, *Vedanta v India*.[52] *Vodafone II* is still pending whereas *Vedanta v India* has been reportedly settled.[53] The other two – *Vodafone I* and *Cairn Energy v India* – have been decided in the favour of the investor.

India's retroactive tax story started with a domestic tax battle involving Vodafone and the Indian tax department. In 2007, Vodafone BV International (Vodafone's Netherland entity) purchased a single share in CGP Investments (hereinafter CGP), a company incorporated in the Cayman Islands

43 ibid para 177.
44 *Burlington Resources Inc v Republic of Ecuador* (n 20).
45 ibid para 392. See also Davie (n 9) 202.
46 *Glencore v Colombia* (n 28).
47 ibid para 1625.
48 ibid paras 1626–27.
49 *Vodafone International Holdings BV v Government of India* [I], PCA Case No 2016-35, Award, 25 September 2020.
50 *Vodafone Group Plc and Vodafone Consolidated Holdings Limited v Government of India [II]*, UNCITRAL.
51 *Cairn Energy* (n 10).
52 *Vedanta Resources PLC v India*, PCA Case No 2016-5.
53 UNCTAD, 'Investment Dispute Settlement Navigator – *Vedanta v India*' (*Investment Policy Hub*) <https://investmentpolicy.unctad.org/investment-dispute-settlement/cases/733/vedanta-v-india> accessed 1 July 2023.

from another Cayman Island incorporated company known as Hutchison Telecommunications International (HTIL) Ltd for US$11.1 billion.[54] CGP indirectly owned 67 per cent of Hutchison Essar Limited (HEL), an Indian entity that conducted telecommunications business in India. Thus, this transaction involved a sale by a company not resident in India of an interest in a non-Indian company that indirectly (not directly) derived value from its capital assets in India.[55] The Indian tax authorities contended that this transaction involved an indirect transfer of rights in HEL held by HTIL. Accordingly, it was claimed that this was a case of accrual or deemed accrual of income for HTIL from a source of income in India.[56] On this basis, India contended that HTIL's capital gains were taxable in India since it was deemed to accrue or arise in India under Section 9(1)(i) of the Income Tax Act, 1961, which provides as follows:

> *The following incomes shall be deemed to accrue or arise in India: –*
>
> *(i) all income accruing or arising, whether directly or indirectly, through or from any business connection in India, or through or from any property in India, or through or from any asset or source of income in India, or through the transfer of a capital asset situate in India.*

Accordingly, under Section 201[57] of the Income Tax Act, Vodafone was held to be an assessee-in-default for failing to deduct tax on the money remitted to HTIL and thus liable under Section 195 of the Income Tax Act. Section 195 obligates a payer to deduct tax at source from the payments made to non-residents if that payment is taxable.[58] The government imposed a tax

54 *Cairn Energy* (n 10) para 103; *Marvin Roy Feldman Karpa v United Mexican States*, ICSID Case No ARB(AF)/99/1, Award, 16 December 2002.

55 See also Meyyappan Nagappan and Srikanth Vasudevan, 'Indirect Transfer Taxation in India: From Vodafone to Cairn' (2017) 45(10) Intertax 665.

56 *Cairn Energy* (n 10) para 109.

57 Section 201(1) of the Income Tax Act, 1961 states – "Where any person, including the principal officer of a company,

> (a) who is required to deduct any sum in accordance with the provisions of this Act; or (b) referred to in sub-section (1A) of section 192, being an employer, does not deduct, or does not pay, or after so deducting fails to pay, the whole or any part of the tax, as required by or under this Act, then, such person, shall, without prejudice to any other consequences which he may incur, be deemed to be an assesses in default in respect of such tax".

58 Section 195(1) of the Income Tax Act, 1961 states, "Any person responsible for paying to a non-resident, not being a company, or to a foreign company, any interest (not being interest referred to in section 194LB or section 194LC) or section 194LD or any other sum chargeable under the provisions of this Act (not being income chargeable under the head 'Salaries') shall, at the time of credit of such income to the account of the payee or at the time of payment thereof in cash or by the issue of a cheque or draft or by any other mode, whichever is earlier, deduct income-tax thereon at the rates in force".

of US$2.2 billion on Vodafone.[59] On the other hand, Vodafone reasoned that the share of CGP that it acquired was a capital asset based outside India. Therefore, no income had arisen or could be deemed to have arisen in India even if CGP indirectly owned capital assets situated in India.

The matter went before the Bombay High Court, which decided the case against Vodafone in 2010.[60] Vodafone challenged this decision in the Supreme Court of India. This was the Supreme Court's first hearing of a case of this nature. It reversed the Bombay High Court ruling. In a ground-breaking decision rendered on 20 January 2012, the apex court held that the off-shore transaction involving Vodafone was not taxable in India.[61] The transfer of a Cayman Islands company shares would not be subject to the capital gains tax in India under Section 9(1)(i) of the Income Tax Act since the shares were not located in India.[62] In this case, the real issue was whether the income arose "through the transfer of a capital asset situated in India". If it did, it was taxable in India. The court examined the scope of Section 9(1)(i). According to Section 9(1)(i), income that accrues to a non-resident, directly or indirectly, is "fictionally deemed to accrue or arise in India if such income accrues or arises as a sequel to the transfer of a capital asset situate in India".[63] Thus, Section 9(1)(i) is a 'deeming provision' which creates a legal fiction to tax as if the income accrued in India. The tax department argued that Section 9(1)(i) is a 'look through' provision. In other words, the contention is that one can 'look through' the transfer of shares of a foreign company that holds shares in an Indian company and treat such a transfer as alike to the transfer of the shares of the Indian company.[64] The assumption to make this argument is that Section 9(1)(i) covers direct and indirect transfers of capital assets.[65]

However, the Supreme Court rejected this argument because Section 9(1)(i) cannot be extended to cover the indirect transfer of capital assets.[66] The apex court held that Section 9(1)(i) talks of capital assets situated in India. This means only direct transfers of capital assets and not indirect transfers.[67] Including indirect transfers within Section 9(1)(i) would mean rewriting

59 S Vasudevan and T Bhatnagar, 'Rollback of Retro Tax: Too Late and Little to Heal the Wounds?' *The Times of India* (16 August 2021) <https://timesofindia.indiatimes.com/blogs/voices/rollback-of-retro-tax-too-late-and-little-to-heal-the-wounds/> (accessed 25 August 2023).

60 *Vodafone International Holdings BV v Union of India* (3 December 2008), WP No 2550 of 2007.

61 *Vodafone International Holdings BV v Union of India* (2012) 6 SCC 613. See also Prabhash Ranjan, *India and Bilateral Investment Treaties: Refusal, Acceptance, Backlash* (OUP 2019).

62 *Vodafone International Holdings v Union of India* (n 61) para 82.

63 ibid para 71.

64 ibid.

65 ibid.

66 ibid.

67 ibid.

the provision and altering its scope and content.[68] In simpler terms, the offshore transaction involving Vodafone did not fall under Section 9(1)(i) of the Income Tax Act.

On the issue of applicability of Section 195 of the Income Tax Act, the Supreme Court held that Section 195 did not apply to the transaction between Vodafone and HTIL because it was a case of an 'outright sale' between two non-residents for a capital asset situated outside India.[69] Thus, there was no obligation to deduct tax at the source.[70] Accordingly, the court concluded that the Indian tax authority "had no territorial tax jurisdiction to tax the said offshore transaction".[71] The Supreme Court quashed the tax demand on Vodafone and ordered the refund of the alleged tax that it was asked to deposit with the Income Tax Department.

4.3.1 The 2012 amendment: retrospective or retroactive?

India amended the Income Tax Act before the ink could dry on the Supreme Court's decision.[72] This amendment, which came into force on 28 May 2012, inserted Explanation 5 to Section 9(1)(i) of the Income Tax Act.[73] This explanation provides:

> *For the removal of doubts, it is hereby clarified that an asset or a capital asset being any share or interest in a company or entity registered or incorporated outside India shall be deemed to be and* ***shall always be deemed to have been*** *situated in India, if the share or interest derives, directly or indirectly, its value substantially from the assets located in India.*
>
> (*emphasis added*)

In addition to amending the Income Tax Act, Section 119 of the Finance Act of 2012 introduced another major legal change. It validated all the tax demands made concerning 'indirect transfers' notwithstanding any court order or decision. Section 119 of the Finance Act provides as follows:

> *Notwithstanding anything contained in any judgment, decree or order of any Court or Tribunal or any authority, all notices sent or purporting to have been sent, or taxes levied, demanded, assessed, imposed, collected or recovered or purporting to have been levied, demanded, assessed, imposed, collected or recovered under the provisions of Income-tax Act, 1961 (43 of*

68 ibid.
69 ibid para 89.
70 ibid.
71 ibid para 90.
72 See Finance Act 2012 (28 May 2012) <http://www.bareactslive.com/ACA/act3538.htm#119> (accessed 25 August 2023).
73 ibid s 4.

> *1961) in respect of income accruing or arising through or from the transfer of a capital asset situate in India in consequence of the transfer of a share or shares of a company registered or incorporated outside India or in consequence of an agreement, or otherwise, outside India, shall be deemed to have been validly made, and the notice, levy, demand, assessment, imposition, collection or recovery of tax shall be valid and* ***shall be deemed always to have been valid*** *and shall not be called in question on the ground that the tax was not chargeable or any ground including that it is a tax on capital gains arising out of transactions which have taken place outside India, and accordingly, any tax levied, demanded, assessed, imposed or deposited before the commencement of this Act and chargeable for a period prior to such commencement but not collected or recovered before such commencement, may be collected or recovered and appropriated in accordance with the provisions of the Income-tax Act, 1961 as amended by this Act, and the rules made thereunder and there shall be no liability or obligation to make any refund whatsoever.*
>
> (*emphasis added*)

These changes were made to address Vodafone-type off-shore transactions or 'indirect transfers' and bring them under the net of the Indian income tax law. India claimed that these changes were clarificatory in nature, that is, the changes aimed to clarify a point of law and the intention of the Parliament. However, the usage of words like "shall always be deemed to have been" in Explanation 5 and "shall be deemed always to have been" in Section 119 of the Finance Act, show that the amendments cover past transactions going back in time till 1 April 1962 when the Income Tax Act came into force. In one stroke, the so-called clarification stretched back in time by almost five decades. It's pretty intriguing to note that the Parliament in 2012 was clarifying the intent behind the Income Tax Act on behalf of the parliamentarians of 1961. These changes went back almost five decades, so the amendments went beyond merely expounding the existing law or elucidating parliamentary intention.

In India, these amendments have been referred to as retrospective changes. For instance, the expert committee's report that the Indian government constituted in 2012 to study the changes made to tax laws on indirect transfers referred to these amendments as 'retrospective'.[74] However, terms like 'retrospective' have often been used without a proper definition. Also, 'retrospective' has frequently been used interchangeably with 'retroactive' to describe the changes made to the income tax law on indirect transfers. This aspect

74 Expert Committee, 'Draft Report on Retrospective Amendments Relating to Indirect Transfers' (2012) <https://www.incometaxindia.gov.in/Lists/Press%20Releases/Attachments/21/Draft_Report.pdf>.

needs some explanation because a retroactive legal change differs from a retrospective one.

A 'retroactive' legal provision is something that "changes the past legal consequences of facts that occurred before the provision was officially published".[75] In other words, "a retroactive statute operates as of a time prior to its enactment".[76] This should be distinguished from a retrospective statute which "is prospective, but it imposes new results in respect of a past event".[77] In the specific context of tax legislation, retroactive legislation refers to legislation whereby a tax or a higher tax burden is imposed on earned income.[78] Put another way, a retroactive tax law encompasses those situations where the law set no or a lower tax burden when the income was earned, and the amendment changed this to impose a new or a higher tax burden. This needs to be contrasted with 'retrospective' legislation whereby a tax burden, including a higher burden, is imposed on future income arising from a transaction that has already been finalized.[79] Following this logic, a tax amendment will be 'prospective' if it imposes a higher or a new tax burden on the transactions that will take place from the date the law is amended. That is, the law applies prospectively by covering only prospective events, not events that have already occurred, even if the income is yet to be generated.

One can understand this with the help of a simple example. Assume, A and B signed a contract on 1 May 2023. This contract would result in A paying B a fee for his services on 1 October 2023. The tax rate on such a fee on 1 May 2023 is 10 per cent. Further, assume that on 1 June 2023, the law changes stating that the new tax rate on income generated from the kind of transaction involving A and B will be 20 per cent. If this change applies to past transactions (such as the one involving A and B) and future transactions, the amendment will be 'retrospective'. However, if this change is restricted to future transactions, that is, transactions that take place on or after 1 June 2023, it will be 'prospective'. Thus, incomes that arise after 1 June 2023 due to transactions entered before 1 June, will still be taxed at 10 per cent. Now, if the completed transaction between A and B had already generated an income before 1 June 2023 taxed at 10 per cent, and the law enacted on 1 June 2023 says that the past income will now be taxed at 20 per cent, it will be a case of 'retroactive' amendment.

Applying these concepts to the Indian scenario, the Indian tax law amendment on 'indirect transfers' can be classified as 'retroactive' because it aimed to cover past 'indirect transfer' transactions and incomes that had already arisen

75 JLM Gribnau and MRT Pauwels (eds), 'Retroactivity of Tax Legislation' (2013) EATLP International Tax Series No 9, EATLP/IBFD.

76 E Driedger, 'Statutes: Retroactive Retrospective Reflections' (1978) 56 Canadian Bar Review 264, 268–69.

77 ibid 268.

78 Philip Baker, 'Retroactive Tax Legislation' (2012) 6(48) International Taxation 780.

79 ibid.

and earned from such transactions. Stated differently, the 2012 amendment created a fresh tax obligation on a completed transaction in the past, which, as the law stipulated at that time, was not taxable. This clearly falls in the bracket of retroactive tax legislation as described earlier. Although it is important to bear in mind that in India, the terms 'retroactively' and 'retrospectively' have been used interchangeably.[80]

India amended the law to nullify the Supreme Court decision in favour of Vodafone. As a result, the tax demand that the apex court struck down was resurrected. Section 119 of the Finance Act made it abundantly clear that India intended to continue the tax claim against Vodafone, notwithstanding the Supreme Court ruling. As was widely expected, this move spooked foreign investors and attracted extensive reproach.[81] One commentator described retroactive taxation as 'fiscal plunder'[82] while another referred to it as 'tax terrorism'.[83]

Having understood the character of India's tax amendment, we now turn our attention to the ISDS claims brought by Vodafone and Cairn Energy.

4.3.2 Vodafone's ISDS claim

Vodafone challenged the imposition of the retroactive tax before an ISDS tribunal under the India-Netherlands BIT (*Vodafone I*)[84] followed by an ISDS claim under the India-UK BIT (*Vodafone II*).[85] While the claim under the India-UK BIT is pending, the ISDS tribunal under the India-Netherlands BIT handed down an award on 25 September 2020, ruling in favour of Vodafone. The tribunal pronounced that India's retroactive tax violated the FET provision. The award is not publicly available, barring the operative part of the ruling. In the part of the ruling publicly available, the tribunal held that India's

> *conduct in respect of the imposition of the Claimant of an asserted liability to tax notwithstanding the Supreme Court Judgement is in breach of the guarantee of fair and equitable treatment laid down in Article 4(1) of the BIT, as is the imposition of interest on the sums in question and the imposition of penalties for non-payment of the sums in question.*[86]

80 India made this argument before the *Cairn Energy* tribunal. See *Cairn Energy* (n 10) para 1080.

81 See *Draft Report on Retrospective Amendments Relating to Indirect Transfers* (n 74).

82 J Rao, 'Whither India's Economic Reforms?' in Atul Thakur (ed), *India Now and in Transition* (Niyogi Books 2017) 215.

83 Sadanand Dhume, 'Tax Terrorism Returns to India' *The Wall Street Journal* (7 May 2015) <https://www.wsj.com/articles/tax-terrorism-returns-to-india-1431015852> accessed 1 July 2023.

84 *Vodafone v India* [I].

85 *Vodafone v India [II].*

86 ibid para 363.

Article 4(1) of the India-Netherlands BIT provides as follows:

> *Investments of investors of each Contracting Party shall at all times be accorded fair and equitable treatment and shall enjoy full protection and security in the territory of the other Contracting Party.*

Thus, Article 4(1) obligates the host State to provide FET and full protection and security (FPS) to foreign investments. The BIT does not define FET and FPS. Since the *Vodafone* award is not in the public domain, we do not know how the ISDS tribunal interpreted the FET provision, which has otherwise been subjected to expansive interpretation by ISDS tribunals.[87]

An essential point in the context of India-Netherlands BIT is Article 4(4), which provides as follows:

> *The provisions of paragraphs 1 and 2 in respect of the grant of national treatment and most favoured nation treatment shall also not apply in respect of any international agreement or arrangement relating wholly or mainly to taxation or any domestic legislation or arrangements consequent to such legislation relating wholly or mainly to taxation.*

Article 4(4) exempts taxation measures from certain substantive rights that foreign investors enjoy. It specifically mentions that national treatment and MFN, mentioned in paragraph 2, do not apply to taxation measures. Paragraph 2 of Article 4 refers to national treatment and most favoured nation (MFN) provision.[88]

In other words, even if taxation measures provide less favourable treatment to a foreign investor *vis-a-vis* another foreign investor or a domestic investor, it will not be a violation of the MFN and national treatment provision, respectively. Interestingly, Article 4(4) also mentions paragraph 1 but does not mention FET and FPS – the two standards that paragraph 1 of Article 4 contains. Thus, while paragraphs 1 and 2 are mentioned in Article 4(4), the two substantive standards mentioned are MFN and national treatment (the ones given in paragraph 2). Article 4(4) does not mention FET and FPS (the substantive standards provided in paragraph 1).

This vague drafting of Article 4(4) makes it open to two plausible interpretations. First, despite mentioning paragraph 1, Article 4(4) exempts taxation measures only from the application of the MFN and national treatment that

87 For a detailed discussion on the FET provision see Rumana Islam, *The Fair and Equitable Treatment Standard in International Investment Arbitration* (Springer 2018).

88 Article 4(2) of India-Netherlands BIT provides as follows: *"Each Contracting Party shall accord to such investments, including their operation, management, maintenance, use, enjoyment or disposal by such investors, treatment which shall not be less favourable than that accorded either to investments of its own investors or to investments of investors of any third State, whichever is more favourable to the investor concerned".*

are explicitly listed. After all, if the countries wanted to exclude taxation measures from the ambit of FET and FPS, they would have said so unequivocally as they do for MFN and national treatment. If this argument is accepted, the FET provision will continue to apply to taxation measures. Second, even if FET and FPS are not mentioned in Article 4(4), the inclusion of paragraph 1 makes it copiously clear that taxation measures are also excluded from the ambit of FET and FPS.[89] The first interpretation would make the words 'paragraphs 1' in Article 4(4) redundant.

Thus, one can say that the meaning of Article 4(4) is ambiguous or obscure, which could be the trigger to refer to Article 32 of the Vienna Convention on Law of Treaties (VCLT). Article 32 states:

> *Recourse may be had to supplementary means of interpretation, including the preparatory work of the treaty and the circumstances of its conclusion, in order to confirm the meaning resulting from the application of article 31, or to determine the meaning when the interpretation according to article 31: (a) leaves the meaning ambiguous or obscure; or (b) leads to a result which is manifestly absurd or unreasonable.*

Article 32 recognizes the preparatory work of a treaty – materials produced during treaty negotiations, also called *travaux préparatoires* ('*travaux*') – as a supplementary means of treaty interpretation. The treaty interpreter can turn to Article 32 either to confirm the meaning she gets after applying Article 31 of the VCLT – the primary means of treaty interpretation – or if the application of Article 31 yields an interpretation that is either ambiguous or manifestly absurd. Several ISDS tribunals have referred to the preparatory work of the treaty as part of the treaty interpretation process.[90] The tribunals refer to the preparatory work to confirm the meaning they get after applying Article 31 of the VCLT,[91] or if the meaning of a treaty provision is ambiguous.[92]

89 Promod Nair and Shivani Singhal, 'Why India Should Challenge the Vodafone-India BIT Award' *Bar and Bench* (24 October 2023) <www.barandbench.com/columns/why-india-should-challenge-the-vodafone-india-bit-award> accessed 1 July 2023.

90 See *Churchill Mining and Planet Mining Pty Ltd v Republic of Indonesia*, ICSID Case No ARB/12/14 and 12/40, Decision on Jurisdiction, 24 February 2014.

91 For example, see *Philip Morris Brands v Oriental Republic of Uruguay*, ICSID Case No ARB/10/7, Decision on Jurisdiction, 2 July 2013, para 34; *Togo Electricité et GDFSuez Energie Services v La Republique Togolaise*, ICSID Case No ARB/06/07, Decision on Annulment, 6 September 2011, paras 45–46; *Aguas del Tunari SA v Republic of Bolivia*, ICSID Case No ARB/02/3, Decision on Respondent's Objections to Jurisdiction, 21 October 2005, paras 266, 283.

92 For a detailed discussion on how the ISDS tribunals have referred to the preparatory work of the treaty under Article 32 of the VCLT see Esme Shirlow and Michael Waibel, 'A Sliding Scale Approach to Travaux in Treaty Interpretation: The Case of Investment Treaties' [2021] British Yearbook of International Law <https://academic.oup.com/bybil/advance-article-abstract/doi/10.1093/bybil/brab001/6169509>. See also *Compañia de Aguas and*

Since the meaning of Article 4(4) is ambiguous, one can turn to the preparatory work of the India-Netherlands BIT. However, the preparatory work is not publicly available. The first-generation BITs generally did not generate many negotiating documents. Interestingly the *Cairn Energy* tribunal briefly referred to the negotiating history of India-Netherlands BIT to deal with India's argument that taxation measures are not arbitrable under Dutch law[93] – a point discussed later in the chapter. The tribunal examined the India-Netherlands BIT to show that tax-related investment disputes are arbitrable under the BITs that the Netherlands has signed.[94] The tribunal said that the negotiating history indicates that the Netherlands considered taxation measures to fall within the scope of the BIT, barring a limited carve-out for MFN and national treatment provisions.[95] From this, it appears that the parties intended to exclude only MFN and national treatment, not FET and FPS, from the purview of taxation measures. This view aligns with the first interpretation of Article 4(4) advanced earlier.

For the sake of argument, let's assume that taxation measures are carved out from the scope of the FET provision. Does this mean that countries are free to enact any tax legislation and that there are no limits on State power? A carve-out cannot be read as giving countries a free pass to act as they please. If a host State imposes disproportionate costs on the investor compared to the public policy objective it seeks to achieve, it will be a case of misusing the exception. Imposing a retroactive change in tax law after losing the case in the country's apex court and thus diluting the benefit the investor would have received, undoubtedly reek of abuse of public power. An ISDS tribunal should hold a host State accountable for the same. As it was held in *Yukos Universal v Russia*,[96] if States act in bad faith towards foreign investors, abuse their right to tax, or adopt mala fide taxation measures, they won't be able to benefit from the carve-out provision.[97]

Since the *Vodafone* award is not in the public domain, one does not know how the tribunal dealt with this issue. Nonetheless, we know that the tribunal found India's retroactive taxation in breach of the FET provision in Article 4(1). Thus, it is evident the tribunal managed to get around the interpretative challenge posed by Article 4(4). However, we do not know

---

Vivendi Universal SA v Argentine Republic, ICSID Case No ARB/97/3, Decision on the Challenge to the President of the Committee, 3 October 2001, paras 7–24; *HICEE BV v The Slovak Republic*, UNCITRAL, PCA Case No 2009-11, Partial Award, 23 May 2011, para 116.

93 *Cairn Energy* (n 10) paras 823–27.

94 ibid para 827.

95 ibid.

96 *Yukos Universal Limited (Isle of Man) v The Russian Federation*, UNCITRAL, PCA Case No 2005-4/AA227.

97 ibid para 1407. See also *Belenergia SA v Italian Republic*, ICSID Case No ARB/15/40, paras 377–78.

whether it applied Article 32 of the VCLT or held that India abused the exception for taxation measures.

4.3.3 Cairn Energy's ISDS claim

Let us now turn to examine the *Cairn Energy* award, which is significant not just from the Indian standpoint but also from the perspective of international investment law and its interface with taxation. Although the trigger for the 2012 amendment to the Income Tax Act was the Indian government's legal loss in the *Vodafone* case before the Indian Supreme Court, the amendment re-opened many old and closed 'indirect transfer' transactions, such as Cairn Energy's internal corporate restructuring in India.

Retroactive tax on Cairn Energy

Between 1996 and 2006, Cairn Energy acquired many interests in India's oil sector that were held by 27 subsidiaries incorporated abroad.[98] Cairn Energy, in 2006, decided to consolidate the 27 subsidiaries under a new entity in India, Cairn India Limited (CIL).[99] CIL's 31 per cent of shares were sold to the public, and Cairn UK Holdings Limited (CUHL), the second claimant, held the remaining 69 per cent of shares.[100] The 27 subsidiaries were transferred to CUHL. Subsequently, they were transferred to Cairn India Holdings Limited (CIHL), a wholly owned subsidiary of Cairn Energy and incorporated in Jersey. Finally, CIL acquired CIHL from CUHL.[101] This acquisition, that is, CIL acquiring CIHL, included the capital gains realized by CUHL, which became the focus of India's taxation measures.[102]

In 2014, the tax authorities launched their investigation into Cairn's restructuring from 2006, preventing CUHL from selling its shares in CIL. In 2016, a tax demand notice of approximately US$4.4 billion (including interest) was issued to CUHL on the 2006 transactions.[103] India's Income Tax Appellate Tribunal upheld the tax demand; however, CUHL did not pay the tax despite several notices. Finally, India engaged in the forced sale of CUHL's shares in CIL, which by November 2018, amounted to 98.72 per cent of CUHL's shareholding in CIL.[104] Simultaneously, Cairn Energy sued India, alleging that

98 *Cairn Energy* (n 10) para 25. For facts of this case see also Prabhash Ranjan, '*Cairn Energy v India*: Continuity in the Use of ILC Articles on State Responsibility' (2022) 37(1) ICSID Review 543–51.
99 *Cairn Energy* (n 10) paras 29–30.
100 ibid para 73.
101 ibid paras 32–43, 67–78.
102 ibid paras 146–84.
103 ibid para 186.
104 ibid para 205.

the imposition of taxes retroactively violates several provisions of the India-UK BIT, including the FET standard.

Characterisation of India's tax law amendment: clarificatory or retroactive?

One of the first issues before the *Cairn Energy* tribunal was classifying India's tax law amendment. As already pointed out, the amendment to the Income Tax Act was retroactive in nature. The *Cairn Energy* tribunal held the same. Let us understand how. The tribunal first defined retroactive law. It said that it would consider a law to be retroactive "if it changes the content of the law in the past, so that the law is deemed to have always had such (new) content, and applies to transactions that took place in the past".[105]

Next, the tribunal elucidated the meaning of the term 'clarificatory'. It held that to 'clarify' means "to make something clear or easier to understand".[106] Put differently, the tribunal held that a clarificatory amendment to the law would endeavour to make the meaning of the law more precise and lucid to get rid of its equivocal nature without changing the sense of the law or its scope.[107]

With these conceptual understandings in mind, the tribunal proceeded to analyse whether the amendment to Section 9(1)(i) of the Income Tax Act brought out by the 2012 amendment was retroactive or clarificatory. To answer this question, the tribunal studied the Indian tax law, the legislative debates, and most importantly, the decision of the Supreme Court in the *Vodafone* case[108] – the sole instance where the apex court interpreted Section 9(1)(i) of the Income Tax Act as it stood before the 2012 amendment. As already discussed, the Supreme Court interpreted Section 9(1)(i) to mean that it did not cover indirect transfers. After elaborately debating the Supreme Court's *Vodafone* ruling,[109] as it represented the Indian law on the issue of imposing capital gains tax on indirect transfers, the tribunal concluded that the Indian law as it existed till the day it was amended in 2012 did not allow for imposing capital gains tax on indirect transfers.[110] The 2012 amendment, by making indirect transfers taxable, expanded the scope of Section 9(1)(i) not just for future transactions and incomes but also for past transactions and incomes going back to 1 April 1962, the year the Income Tax Act was enacted.[111] The 2012 amendment changed the content of Section 9(1)(i) as it existed in the past and did so with effect on all such transactions dating back to 1 April 1962. This was much more than just clarifying the law. Put differently,

105 ibid para 1080.
106 ibid para 1081.
107 ibid.
108 *Vodafone International Holdings BV v Union of India* (n 61).
109 *Cairn Energy* (n 10) paras 1204–49.
110 ibid para 1250.
111 ibid para 1258.

this amendment created or imposed a new tax obligation on past income that was not taxable according to the law at that time – a point that the Supreme Court of India clarified.

The constitutionality argument

Next, India argued that the 2012 amendment was constitutional because the Indian legal system permitted enacting tax legislation that had a retroactive effect.[112] While this is true, it does not mean the parliament's power to amend tax laws retroactively is limitless. The Supreme Court has clarified that a retroactive tax legislation that imposes a startling financial burden on a taxpayer or broadens the meaning of a provision in an unforeseeable manner will not be constitutional.[113]

At any rate, as the tribunal held, whether the 2012 amendment was constitutional might be a factor in considering whether India has breached its BIT obligations, but it is not dispositive of it.[114] Besides, assuming the 2012 amendment was constitutional, does not answer the fundamental question of whether India breached its international law obligations contained in the BIT. As the tribunal held, parliaments worldwide have the right to change any law, including the Constitution itself.[115] From the standpoint of international law, the question is whether such a change in the law is consistent with that country's international obligations. The fact that a law enacted or amended is constitutional or legal as per the country's municipal legal system does not preclude a finding that the State may have breached its international law obligations.[116] Therefore, even if the 2012 amendment is constitutional under the Indian legal system, it could still breach India's BIT obligations.[117] The determination of whether India has breached its obligations under the India-UK BIT has to be answered by primarily applying international law.[118]

Exclusion of taxation measures from the scope of the BIT

Another argument India advanced to defend its tax measures was that taxation matters are beyond the ambit of the BIT arbitration.[119] This argument aimed to prove that the *Cairn Energy* tribunal does not have jurisdiction. One part of

112 ibid paras 838–46.
113 *Jayam and Company v Assistant Commissioner & Anr* (2016) 15 SCC 125. See also *Cairn Energy* (n 10) paras 1682, 1683.
114 *Cairn Energy* (n 10) paras 1688–92.
115 ibid para 1064.
116 ibid.
117 ibid.
118 ibid para 863.
119 ibid para 792.

India's argument originated from that school of thought, which, as discussed in the chapter before, believes that there is something special or unique about a State's right to tax, and thus, it cannot be arbitrated before an ISDS tribunal as part of international public policy. The second part of India's argument was textual, based on the text of the India-UK BIT.[120]

Let us see how the tribunal dealt with these parts of India's core argument. On the issue of taxation measures being not arbitrable due to it being a part of international public policy, the tribunal first clarified that the dispute before it was not a taxation dispute but a tax-related investment dispute.[121] This point has been discussed before in the chapter. Arguably, this distinction is unnecessary. It is unlikely that a foreign investor will bring a tax dispute proper before an ISDS tribunal, that is, a row about the taxability of a specific transaction. The investor will likely bring a claim alleging that the State's taxation measure breaches one or more substantive treaty protection standards contained in the BIT. Thus, most, if not all, tax disputes before ISDS tribunals will be tax-related investment disputes. Nonetheless, the distinction between tax and tax-related investment disputes is essential conceptually.

Hence, the *Cairn Energy* tribunal framed the issue as whether taxation-related investment disputes are not arbitrable as part of international public policy.[122] The tribunal held that they are. Several international instruments were referred to buttress this point, such as the scores of investment treaties that European Union (EU) member countries have signed that allow tax-related investment disputes to be arbitrated;[123] and OECD's Multilateral Convention to Implement Tax Treaty-Related Measures to Prevent Base Erosion and Profit Shifting, which permits arbitration of tax-related claims.[124]

Another important contribution that the tribunal made is the distinction between dealing with tax-related investment disputes related to the tribunal's jurisdiction and merits stage. International law calls for deferential scrutiny of taxation or fiscal measures because they are undistinguishably linked to a State's sovereign exercise of police powers.[125] However, this issue is related to the merits stage, when an international tribunal will adjudicate whether taxation measures breach the treaty standards. The fact that taxation measures are an integral part of the State's police powers cannot be the basis to say that tax-related investment disputes are not arbitrable. At any rate, as already discussed at the beginning of this chapter, there is no automatic immunity to taxation measures from the purview of BIT claims.

120 ibid.
121 ibid paras 793–94.
122 ibid para 828.
123 ibid para 830.
124 ibid para 833.
125 ibid.

On the textual point, whether the India-UK BIT excludes tax-related investment disputes from its coverage, the tribunal analysed several provisions of the BIT. First, the tribunal referred to the issue of India's consent for arbitration located in Article 9 of the BIT. Article 9(1) provides:

> *Any dispute between an investor of one Contracting Party and the other Contracting Party in relation to an investment of the former under this Agreement shall, as far as possible, be settled amicably through negotiations between the parties to the dispute.*

Article 9(2) provides:

> *Any dispute which has not been amicably settled within a period of six months from written notification of a claim may be submitted to international conciliation under the Conciliation Rules of the United Nations Commission on International Trade Law, if the parties to the dispute so agree.*

Article 9 uses the words "any dispute". Thus, it is a broad jurisdictional clause. The signatory countries have consented to arbitration for all disputes between the foreign investor and the host State, including tax-related investment disputes.[126] There is no explicit exclusion for any category of disputes from the jurisdiction of ISDS tribunals.

Second, the tribunal looked at Article 4(3)(b), which provides:

> *The provisions of this Agreement relative to the grant of treatment not less favourable than that accorded to the investors of either Contracting Party or of any third State shall not be construed so as to oblige one Contracting Party to extend to the investors of the other the benefit of any treatment, preference or privilege resulting from:*
>
> . . .*(b) any international agreement or arrangement relating wholly or mainly to taxation or any domestic legislation relating wholly or mainly to taxation.*

Article 4(3)(b) carves out taxation measures for two substantive standards – MFN and national treatment. In other words, if the host State treats a foreign investor less favourably in terms of taxation *vis-à-vis* another foreign investor (MFN) or a domestic investor (national treatment), such regulatory conduct will not give rise to a tax-related investment claim as far as these two standards are concerned. However, there is no exception for other substantive treaty

126 ibid paras 796–98.

standards, such as the FET provision. In other words, Article 4(3)(b) is a limited tax-related exception in the BIT.[127]

Thus, it is quite clear that there is no exclusion of taxation measures from the scope of the BIT, either as part of public policy or textually. Like several other ISDS tribunals on taxation measures, the *Cairn Energy* tribunal stated that it would not comment on India's sovereign powers to tax indirect transfers; however, an absolute and unquestioning deference cannot be provided for such matters because there are limits on it.[128]

After having discussed that taxation measures are not *per se* excluded from the purview of the BIT, we will now examine how the tribunal dealt with the retroactivity of the tax amendment. Specifically, the question is whether a retroactive application of law breaches the FET standard. The FET standard in India-UK BIT is given in Article 3(2) as follows:

> *Investments of investors of each Contracting Party shall at all times be accorded fair and equitable treatment and shall enjoy full protection and security in the territory of the other Contracting Party.*

The normative content of the FET provision is missing in Article 3(2). Thus, like several other FET provisions, especially those present in the first-generation BIT, the onus of finding out the meaning of the FET provision is on the ISDS tribunal.

The handling of the retroactive tax measure

Before examining how the *Cairn Energy* tribunal dealt with the retroactivity issue, it will be useful to briefly sketch the scholarly and arbitral landscape on this issue, whether a retroactive change in the law (not restricted to tax law) breaches the FET provision. Numerous ISDS tribunals have held that a core component of the FET provision is legitimate expectations,[129] as also discussed in Chapter 2. The investor's legitimate expectations are based on the undertakings and representations that a host State makes, explicitly or implicitly, to the investor.[130] Much more than implicit, explicit representations or specific commitments are the strongest basis of legitimate expectations.[131] These

127 ibid para 799.

128 ibid at 1794.

129 See *Novenergia II – Energy & Environment (SCA), SICAR v Kingdom of Spain*, SCC Case No 063/2015, Final Award, 15 February 2018, para 648. *Watkins Holdings SÀRL and others v Kingdom of Spain*, ICSID Case No ARB/15/44, Award, 21 January 2020, para 518. See also Rudolf Dolzer, Ursula Kriebaum and Christoph Schreuer, *Principles of International Investment Law* (3rd edn, OUP 2022) 208–12.

130 ibid 208.

131 ibid 209. See also *Union Fenosa Gas, SA v Arab Republic of Egypt*, ICSID Case No ARB/14/4, Award, 31 August 2018, para 9.83.

explicit representations could include a specific commitment that the regulatory or legislative framework that existed at the time of investment shall not be altered. Put differently, foreign investors cannot legitimately expect, absent specific commitments, that a country will not change its laws. The assumption here is that one is talking about changing laws prospectively. But what happens when a law is changed retroactively? Stephan Schill argues that enacting legislation that has a retroactive effect may breach the foreign investor's legitimate expectations.[132] In other words, while foreign investors cannot legitimately expect that the host State will not change the laws minus specific commitments not to do so, this is only for changing the law prospectively, not retroactively. If the change were retroactive, it would arguably breach the FET provision even if the foreign investor has not made specific commitments.

Barring a few instances, the issue of retroactive legislation or measures has not been raised before ISDS tribunals. One such instance was in *ATA v Jordan*.[133] In this case, the foreign investor obtained a favourable decision against a State-owned company in Jordan. However, the Jordanian courts annulled this award. The Jordanian arbitration law, at that point in time, allowed the investor to initiate another arbitration if the court later annulled an award. In 2001, Jordan amended its arbitration law retroactively to extinguish the foreign investor's right to initiate another arbitration in case of annulment of a previous award.[134] Hence, this amendment denied the foreign investor the right to initiate a new arbitration, which it was earlier entitled to do. The tribunal held that this retroactive legislation violated the FET provision.[135]

Arguably, Jordanian law was not retroactive but retrospective because it was prospective in nature but looked backwards. It attached a new consequence in the future (not allowing the foreign investor to initiate new arbitration) to acts that happened before (the foreign investor bringing the original arbitration claim against Jordan's State-owned company) the law was enacted.[136]

In *Eiser v Spain*,[137] Spain changed its energy sector regulations retroactively. This was held to be a breach of the FET provision of the Energy Charter Treaty. The tribunal held that the FET provision cannot be interpreted to mean regulatory stability and, thus, the host State has the right to regulate the

132 S Schill, 'Fair and Equitable Treatment under Investment Treaties as an Embodiment of the Rule of Law' (2006) IILJ Working Paper 2006/6 (Global Administrative Law Series) <https://iilj.org/wp-content/uploads/2016/08/Schill-Fair-and-Equitable-Treatment-under-Investment-Treaties-as-an-Embodiment-of-the-Rule-of-Law-2006-2.pdf> accessed 1 July 2023.

133 *ATA Construction, Industrial and Trading Company v The Hashemite Kingdom of Jordan*, ICSID Case No ARB/08/2, Award, 18 May 2010.

134 ibid paras 116, 126.

135 ibid paras 121–29.

136 *Cairn Energy* (n 10) para 1778.

137 *Eiser Infrastructure Limited and Energia Solar Luxembourg SARL v Kingdom of Spain*, ICSID Case No ARB/13/36, Award, 4 May 2017, para 362.

evolving circumstances.[138] However, retroactive regulations that completely change the legal and regulatory framework amount to a radical and impermissible change, thus violating the FET provision.[139] Likewise, another ISDS tribunal, in *Bilcon of Delaware v Canada*,[140] observed that changes in legal or policy framework that have a retroactive effect would amount to a breach of the international minimum standard[141] under customary international law often considered equivalent to the FET standard in the BIT.

These tribunals did not scrutinize the retroactive measures in detail and proceeded on the assumption that retroactivity *per se* violates the FET provision. On the other hand, the *Cairn Energy* tribunal offered a detailed and nuanced analysis of the retroactive tax measure. Although this analysis is in the context of the retractive tax legislation, it will also hold good for other retroactive measures.

The *Cairn Energy* tribunal examined the validity of retroactive taxation *vis-à-vis* the FET provision. The tribunal stated that an important element of the FET standard is the principle of legal certainty, an aspect of the rule of law.[142] Several tribunals have documented certainty or stability in the legal framework as part of the FET provision.[143] The vexed question is whether legal certainty or stability means the immutability of the regulatory framework that existed when the investment was made. Federico Ortino traces the evolution of arbitral practice on this issue. He shows that older tribunals followed a 'strict stability obligation' whereby any alteration in the regulatory regime was understood as a change in the legal framework that the investor considered while investing, and thus, a breach of the FET provision.[144] The tribunals did not examine any justifications or rationale for making such a

138 ibid para 362.

139 ibid paras 382, 414. See also Y Kryvoi and S Matos, 'Non-Retroactivity as a General Principle of Law' (2021) 17(1) Utrecht Law Review 46–58.

140 *Clayton and Bilcon of Delaware Inc v Government of Canada*, PCA Case No 2009-4, Award on Jurisdiction and Liability, 17 March 2015.

141 ibid para 572.

142 *Cairn Energy* (n 10) paras 1741–47. For a critical discussion on the tribunal's methodology to determine the content of the FET provision, See J Paine, '*Cairn Energy v India*: Retroactive Taxation, Fair and Equitable Treatment and the General Principles Method' (*EJIL: Talk*, 13 January 2021) <https://www.ejiltalk.org/cairn-energy-v-india-retroactive-taxation-fair-and-equitable-treatment-and-the-general-principles-method/> accessed 1 July 2023.

143 See *PSEG Global, Inc, The North American Coal Corporation, and Konya Ingin Electrik Uretim ve Ticaret Limited Sirketi v Republic of Turkey*, ICSID Case No ARB/02/5, Award, 19 January 2007, para 250. See *Murphy Exploration and Production Company International v Republic of Ecuador (II)*, PCA Case No 2012-16 (formerly AA 434), Partial Final Award, 6 May 2016, para 207.

144 See F Ortino, 'The Obligation of Regulatory Stability in the Fair and Equitable Treatment Standard: How Far Have We Come?' (2018) 21(4) Journal of International Economic Law 845–65.

change.[145] The later tribunals have adopted what Ortino calls conceptually a 'softer stability obligation' where merely an alteration in the regulatory regime does not mean that stability and predictability of the legal framework have been modified, resulting in a violation of the FET provision.[146]

The justifiable reason for the 'softer stability approach' is that if States are held liable for merely changing their laws in good faith, it will have a chilling effect on their right to regulate in the public interest.[147] As the tribunal held in *9REN v Spain*, there is a "need to balance a State's regulatory autonomy against international obligations freely undertaken".[148] Often, States are required to respond to new imperatives and challenges, which, in turn, might require modifications in the legal framework. Countries should have the regulatory freedom to do so.[149] Therefore any change in the legal and regulatory framework cannot be interpreted to mean that the State has failed to honour the principle of legal certainty and thus breached the FET provision.[150]

At the same time, the tribunals have also held that the changes made by the host State to its legal framework should bear a "reasonable relationship to rational policies".[151] In other words, amendments to the legal framework will not violate the requirement of legal stability, provided the regulatory measures are reasonably related to a legitimate public policy objective or are proportionate.[152]

While recognizing that legal certainty is a part of the FET provision, the *Cairn Energy* tribunal followed the 'softer stability obligation' approach and held that legal certainty is not absolute. While many tribunals, as discussed, have held that countries can change their laws, meaning thereby that changes will be made to the legal framework prospectively, the *Cairn Energy* tribunal recognized that even retroactive changes are permissible provided they were proportional to the public purpose sought to be achieved.[153] Thus, according to the tribunal, the State's public purpose in enacting retroactive law should

145 ibid. A good example of this is *Occidental Exploration and Production Company v Republic of Ecuador (I)*, LCIA Case No UN3467, Award, 1 July 2004, para 183.

146 See Ortino (2018) (n 144); See also *Saluka Investments BV v Czech Republic*, UNCITRAL, Partial Award, 17 March 2006, paras 302–5.

147 See *Impregilo SpA v Argentine Republic*, ICSID Case No ARB/07/17, Award, 21 June 2011.

148 *9REN Holding SARL v Kingdom of Spain*, ICSID Case No ARB/15/15, 31 May 2019, para 254.

149 See *Voltaic Network GmbH v Czech Republic*, PCA Case No 2014-20, Award, 15 May 2019, para 488; *Charanne v Spain* (n 24) paras 510, 513.

150 See *Masdar Solar & Wind Cooperatief UA v Kingdom of Spain*, ICSID Case No ARB/14/1, Award, 16 May 2018.

151 *Saluka v Czech Republic* (n 146) para 305.

152 See *Jan Oostergetel and Theodora Laurentius* v *Slovak Republic*, UNCITRAL, Final Award (23 April 2012) para 224; *Charanne v Spain* (n 24) para 514.

153 *Cairn Energy* (n 10) paras 1788–89.

be balanced with the investor's interest in legal certainty.[154] The *Cairn Energy* tribunal's contribution in this regard is the following. First, the tribunal added a new dimension to the test: 'regulatory changes are permissible if proportionate'. This new dimension extends the proportionality argument to retroactive amendments. Thus, retroactive amendments are also permissible if they are proportionate. Second, the *Cairn Energy* tribunal brought a new nuance to the debate that retroactive change *per se* is to be condemned. According to the *Cairn Energy* tribunal, just because a change in law has been made retroactively, that, on its own, does not mean that the host State has breached the principle of legal certainty, and thus the FET provision.

In the context of India's retroactive tax law, the issue was whether a specific public purpose justified India's decision to impose taxes retroactively that could not be attained by applying taxes prospectively.[155] The tribunal stated that there is a reasonable presumption that laws will be applied prospectively. Therefore, the public purpose that justifies the prospective application of law will usually be insufficient to justify its retroactive application.[156] There must be an additional public purpose demonstrating sufficient legal reasoning for the retroactive application of the law.[157] Thus, the tribunal laid down a stricter proportionality test to justify a retroactive change in the law. This is entirely justifiable because the more severe or drastic a legal change, the greater its justification to legitimize it.

The tribunal applied this stricter standard to various justifications advanced by India. For example, India argued that the legislative change was intended to ensure that foreign corporations that use tax havens to indirectly transfer underlying Indian assets pay taxes. However, the tribunal held that this objective could be accomplished by amending the income tax law prospectively and not retroactively.[158] Likewise, India attempted to justify retroactive taxation by contending that it aimed at combating foreign corporations' systemic tax abuse. The tribunal did not agree and held that India failed to demonstrate that there was any such systemic abuse. Furthermore, in the event of abusive taxation, India had other tools to attempt to address it effectively.[159] Thus, the tribunal reasoned that India's decision to apply the law without specific justification retroactively created a new tax burden on a transaction that was not taxable when it occurred, that is, in 2006.[160] By doing so, India deprived Cairn of its ability to plan its activities, keeping in mind the legal consequences of its conduct.[161] The tribunal thus concluded that India's decision to retroactively apply the law disproportionately undermined the principle of legal certainty,

154 ibid.
155 ibid para 1790.
156 ibid.
157 ibid paras 1794, 1801.
158 ibid paras 1809–10.
159 *Cairn Energy* (n 10) paras 1812–15.
160 ibid para 1816.
161 ibid.

violating the FET standard. The tribunal ordered India to pay US$1.2 billion to Cairn plus interest, totalling approximately US$1.7 billion.[162]

India refused to comply with the award because it believes that the award is "highly flawed".[163] India not complying with the awards, led Cairn to commence enforcement proceedings against India globally to recover the compensation awarded by the tribunal. For example, Cairn commenced an enforcement petition in a court in the United States against India's national airline carrier, Air India, to seize the aircraft and other assets to enforce the award.[164] Cairn also pleaded with a French court to seize Indian assets to recover the amount due.[165]

Nonetheless, in 2021, India amended its Income Tax Act to do away with the retroactive changes introduced by the 2012 amendment. We discuss the 2021 amendment next.

4.3.4 2021 amendment

In late 2021, India amended the Income Tax Act to eliminate the 2012 retroactive application of tax laws on indirect transfers.[166] A new proviso has been added to Explanation 5 in Section 9(1)(i) of the Income Tax Act.[167] This proviso states that any claim for a capital gains tax will not apply to indirect transfers of Indian assets made on or before 28 May 2012, when the 2012 amendment entered into force. By making the 2012 amendment prospective in nature, the 2021 amendment ensures that Section 9(1)(i) shall not apply to transactions like those of Vodafone and Cairn Energy.

Section 119 of Finance Act 2012, which validated the tax demands retroactively after the Supreme Court judgement in favour of Vodafone, has been jettisoned.[168] However, the nullification of tax demands on indirect transfers that took place before 28 May 2012 is subject to certain riders. First, India will return only the principal amount in tax collected due to the application

162 A Ranade, 'How India Ended Up Owing $1.7 Billion to Cairn' *The Times of India* (23 July 2021) <https://timesofindia.indiatimes.com/india/how-india-ended-up-owing-1-7-billion-to-cairn/articleshow/84611453.cms> accessed 25 August 2023.

163 Ministry of Finance, 'Government of India Condemns False Reporting on Cairn Legal Dispute' (23 May 2021) <https://pib.gov.in/PressReleaseIframePage.aspx?PRIBID=1721039> accessed 25 August 2021.

164 C Shah and M Rodin, *Cairn Energy v Air India: A New Approach to "Flight Risk" in Enforcement Terms?* (Thomson Reuters, 16 July 2021) <http://arbitrationblog.practicallaw.com/cairn-energy-v-air-india-a-new-approach-to-flight-risk-in-enforcement-terms/> accessed 1 July 2023.

165 P Upadhyay, 'Retrospective Tax on Indirect Transfers to Be Made Prospective: New Bill' (*Bloomberg Quint*, 5 August 2021) <https://www.bloombergquint.com/business/retrospective-tax-on-indirect-transfers-to-be-made-prospective-new-bill> accessed 25 August 2023.

166 Taxation Laws (Amendment) Act, 2021.

167 ibid s 2.

168 ibid s 3. This adds a proviso to Section 119 of the Finance Act, 2012.

of retroactive taxation and not the interest. The decision not to return the interest but only the principal is profoundly problematic. It contradicts the clear statutory provision under section 244A of the Income Tax Act by which the government is obliged to pay interest if any amount is to be refunded to the assessee.[169] However, in the instant amendment, the government has sidestepped the requirement provided in section 244A without offering any plausible justification. In the specific case of Cairn Energy, only returning the principal amount would mean that Cairn would receive much less money than what the ISDS tribunal under the India-UK BIT ordered.

Second, the company or entity that was subjected to retroactive taxation will have to withdraw all cases regarding retroactive tax that are filed either in domestic courts or before international arbitration. Third, the company or the entity concerned shall also have to waive their right to seek a legal remedy against retroactive taxation in domestic courts and before international arbitration tribunals.

Stated differently, the 2021 amendment offers conciliation to investors such as Vodafone and Cairn to settle their longstanding tax disputes. Vodafone and Cairn will have to accept the principal amount, forego the interest, and cease all of the legal proceedings under the ISDS, including the attempts to enforce the tribunal's decision in different jurisdictions. They will also have to waive their right to bring an ISDS claim in the future on this matter. This also means that retroactive taxation will continue to apply if Vodafone and Cairn did not adhere to these prescribed conditions.

It is important to note that India has not incorporated this amendment into the Income Tax Act and the Finance Act to comply with the two adverse ISDS awards or its international law obligations enshrined in the BIT; however, the defeats at the two ISDS tribunals instigated its inclusion. If India intended to comply with the adverse ISDS awards, it would have indicated this in the 'statement of objects and reasons' of the 2021 amendment.[170] Additionally, India should have offered to pay the interest on the taxes it had collected from foreign investors by applying the tax law retroactively. The 'statement of objects and reasons' of the 2021 amendment states that this change is being made as part of domestic legal reforms in India to provide tax stability and certainty to foreign investors.[171] India, however, continues to believe that taxation matters are beyond the purview of BIT arbitration.[172]

169 Section 244A(1) of Income Tax Act, 1961 provides: "Where refund of any amount becomes due to the assessee under this Act, he shall, subject to the provisions of this section, be entitled to receive, in addition to the said amount, simple interest thereon' calculated as per the method given in the section".

170 Taxation Laws (Amendment) Act 2021, 'Statement of Objects and Reasons'.

171 ibid.

172 R Jayaswal and R Singh, 'Retro Tax Ban Won't Dilute Sovereign Right to Tax: FM' *Hindustan Times* (10 August 2021) <https://www.hindustantimes.com/business/retro-tax-ban-won-t-dilute-sovereign-right-to-taxfm-101628558797665.html> accessed 25 August 2021.

4.4 Conclusion

Benjamin Franklin famously said that nothing in this world is certain but death and taxes. Undoubtedly, India has the sovereign power to impose taxes on foreign corporations. However, this power should be exercised within the due limits, including the boundaries imposed by international law. The *Vodafone* and *Cairn Energy* cases would not have arisen had India not retroactively amended its tax law with the specific objective of overruling the decision of the Supreme Court in favour of Vodafone. The retroactive saga falls under the Yukos narrative. It is a classic case of the State, after losing a case to a foreign investor in the country's apex court, using its sovereign power to change the rules of the game, overturning the outcome, which was in the favour of the foreign investor. It gives the impression that India was targeting one particular company to pay taxes overlooking its own judicial decisions. It also shows a certain degree of malice. Thus, in one stroke, amending the IT Act in 2012, India wiped out Vodafone's benefit from the Supreme Court and converted an illegal tax demand into a lawful one. This new tax law re-opened the *Vodafone* case and all the concluded transactions dating back to 1962, including Cairn Energy's internal restructuring.

The government admitted that the 2012 amendment was a mistake when it decided to amend the Income Tax Act in 2021. Prime Minister Narendra Modi said: "Recently, fixing mistakes of the past, we have decided to end retrospective taxation. The way in which this is being appreciated by the industry makes me believe that this will lead to the trust between industry and Government being strengthened".[173] Thus, it was a mistake that triggered these ISDS claims against India.

The government did a commendable job when it decided to amend the Income Tax Act in 2021, though this should have been done before. While the amendment doing away with the imposition of taxes retroactively will reinforce foreign investors' confidence to invest in India, it would have been better if it had made this change to its tax laws to comply with the *Vodafone I* and *Cairn Energy* tribunals' awards. That would have promoted India's image much more as a liberal democracy that respects and abides by the decisions of international tribunals. A more fundamental question is, what did India gain from this misadventure that lasted more than nine years? It spent considerable resources in fighting legal battles in international tribunals. It will not receive the revenue it wanted to earn through retroactively applying tax laws. Moreover, the decision to retroactively impose taxes severely besmirched India's reputation as a prime destination for foreign investment and a country based on the rule of law.

173 'CII Meet: Fixing Mistakes of Past, Retrospective Tax Move Will Build Trust, Says PM Modi' *The Indian Express* (12 August 2021) <https://indianexpress.com/article/business/economy/cii-meet-fixing-mistakes-of-past-retrospective-tax-move-will-build-trust-says-pm-modi-7449594/> accessed 2 August 2023.

The important lessons that India can learn are as follows. First, if India's objective was to ensure that transnational corporations that use tax havens for selling or buying capital assets that derive their value from assets based in India, it could have amended Section 9(1)(i) of the Income Tax Act prospectively. Second, countries need to internalize and consider their BIT obligations while undertaking massive changes in their taxation regime. There is no evidence that India considered its BIT obligations while changing the tax laws retroactively. Third, and most importantly, a liberal democracy like India should exercise its public power in a manner compatible with the letter and spirit of the rule of law, that is, imposing taxes without oppressing anyone.

5 The Nissan Saga

ISDS claims due to the actions of sub-national governments

5.1 Introduction

An important ISDS claim brought against India was by the Japanese automaker Nissan.[1] This claim – *Nissan v India*[2] – arose against India due to the actions of the government of Tamil Nadu, a State in South India where Nissan had invested in a vehicle manufacturing plant.[3] This investment was made through a consortium known as the R&N Consortium, which comprised of Nissan and another company, Renault.[4] This consortium also consisted of other entities such as Nissan Motor India Private Limited (NMIPL) – a wholly owned subsidiary of Nissan International Holding B.V.,[5] and a jointly owned entity by Renault and Renault B.V. called Renault Indian Private Limited (RIPL).[6] A memorandum of understanding (MoU) was entered into between the R&N consortium and the government of Tamil Nadu.[7] As per this MoU, the R&N Consortium agreed to invest in the State for seven years in return for various investment incentives, including fiscal incentives the Tamil Nadu government promised the investors.[8]

Nissan invested approximately US$890 million toward erecting a vehicle manufacturing plant.[9] However, the Tamil Nadu government failed to pay the promised incentives. Further, the State of Tamil Nadu amended the Tamil Nadu Value Added Tax (TN VAT) Act to deny the tax benefits that Nissan claimed and adopted other government orders.[10] Subsequently, NMIPL and

1 *Nissan Motor Co, Ltd v Republic of India*, PCA Case No 2017-37, Decision on Jurisdiction, 29 Apr 2019. (hereinafter '*Nissan v India*').
2 ibid.
3 ibid para 54.
4 ibid.
5 ibid.
6 ibid.
7 ibid para 55.
8 ibid.
9 ibid.
10 ibid para 165.

DOI: 10.4324/9781003324379-5

RIPL brought claims against the Tamil Nadu government at the Madras High Court, challenging the constitutionality of these actions.

Additionally, Nissan brought an ISDS claim alleging that the denial of promised value-added tax (VAT) refunds or fiscal incentives violated the fair and equitable treatment (FET) clause in Article 87(1) of the India-Japan FTA.[11] In other words, Nissan brought a claim against India for the alleged failure of the Tamil Nadu government to pay as per their promise and claimed approximately US$770 million in damages.[12] Nissan also argued that India breached the umbrella clause in Article 87(2) of the India-Japan FTA.

This case falls in the category of ISDS disputes initiated against a country for the actions of one of its sub-national governments because the latter's activities can be attributed to the former. An additional ISDS claim has been lodged against India due to the actions of a sub-national or federal government – *RAKIV v India*.[13] RAKIA or Ras Al Khaimah Investment Authority is a UAE company that sued India under the India-UAE BIT due to the deeds of the government of Andhra Pradesh, a State in Southern India.[14] RAKIA brought this claim because the Andhra Pradesh government had cancelled an agreement to supply bauxite to an aluminium refinery that the former controlled.[15] In May 2022, an ISDS tribunal dismissed the case on jurisdictional grounds.[16] However, since the arbitral award is not available in the public domain, one does not know the reasoning of the ISDS tribunal. This impedes our ability to deal with this case in detail. Consequently, the emphasis of the chapter will be on the *Nissan* case.

Given that both these cases were brought against India due to the actions of the regional governments, and considering that India has 28 States, each with its own sub-national administration capable of influencing foreign investments, it becomes crucial to understand this matter comprehensively. Hence, in Section 5.2, the chapter discusses the rules of attribution under international law before focussing on the *Nissan* case and its issues in detail. After discussing the rules of attribution, the chapter will emphasize three specific arguments that cropped up in the *Nissan v India* case. In Section 5.3, the

11 ibid para 56.

12 ET Bureau, 'Nissan Sues India Over Outstanding Dues Seeks Over $770 Million' *Economic Times* (1 December 2017) <https://economictimes.indiatimes.com/industry/auto/news/nissan-sues-india-over-outstanding-dues-seeks-over-770-mln/articleshow/61875710.cms> accessed 27 August 2023.

13 Ras-Al-Khaimah Investment Authority v. India, PCA Award, 11 May 2022.

14 Zoe Williams, 'Emirati Investor Files UNICITRAL BIT Arbitration Against India' *IAReporter* (12 January 2017) <https://www.iareporter.com/articles/emirati-investor-files-uncitral-bit-arbitration-against-india/> accessed 27 August 2023.

15 ibid.

16 V Raghavendra, 'Bauxite Mining Dispute | IDRC Dismisses UAE Body's Claim for Damages from Andhra Govt' *The Hindu* (19 May 2022) <https://www.thehindu.com/news/national/andhra-pradesh/bauxite-mining-dispute-idrc-dismisses-uae-bodys-claim-for-damages-from-andhra-govt/article65429248.ece> accessed 27 August 2023.

chapter will examine India's assertion that Nissan cannot bring a claim against India due to 'lack of privity'. Next, in Section 5.4, the focus will shift to India's argument that the tribunal lacked jurisdiction due to a fork-in-the-road provision in the India-Japan FTA. In Section 5.5, the chapter will examine India's view that the tribunal does not have jurisdiction because the dispute involves taxation measures. Section 5.6 offers the concluding remarks.

5.2 Rules of attribution

Rules of attribution are critical in international law to decide the accountability of States. States can be held accountable under international law for an action only if that action can be attributed to that State. The most important instrument here is the International Law Commission's (ILC's) Articles on the Responsibility of States for Internationally Wrongful Acts (ARSIWA). Article 2 of ARSIWA states that for an internationally wrongful act of a State to occur, two conditions must be satisfied: first, the action or the omission should be attributable to the State under international law; and second, such action or omission should constitute a breach of an international obligation of the State.[17] Therefore, one of the most critical requirements of Article 2 is that the conduct in question should be attributable to the State.[18] Chapter II of ARSIWA (Articles 4 to 11) elucidates the circumstances when the conduct of an act or omission is considered the conduct of the State.[19] In particular, we focus on Article 4(1) of ARSIWA, which provides as follows:

> *The conduct of any State organ shall be considered an act of that State under international law, whether the organ exercises legislative, executive, judicial or any other functions, whatever position it holds in the organization of the State, and whatever its character as an organ of the central Government or of a territorial unit of the State.*

As per the ILC commentaries on ARSIWA, Article 4(1) provides the "first principle of attribution" to establish State responsibility in international law.[20] This first principle is that "the conduct of an organ of the State is attributable to that State".[21] Alternatively known as the 'State unity' theory, this principle recognizes that any State action regardless of the level at which it occurs, is attributed to the respective State that is a subject of

17 See International Law Commission, 'Draft Articles on Responsibility of States for Internationally Wrongful Acts' (November 2001) Supplement No 10 (A/56/10) chp.IV.E.1 <https://legal.un.org/ilc/texts/instruments/english/commentaries/9_6_2001.pdf > accessed 27 August 2023. (hereinafter 'ILC Commentaries').

18 ibid 38.

19 ibid.

20 ibid 40.

21 ibid.

international law.[22] The "organ of a State" here includes all entities irrespective of whether they perform executive, legislative, or judicial functions and regardless of the position they hold in the State's organization. It is important to note, for the purposes of this chapter, the conduct of a territorial unit of a State such as a sub-national or a provincial government or regional and local units is also attributable to that State.[23] The actions of a sub-national government are attributable to the State because federal countries have diverse structures and varying power distribution. Further, these constituent units neither have a separate international legal personality nor treaty-making power.[24]

Various ISDS tribunals have also held that actions of territorial units, provincial governments, or bodies are attributable to the State.[25] In one case, *UAB Energija (Lithuania) v Latvia*,[26] the tribunal held that the conduct of a municipality (local government) is attributable to the State.[27] In other words, under international law, the central government is responsible for the actions of its territorial units such as provinces, constituent States, and municipalities.[28] This is true even if the provincial governments or territorial units in a State have a separate legal personality under that country's municipal law.[29] For

22 Arwel Davies, 'State Liability for Judicial Decisions in European Union and International Law' (2012) 61 International & Comparative Law Quarterly 585–611; Robet Kolb, *The International Law of State Responsibility* (Edward Elgar 2017) 70–102.

23 ILC Commentaries (n 17) 41. See also *LaGrand (Germany v United States of America)*, Judgment, ICJ Reports (2001) 466 at 495, para 81.

24 ILC Commentaries (n 17) 42.

25 *Resolute Forest Products Inc v Canada*, PCA Case No 2016-13, paras 298–300, 306. See also Carlo de Stefano, 'Attribution of Conduct to a State' (2022) 37 ICSID Review – Foreign Investment Law Journal 20, 35–36; Yannick Radi, *Rules and Practices of International Investment Law and Arbitration* (CUP 2020) 430–32.

26 *UAB Eenergija (Lithuania) v Republic of Latvia*, ICSID Case No ARB/12/33. See also *Metalclad Corporation v The United Mexican States*, ICSID Case No ARB(AF)/97/1, Award, 30 August 2000, para 73.

27 *UAB Eenergija (Lithuania) v Republic of Latvia*, paras 799–800.

28 *Stabil, Crimea-Petrol LLC, Elefteria LLC, Novel-Estate LLC and others v The Russian Federation*, PCA Case No 2015-35, paras 168, 173; *Enron Creditors Recovery Corporation (Formerly Enron Corporation) and Ponderosa Assets, LP v Argentine Republic*, ICSID Case No ARB/01/3 (also known as *Enron Creditors Recovery Corp and Ponderosa Assets, LP v The Argentine Republic*), Decision on Jurisdiction, 14 January 2004, para 32; *Parkerings-Compagniet AS v Republic of Lithuania*, ICSID Case No ARB/05/8, Award, 11 September 2007, paras 259–65; *Compañía de Aguas del Aconquija SA (Formerly Aguas del Aconquija) and Vivendi Universal SA (Formerly Compagnie Générale des Eaux) v Argentine Republic (I)*, ICSID Case No ARB/97/3 Award, 21 November 2000, para 49 (hereinafter '*Vivendi v Argentina I*'); *Mytilineos Holdings SA v The State Union of Serbia & Montenegro and Republic of Serbia (I)*, Partial Award on Jurisdiction, 8 September 2006, paras 173, 175, 176.

29 *Tethyan Copper Company Pty Limited v Islamic Republic of Pakistan*, ICSID Case No ARB/12/1, para 727. See also *Muhammet Çap & Sehil Inşaat Endustri ve Ticaret Ltd Sti v Turkmenistan*, ICSID Case No ARB/12/6, para 749; Jorge E Viñuales, 'Attribution of Conduct to States in Investment Arbitration' (2022) 20 ICSID Reports 13, 43.

example, in *Tethyan Copper v Pakistan*,[30] the conduct of Pakistan's Balochistan province was attributed to Pakistan by relying on Article 4 of ARSIWA. Likewise, in *Casinos Austria v Argentina*, the conduct of the Argentinean province of Salta was attributed to Argentina.[31]

In addition to the international legal principle of attribution, an ISDS tribunal justified attributing a province's action to the State by holding that investment treaties would be rendered meaningless if they applied only to national governments and not to the actions of the territorial governments.[32] When a foreign investor invests in a country, the concerned investment might be made in a province of that nation. Such a province might not be directly governed by the central authority but instead may fall under the jurisdiction of a provincial or territorial government. This could be due to the country's internal governance and constitutional structures. In such a situation, the foreign investor will be subjected to the provincial government's actions. Such actions will have a far more significant impact on foreign investment than the conduct of the national government. Arguing that regulatory measures of the provincial government are not attributable to the central government will essentially mean suspending the application of the investment treaty thereby exposing foreign investment to high regulatory risks. This outcome would undermine the fundamental intent behind States signing BITs.

However, there is an important caveat to the preceding discussion. The customary international law rule codified in Article 4(1) of ARSIWA will not apply if countries have agreed to special regimes of responsibility, for example, as part of a treaty.[33] This is recognized in Article 55 of ARSIWA, titled *lex specialis*, which states as follows:

> *These articles do not apply where and to the extent that the conditions for the existence of an internationally wrongful act or the content or implementation of the international responsibility of a State are governed by special rules of international law.*

In other words, countries are free to follow an approach to State responsibility that differs from ARSIWA.[34] This makes ARSIWA residual in their

30 *Tethyan Copper* (n 29) para 727.

31 *Casinos Austria International GmbH and Casinos Austria Aktiengesellschaft v Argentine Republic*, ICSID Case No ARB/14/32, Decision on Jurisdiction, 29 June 2018, para 288.

32 *Zhongshan Fucheng Industrial Investment Co Ltd v Federal Republic of Nigeria*, Final Award, 26 March 2021 para 73.

33 See Martii Koskenniemi, 'Fragmentation of International Law: Difficulties Arising from the Diversification and Expansion of International Law' (13 April 2006) Report of the Study Group of the International Law Commission, Document A/AC.4/L.682, para 142.

34 See Katja Creutz, 'The Tenacity of the Articles on State Responsibility as a General and Residual Framework: An Appraisal' in Federica Paddeu and Christian J Tams (eds), *The ILC Articles at 20* (Working Paper Series Vol 11, GCILS 2021).

application.[35] ISDS tribunals have also upheld the residual nature of ARSIWA, indicating that the unique attribution framework provided by the investment treaty will take precedence over the general principles of attribution.[36] An excellent example of following a *lex specialis* approach is countries signing treaties that define 'State' in narrower terms or in a manner that may produce results different from what would happen if the ARSIWA's attribution rules are applied.[37] Countries may agree to a special regime by including the so-called federal clauses in treaties[38] that limit the application of the treaty obligations to the federal or central government or federal or central legislature and exclude the applicability of the treaty provisions to certain tiers of governments.[39] In the presence of such federal clauses, the treaty obligations will not bind that State's territorial units or provincial governments.

5.2.1 Federal clauses in India's BITs

It is in this context we turn to examine India's new investment treaty practice on the issue of attribution. Before one looks at the 2016 Model BIT and the subsequent investment treaties, it will be instructive to look at the draft 2015 Model BIT. Before India adopted a Model BIT in late 2015, early 2016, it issued a draft Model BIT in the early part of 2015. The final version was quite different from the draft 2015 Model BIT. Article 1.3(i) of the draft 2015 Model BIT defines "government" as "only the Central Government and State Governments in the case of India". Thus, the actions of local governments, that is, governmental structures beneath the State or territorial governments cannot be attributed to the Indian State. Such local governments include municipal authorities, district authorities, and other authorities at the village level. This marks a clear departure from the 'State unity' theory envisaged in Article 4(1) of ARSIWA previously discussed.

Although the actions of federal or provincial governments are attributable to the Indian State, an exception is created for the national treatment provision. Article 4.3 states that the national treatment provision "shall not apply to any law or measure of a regional or local government". Regional government

35 Stefano (n 25) 22; ILC Commentaries (n 17) 32.

36 *Mesa Power Group LLC v Government of Canada*, PCA Case No 2012-17, Award, 24 March 2016, paras 362, 364; *United Parcel Service of America Inc (UPS) v Government of Canada*, UNCITRAL, Award on the Merits, 24 May 2007, paras 59, 62–63; *Adel A Hamadi Al Tamimi v Sultanate of Oman*, ICSID Case No ARB/11/33, Award, 3 November 2015, para 324.

37 ILC Commentaries (n 17) 140.

38 See Henry Burmester, 'Federal Clauses: An Australian Perspective' (1985) 34 International & Comparative Law Quarterly 522.

39 See Article 34 of the Convention for the Protection of the World Cultural and Natural Heritage (adopted on 16 November 1972); Article 41 of the Geneva Convention Relating to the Status of Refugees, United Nations, Treaty Series, Vol 189, p. 137 (entered into force 22 April 1954); Article 11 of the Convention on the Recovery Abroad of Maintenance, UN Conference on Maintenance Obligations (entered into force 25 May 1956).

includes State governments.[40] Thus, for alleged breaches of national treatment, the conduct of the regional or State governments is not attributable to the central government.

Moreover, Article 16.3, which is part of the general exception clauses of the treaty, provides:

> *Nothing in this Treaty shall apply to any Measure taken by a local body or authority at the district, block or village level in the case of India. For avoidance of doubt, a local body or authority shall include the Municipal Corporation, district level officers, gram panchayats and Gram Sabha.*

Article 16.3 is not a typical non-attribution clause, yet it accomplishes a similar outcome. By stating that treaty provisions do not apply to the actions of local governments, it implies that the actions or conduct of local bodies or authorities, that is, governmental agencies beneath the State government, are not attributable to the Indian State. Consequently, India would not bear responsibility for their actions under the scope of the BIT.

The final 2016 Model BIT has watered down some of these provisions. It does not provide a definition of 'government' restricted to only central and State governments. This arguably means that the actions of governments at all levels can be attributed to the central government. However, like Article 16.3 in the draft Model BIT, Article 2.4(i) of the final 2016 Model BIT states that the treaty shall not apply to "any measure by a local government". Again, while this deviates from the conventional non-attribution clauses, it achieves the same effect by shielding the actions of local governments from treaty breaches. India's subsequent BITs with Belarus,[41] Taiwan,[42] and Kyrgyzstan[43] contain similar provisions. The provision in the India-Brazil BIT is slightly different. Article 3.6(a) of the India-Brazil BIT states that the treaty shall not apply to "any measure by a local government, provided that it is consistent with Article 5 of this Treaty" and Article 5 contains the national treatment principle. Thus, Article 3.6(a) of the India-Brazil BIT excludes the applicability of the treaty to the actions of the local government provided they meet the requirements of national treatment. Essentially, if the action of a local government violates the national treatment principle as defined in Article 5, such an action will not be outside the purview of the BIT. In such instances, the conduct of the regional government will be imputable to the Indian State.

40 Article 1.15, Draft 2015 Model Text for the Indian Bilateral Investment Treaty (hereinafter 'Draft 2015 Model BIT') <https://www.mygov.in/sites/default/files/master_image/Model%20Text%20for%20the%20Indian%20Bilateral%20Investment%20Treaty.pdf>.

41 Article 2.4(i) of the India-Belarus BIT.

42 Article 2.4(a) of the India-Taiwan BIT.

43 Article 2.4(i) of the India-Kyrgyzstan BIT.

In Article 1.7 of the final 2016 Model BIT, the term "local government" encompasses two aspects: first, an "urban local body, municipal corporation, or village-level government"; second, an "enterprise owned or controlled by an urban local body, a municipal corporation, or a village-level government". Thus, local government includes not just an urban or a municipal body but also the enterprises owned or controlled by them. Article 1.7 is inclusive, not exhaustive. Consequently, entities not explicitly mentioned can also fall under the local government category. Similar provisions are also present in India-Belarus BIT,[44] India-Kyrgyzstan BIT,[45] India-Taiwan BIT,[46] and India-Brazil BIT.[47]

The 2016 Model BIT, unlike Article 4.3 of the draft 2015 Model, does not exclude the actions of the regional or sub-national governments from the purview of the national treatment provision. The actions of a sub-national government[48] are attributable to the central government for all regulatory measures, including a potential breach of the national treatment provision. The only caveat here is that the impugned action of the sub-national government should be compared with how that sub-national government has treated domestic investors in like circumstances.[49] The actions of a sub-national government in one province of India *vis-à-vis* a foreign investor shall not be compared with how a sub-national government in another province treats domestic investors. A precisely similar provision is present in India-Kyrgyzstan BIT.[50] Article 4.2 of the India-Belarus BIT and the India-Taiwan BIT also contain analogous provisions, with the only difference being that they use the terms 'regional government' and 'regional authority', respectively in place of 'sub-national government'.

Having examined the principles of attribution in international law and the federal provisions within India's recently established BITs, we now turn to dealing with the issues involved in the *Nissan* case brought against India due to the actions of the Tamil Nadu government.

Before delving into these specific matters, it is essential to remember that the available *Nissan* arbitral award pertains to the question of jurisdiction, not the case's underlying merits.

India challenged the tribunal's jurisdiction on several grounds, such as the improper constitution of the ISDS tribunal, the claims of the investor being

44 See Article 1.8(ii) of India-Belarus BIT.

45 Article 1.7 of India-Kyrgyzstan BIT.

46 Article 1.5 of India-Taiwan BIT.

47 Article 2.6 of India-Brazil BIT.

48 Article 1.12 of the Model text for the Indian Bilateral Investment Treaty (hereinafter '2016 Model BIT') defines 'Sub-national government' as "a State Government or a Union Territory administration . . . but does not include local governments".

49 Article 4.2 of the 2016 Model BIT provides: "The treatment accorded by a Party under Article 4.1 means, with respect to a Sub-national government, treatment no less favourable than the treatment accorded, in like circumstances, by that Sub-national government to investors, and to investments of investors, of the Party of which it forms a part".

50 See Article 4.2 of India-Kyrgyzstan BIT.

time-barred, etc.[51] In this chapter, we look at some of these grounds, commencing with the issue of attribution.

5.3 India's lack of privity argument

As pointed out earlier, one of the allegations Nissan made against India was regarding the breach of the umbrella clause in Article 87(2) of the India-Japan FTA. Article 87(2) states:

> *Each Party shall observe any obligation it may have entered into with regard to investment activities in its Area of investors of the other Party.*

Nissan argued that the Tamil Nadu government did not honour the MoU the latter signed with the former, which, in turn, engendered the violation of the umbrella clause.[52] India contested this argument. In this regard, a significant point India raised was that the Tamil Nadu government undertook the contractual obligations, not the central government. Therefore Nissan cannot bring a case of umbrella clause violation against India.[53] According to India, Article 87(2) comes into the picture only when the contracting party to the treaty owes an obligation to an investor.[54] In this case, India argued that since the government of Tamil Nadu, which has a different legal personality, owes an obligation to Nissan, the latter couldn't sue India for the breach of a MoU by the former. India emphasized the word "it" in Article 87(2). It was contended that the word "it" means India, not the actions of sub-national governments. Thus, the argument suggested an absence of privity between Nissan and India, which prevented the former from suing the latter. The crux of India's argument is that the contracting party to the treaty means India's central government and does not include the sub-national governments of India. On the other hand, Nissan argued that since the FTA is an instrument under international law, the rules of attribution apply where the actions of State organs are attributable to the State.[55]

The tribunal did not deal with this question exhaustively because this question was related to the merits of the case rather than the jurisdiction of the tribunal.[56] The tribunal only held that both India and Nissan have an arguable claim.[57] However, India's argument is untenable as India erroneously equates the contracting party with the central government. The central government has signed the treaty, but the treaty binds the whole of India and not just

51 *Nissan v India* (n 1) para 57.
52 ibid paras 251–56.
53 ibid paras 245–50.
54 ibid para 250.
55 ibid para 284.
56 ibid para 284.
57 ibid.

the central government. In the absence of federal clauses in the FTA's investment chapter restricting the meaning of State to the central government, the ARSIWA rules on attribution would apply. As discussed, as per the ARSIWA rules, the actions of sub-national governments are attributable to the central government. Therefore, Nissan was correct in asserting that the actions of the Tamil Nadu government were attributable to the Indian State.

The next issue we deal with is India's objection to the tribunal's jurisdiction on the issue of the fork-in-the-road provision.

5.4 Objection on the ground of fork-in-the-road provision

India argued that the tribunal lacks jurisdiction because Nissan has already initiated proceedings before a domestic court in India. As per the fork-in-the-road provision in Article 96(6) of the India-Japan FTA,[58] the investor cannot raise the same dispute before an ISDS tribunal.[59] The fork-in-the-road provision means that the investor must choose between litigating before the host State's domestic courts and pursuing ISDS and that the choice is final.[60] Countries include fork-in-the-road provisions in their BITs to ensure no multiple proceedings for the same dispute to avoid conflicting decisions or to preclude investors from claiming double remedy for the same cause of action.[61]

Several ISDS tribunals have held that a 'triple identity' test must be satisfied for the fork-in-the-road provision to apply.[62] This 'triple identity' test means that a foreign investor cannot bring a claim before an international arbitration tribunal if the same dispute involving the same cause of action and the same parties has been submitted to the local courts of the host State.[63] This test has

58 Article 96(6) of India-Japan FTA provides, "No investment dispute may be submitted to international conciliation or arbitration referred to in paragraph 4 if the disputing investor has initiated any proceedings for the resolution of the investment dispute before courts of justice or administrative tribunals or agencies. However, in the event that those proceedings are withdrawn within 30 days from the date of filing the case, the disputing investor may submit the investment dispute to such international conciliations or arbitrations".

59 *Nissan v India* (n 1) para 57.

60 See Ursula Kriebaum, Christoph Schreuer and Rudolf Dolzer, *Principles of International Investment Law* (OUP 2022) 384–85.

61 For more on the functions and effect of fork-in-the-road provision see Markus A Petsche, 'The Fork in the Road Revisited: An Attempt to Overcome the Clash Between Formalistic and Pragmatic Approaches' (2019) 18 Washington University Global Studies Law Review 391. See also Ung Sovanmony, 'Loopholes in the Application of the "Fork-in-the-Road" Provisions in Investor-State Dispute Settlement Mechanisms' (*Cambridge Core Blog*, 12 October 2022) <https://www.cambridge.org/core/blog/2022/10/12/loopholes-in-the-application-of-the-fork-in-the-road-provisions-in-investor-state-dispute-settlement-mechanisms/> accessed 27 August 2023.

62 Petsche (n 61) 385.

63 ibid. See also *Khan Resources Inc, Khan Resources BV and Cauc Holding Company Ltd v the Government of Mongolia and Monatom Co, Ltd*, PCA Case No 2011-9, Decision on Jurisdiction, 25 July 2012, paras 390–400; *Víctor Pey Casado and President Allende Foundation v*

been criticized due to its potential complexity and difficulty to satisfy.[64] For instance, the domestic legal system of several countries may not have mechanisms to hear treaty disputes. So when the foreign investor brings a claim before the domestic courts of a country challenging a host State's action, it will not allege a treaty breach but a violation of domestic law. But, formalistically, this means that the dispute is different, even if the cause of action is the same. As a result, the foreign investor can simultaneously bring a BIT dispute. Likewise, if a foreign investor's locally incorporated entity initiates a domestic claim, the foreign investor can formally bring a BIT claim in her name for the same cause of action.

As against the 'triple identity' test, some ISDS tribunals provide a 'fundamental basis' test.[65] As per this test, the real question is whether the fundamental basis of a claim brought before an ISDS tribunal is autonomous of the claims brought before domestic courts or other forums.[66] This test goes beyond a mechanical and formalistic application focused solely on whether the dispute or the involved parties are identical. For example, an ISDS tribunal will not have jurisdiction if the fundamental basis of a treaty-violation claim brought by an investor is the same as a contractual violation claim initiated by the investor before the domestic courts of the host State.[67]

In the *Nissan* case, the investor batted for applying the 'triple identity' test[68] whereas India vehemently argued that the tribunal should apply the 'fundamental basis' test.[69] The tribunal dealt with the fork-in-the-road provision given in Article 96(6) by closely looking at the language of the clause rather than applying the 'triple identity' test or the 'fundamental basis' test.[70] This approach of the *Nissan* tribunal was synchronous with other tribunals that have implied that the actual interpretation of the fork-in-the-road provision

---

Republic of Chile, ICSID Case No ARB/98/2, Award, 8 May 2008, paras 467–95; *Yukos Universal Limited (Isle of Man) v The Russian Federation*, PCA Case No 2005-04/AA227, Interim Award, 30 November 2009, para 598; *FREIF Eurowind Holdings Ltd v Kingdom of Spain*, SCC Case No 2017/060, Final Award, 8 March 2021, para 420; *Zhongshan Fucheng Industrial Investment Co Ltd v Federal Republic of Nigeria*, Final Award, 26 March 2021, paras 83–84; *Addiko Bank AG v Montenegro*, ICSID Case No ARB/17/35, Award, 24 November 2021, paras 402–4.

64 Serena Lee and Myron Phua, 'Supervisión y Control v Costa Rica: Developing the Pantechniki v Albania Standard for "Fork in the Road" Provisions in Investment Treaties' (2019) 34 ICSID Review – Foreign Investment Law Journal 203.

65 *Pantechniki SA Contractors & Eng'rs (Greece) v Republic of Albania*, ICSID Case No ARB/07/21, Award, 29 July 2009.

66 ibid paras 61–67.

67 See *H&H Enterprises Investments, Inc v Arab Republic of Egypt*, ICSID Case No ARB/09/15, Award, 6 May 2014, paras 368–70; *Supervision y Control SA v Republic of Costa Rica*, ICSID Case No ARB/12/4, Award, 18 January 2017, paras 294–318.

68 *Nissan v India* (n 1) para 181.

69 ibid paras 175–80.

70 ibid para 215.

will depend on the actual wording of the clause.[71] The *Nissan* tribunal carefully looked into Article 96(6), which provides as follows:

> *No investment dispute may be submitted to international conciliation or arbitration referred to in paragraph 4 if the disputing investor has initiated any proceedings for the resolution of the investment dispute before courts of justice or administrative tribunals or agencies. However, in the event that those proceedings are withdrawn within 30 days from the date of filing the case, the disputing investor may submit the investment dispute to such international conciliations or arbitrations.*

The tribunal said that Article 96 (6) is very clear in its language and meaning.[72] There are two concepts in Article 96(6), which are of paramount importance: 'investment dispute' and 'disputing investor'. It states that no "investment dispute" can be submitted to international arbitration if the "disputing investor" has already initiated proceedings regarding the same dispute before local courts or tribunals.[73] The definition of 'investment dispute', which is referred to in Article 96(6), is given in Article 96(1), as follows:

> *a dispute between a Party and an investor of the other Party that has incurred loss or damage by reason of, or arising out of,* ***an alleged breach of any obligation under this Chapter and other provisions of this Agreement*** *as applicable with respect to the investor and its investments.*
>
> (*emphasis added*)

An important component of this definition is that there should be an allegation that the host State has breached the substantive obligations of the treaty. In other words, the tribunal held that an 'investment dispute' under Article 96(6) of the India-Japan FTA means a dispute where the foreign investor alleges that the host State has breached the treaty provisions.[74] Thus, the fork-in-the-road provision in Article 96(6) would come into the picture only if the foreign investor brought an 'investment dispute', as defined in the India-Japan FTA, before an Indian court and did not withdraw it within 30 days. The tribunal held that in the current instance, Nissan's claim before the High Court of Madras is not of an alleged treaty breach but the constitutionality of the TN VAT Act.[75] These two claims (one before the ISDS tribunal and the other before the High Court) may have certain common aspects, but they are

71 See *AsiaPhos Limited and Norwest Chemicals Pte Limited v People's Republic of China*, ICSID Case No ADM/21/1, Award, 16 February 2023, para 132; *Jin Hae Seo v Republic of Korea*, HKIAC Case No 18117, Concurring Opinion of Dr Benny Lo, 27 September 2019, para 29.

72 *Asia Phos v China* (n 71) paras 208–9.

73 *Nissan v India* (n 1) para 213.

74 ibid para 211.

75 ibid para 214.

still different. Therefore, the claim before the High Court of Madras is not an 'investment dispute' under the India-Japan FTA.

Likewise, the term 'disputing investor' used in Article 96(6) is defined in Article 96(2) as "an investor who is a party in the investment dispute".[76] This narrow definition does not include the affiliates or other entities controlled by the investor. The dispute brought before the Madras High Court is by a different entity, not by the 'disputing investor'. Based on this clear language and definitions, the tribunal concluded that the fork-in-the-road clause only applies when the same "investment dispute" has been brought before both international arbitration and local proceedings. As a result, India's objection based on Article 96(6) was rejected and the tribunal's jurisdiction to proceed with the arbitration was confirmed.[77] Subsequently, we delve into whether the tribunal lacked jurisdiction due to the nature of the dispute involving taxation.

5.5 Objection on the grounds of taxation measures

India argued that the incentives that Nissan was claiming were tax refunds, which fell outside the scope of the India-Japan FTA. On the other hand, Nissan contended that the claimed incentives were not tax refunds but incentives offered by India to encourage investment.[78] It claimed that the term "refund" was used as a shorthand to describe how the incentives are quantified based on certain taxes paid, but the incentives themselves were not part of the taxation system.[79] Nissan argued that these incentives are not taxation measures as they are not part of the taxation law and were not granted under relevant statutory powers.[80] On the other hand, they are contractual obligations under the 2008 MoU, independent of government orders, and not contingent on taxation measures.[81] Accordingly, Nissan maintained that its claims did not concern "taxation measures" as they do not challenge the tax laws but are based on the validity of the relevant tax laws since the claimed incentives are calculated by reference to them.[82] Nissan argued that disputes relating to contractual entitlements, even if quantified by reference to tax law, were not excluded by the taxation carve-out clause.[83]

The relevant provision here is Article 10(1) of the India-Japan FTA, which provides that "[u]nless otherwise provided for in this Agreement, the provisions of this Agreement shall not apply to any taxation measures". Article 10(1) is an exclusionary clause in the treaty that carves out certain matters,

76 ibid para 212.
77 ibid para 218.
78 ibid para 343.
79 ibid.
80 ibid para 360.
81 ibid para 363.
82 ibid para 369.
83 ibid para 374.

including taxation measures, from the scope of the FTA.[84] The article states that the provisions of the agreement shall not apply to any taxation measures unless otherwise provided for. It means that taxation measures are not subject to FTA-based obligations, and any disputes arising from taxation measures cannot be resolved through FTA-based arbitration.[85]

Many investment treaties contain a carve-out clause for taxation measures, as also discussed in Chapter 4. A very prominent example of a complete carve-out is Article 21(1) of the Energy Charter Treaty, which provides,

> *except as otherwise provided in this Article, nothing in this Treaty shall create rights or impose obligations concerning Taxation Measures of the Contracting Parties. In the event of any inconsistency between this Article and any other provision of the Treaty, this Article shall prevail to the extent of the inconsistency.*

An important issue in interpreting such carve-out clauses is whether the regulatory measure that the State labels as a 'taxation measure' is indeed such a measure or is the State employing the carve-out provision to protect its regulatory actions unrelated to taxation. In other words, when can we say that the measure in question is a taxation measure?[86] This issue arose in several cases brought by investors against the Czech Republic under the Energy Charter Treaty and other BITs of the Czech Republic.[87] The Czech Republic modified its incentive regime for the renewable energy sector, including by imposing a levy on electricity that solar power plants generated.[88] In one of the cases where these regulatory measures were challenged, the issue was whether the solar levy imposed by the Czech Republic is a taxation measure and thus exempt from the tribunal's jurisdiction due to the Energy Charter Treaty's carve-out for taxation measures. The tribunal held that under Article 21 of the Energy Charter Treaty, whether a measure is a 'taxation measure' has to be determined as per the country's domestic law.[89] After carefully assessing Czech law and judicial decisions, the tribunal concluded that the solar levy was not

84 ibid para 377.
85 ibid para 379.
86 Article 21(7)(a) of the ECT provides: "[t]he term 'Taxation Measure' includes: (i) any provision relating to taxes of the domestic law of the Contracting Party or of a political subdivision thereof or a local authority therein; and (ii) any provision relating to taxes of any convention for the avoidance of double taxation or of any other international agreement or arrangement by which the Contracting Party is bound".
87 *WA Investments-Europa Nova Limited v The Czech Republic*, PCA Case No 2014-19, Award, 15 May 2019; *Photovoltaik Knopf Betriebs-GmbH v The Czech Republic*, PCA Case No 2014-21, Award, 15 May 2019; *Antaris Solar GmbH and Dr. Michael Göde v The Czech Republic*, PCA Case No 2014-1, 2 May 2018.
88 *ICW Europe Investments Limited v The Czech Republic*, PCA Case No 2014-22, Award, 15 May 2019.
89 ibid paras 290–93.

a 'taxation measure' and thus not eligible for carve-out from the ECT.[90] The tribunal held that since the main objective of the solar levy was to reduce the incentives granted to the solar investors and not generate revenue for the State, it was not a taxation measure.[91] Likewise, in another Energy Charter Treaty case, *Silver Ridge v Italy*,[92] the question before the tribunal was whether the contested measures were part of taxation measures for the carve-out to kick in. The tribunal held that the measure in question was not a taxation measure.[93]

Outside of the Energy Charter Treaty, too, there have been cases where the issue of interpretation of 'taxation measures' has arisen. One such case is *Encana v Ecuador*, where Article XII (1) of the Canada-Ecuador BIT had to be interpreted. Article XII (1) provides: "except as set out in this article, nothing in this agreement shall apply to taxation measures". However, the term "taxation measures" is not defined in the BIT.[94] The tribunal held that whether "something is a tax measure is primarily a question of its legal operation, not its economic effect".[95] Put differently, a measure that imposes a liability on classes of persons to pay money to the State for public purposes would qualify as a taxation measure.[96] The tribunal in *Burlington v Ecuador* reaffirmed this principle and added that an additional requirement for something to be a taxation measure is that there should be no direct benefit to the taxpayer.[97]

Unlike the Energy Charter Treaty, the term 'taxation measures' is not explicitly defined in the India-Japan FTA.[98] However, the tribunal in *Nissan v India* held that taxation measures can be understood in the context of international law as any measure, including laws, regulations, decisions, administrative actions, or others, that impose liability on classes of persons to pay money to the State for public purposes, without any direct benefit to the taxpayer.[99] Specifically, the tribunal held that to determine whether a measure qualifies as a taxation measure under the domestic law of the host State, the questions of 'who', 'what', and 'why' within the domestic legal framework of the host State would have to be answered.[100] 'Who' means determining

90 ibid paras 294–307.
91 ibid para 317.
92 *Silver Ridge Power BV v Italian Republic*, ICSID Case No ARB/15/37, Award, 26 February 2021.
93 ibid paras 297–311.
94 V Vasudev, 'Interactions Between Taxation Measures and International Investment Agreements' in J Chaisse and others (eds), *Handbook of International Investment Law and Policy* (Springer 2019) 13.
95 *EnCana Corporation v Republic of Ecuador*, LCIA Case No UN3481, Award, 3 February 2006, para 142.
96 ibid.
97 *Burlington Resources, Inc v Republic of Ecuador*, ICSID Case No ARB/08/5, para 159.
98 *Nissan v India* (n 1) para 382.
99 ibid para 384.
100 ibid para 386.

the entities under the host State's laws that are empowered to collect or administer taxes; 'what' deals with the qualitative nature of the measure; and 'why' implies the purpose of the measure, i.e. whether it is inspired principally by tax objectives.[101] On application of the principles on the current factual matrix at hand that involves disputes over non-payment of incentives under a MoU between Nissan and the Government of Tamil Nadu, the tribunal held that it is not in a position to resolve the issue at this preliminary stage.[102] The origin and nature of the incentives, as well as the government conduct in question, were held to be not yet clear. The issue was declared complex, and further factual development was required to ascertain whether the challenged government conduct involved taxation measures subject to exclusion under Article 10(1) of the India-Japan FTA.[103] Thus, the tribunal deferred this issue for further consideration.[104]

5.6 Conclusion

The tribunal dismissed most of India's objections to jurisdiction, including on issues like the improper constitution of the ISDS tribunal, claims of the investor being time-barred, etc.[105] It directed that the claim should proceed to the merits phase. In this way, the tribunal ruled against India; thus, the case counts as a loss to India. But before the case could go to the merits stage, reportedly, India settled the case with Nissan.[106] As part of this settlement, Nissan is expected to get $185 million to $238 million from India.[107]

While the case may have been settled, it is crucial for several reasons. First, like all the previous ISDS claims we discussed, this case did not arise because India adopted a regulatory measure to protect public health, safeguard the environment, or any other lofty public interest imperative, which the investor believed violated its treaty-protected rights. Put differently, there is no Philip Morris dimension to this case. Second, like the previous cases discussed, this case falls closer to the Yukos pole. The Yukos dimension of this case is that the foreign investor sued India due to a lack of good governance. The government of Tamil Nadu promised incentives to lure investors to invest. Nissan relied on these incentives in deciding to invest. Once the investment came in, incentives were allegedly withdrawn. Moreover, it is not evident if there was any public policy justification to withdraw the incentives. This ISDS claim against India

101 ibid.
102 ibid para 396.
103 ibid para 395.
104 ibid para 399.
105 ibid para 57.
106 Aditi Shah and Sudarshan Varadhan, 'Nissan Settles Dispute with Indian State Over Unpaid Dues – Sources' *Reuters* (28 May 2020) <https://www.reuters.com/article/us-nissan-india-arbitration-exclusive-idUKKBN2342AR> accessed 27 August 2023.
107 ibid.

would not have arisen if the Tamil Nadu government had kept its promise. Third, this ISDS case highlights the potential for India to face BIT claims arising due to the conduct of its sub-national governments. While this may not be a significant issue for several smaller countries or those nations that do not have a federal constitution, it is undoubtedly vital for India. The regulations that State governments in India adopt invariably impact foreign investment. For instance, several sub-national governments in India offer additional incentives to foreign investments in the electronics sector, such as waiver of registration duty, stamp duty, reimbursement of VAT (as was the case in the Nissan dispute), etc.[108] Fourth, it is important to sensitize the States about India's investment treaties. Provincial governments should consider India's investment treaty obligations while framing policies and laws that may affect foreign investment. This will require unleashing a process of internalization of investment treaties, that is, formal and informal processes through which a country's international law obligations are taken into account in governmental decision-making.[109] In this regard, it is important to recall the proposal to adopt a Centre-State Investment Agreement whose purpose was to sensitize India's states about BIT obligations and ensure their compliance.[110] However, this initiative was abandoned in 2017 due to concerns about its unworkability.[111] An important takeaway from the Nissan fiasco is that the central government should double down on the effort to educate sub-national governments about investment treaties to avoid Nissan-kind disputes in the future.

108 Ministry of Electronics and Information Technology, Government of India, FAQ's on Foreign Direct Investment & Electronic System Design & Manufacturing (ESDM) <https://www.meity.gov.in/writereaddata/files/FAQ_FDI_ESDM.pdf> accessed 1 August 2023.

109 For more on this issue see Prabhash Ranjan, 'The Impact of Investment Treaties on the Rule of Law in India' in N Jansen Calamita and Ayelet Berman (eds), ***Investment Treaties and Rule of Law Promise*** (CUP 2022) 38.

110 Arun Jaitley, 'Budget Speech 2016–2017' (29 February 2016) para 9(2.2) at 34 <www.indiabudget.gov.in/doc/bspeech/bs201617.pdf>; Ministry of Finance, DEA, 'Annual Report 2016–2017' <www.dea.gov.in/sites/default/files/Annual%20Report-2016-17-E.pdf>; Ranjan (n 109) 302–5.

111 Ranjan (n 109) 303. See also Josef Ostřanský and Facundo Pérez Aznar, 'Investment Treaties and National Governance in India: Rearrangements, Empowerment, and Discipline' (2021) 34 Leiden Journal of International Law 373–96.

6 Missing ISDS in India's new FTAs – towards de-legalization and de-judicialization

6.1 Introduction

As mentioned in Chapter 1, the mounting ISDS claims against India triggered a backlash by the Indian State against international investment law. Although, as Chapters 2 to 5 have shown, many of these ISDS claims originated due to India's poor regulation and mistakes (the Yukos moments), India reacted sturdily to being called out for not honouring its treaty commitments towards foreign investors. It joined the global chorus that the ISDS processes are skewed against the interests of developing countries and that they favour big corporations and developed countries.[1] The clearest indicator of this is India unilaterally terminating almost all its BITs, barring a few.[2] At the same time, at least formally, India, unlike countries like South Africa, hasn't cut itself completely from ISDS or international investment law. As documented in Chapter 1, India adopted a new Model BIT in 2016 containing investment protection features and an ISDS clause. India has shared its Model BIT with all the countries with whom it has unilaterally terminated the BIT and expressed its willingness to sign a new investment treaty based on its Model BIT.[3] In March 2020, the Indian government shared in the Indian parliament that India is renegotiating BITs with 34 States/regional blocks covering 70 countries.[4]

1 See the speech of India's Law Minister on 12 February 2021 in the Indian Parliament: Lok Sabha Debates, 12 February 2021, Seventeenth Series, Vol XI, Fifth Session, p. 820 <https://eparlib.nic.in/bitstream/123456789/800935/1/lsd_17_05_12-02-2021.pdf> accessed 9 August 2023.

2 Answer by the Minister of State in the Ministry of External Affairs, Lok Sabha Unstarred Question No 3947 (24 March 2023) <https://mea.gov.in/lok-sabha.htm?dtl/36405/question_no3947_bilateral_investment_treaties> accessed 9 August 2023.

3 ibid.

4 Answer by the Minister of State in the Ministry of Finance, Lok Sabha Unstarred Question No 3545 (16 March 2020) <https://eparlib.nic.in/bitstream/123456789/972262/1/AU3545.pdf> accessed 9 August 2023. See also Committee on External Affairs, *India and Bilateral Investment Treaties Tenth Report* (Ministry of External Affairs 2021) <http://164.100.47.193/lsscommittee/External%20Affairs/17_External_Affairs_10.pdf> accessed 9 August 2023.

DOI: 10.4324/9781003324379-6

However, the proof of the pudding is in the eating. Despite the claims that India is negotiating BITs with several countries based on the 2016 Model BIT, India has signed only a handful of BITs with Belarus, Kyrgyzstan, Taiwan, and Brazil in the last eight years. Of the four, two treaties (with Kyrgyzstan and Brazil) are yet to be enforced. While the BITs with Belarus, Kyrgyzstan, and Taiwan contain ISDS provisions mirroring India's 2016 Model BIT, there is no ISDS in the investment treaty with Brazil. As noted in Chapter 1, India's commitment to ISDS has waned considerably. While India hasn't cut loose from the ISDS mechanism, it has imposed innumerable stringent procedural requirements on foreign investors' access to international arbitration, as discussed in Chapter 1. All this casts doubt over the effectiveness of the ISDS clause from the point of view of safeguarding foreign investment from capricious and abusive State conduct. It is as good as not having the ISDS mechanism.

While India hasn't been very active in negotiating standalone investment treaties, it seems to be on a free trade agreement (FTA) signing and negotiating spree. In the last few years, India has signed FTAs with Mauritius,[5] the United Arab Emirates (UAE),[6] and Australia.[7] India is also vigorously negotiating FTAs with the United Kingdom (UK),[8] the European Union (EU),[9] Canada,[10] Israel,[11] Bangladesh,[12] the Eurasian Economic Union (EAEU – an

5 Comprehensive Economic Cooperation and Partnership Agreement (CECPA) Between the Republic of India and the Republic of Mauritius (signed on 22 February 2021) <https://commerce.gov.in/wp-content/uploads/2021/08/India-Mauritius-CECPA-Text-for-Upload.pdf>.

6 Comprehensive Economic Partnership Agreement Between the Government of the Republic of India and the Government of the United Arab Emirates (signed on 18 February 2022) <https://commerce.gov.in/international-trade/trade-agreements/comprehensive-economic-partnership-agreement-between-the-government-of-the-republic-of-india-and-the-government-of-the-united-arab-emirates-uae/>.

7 India-Australia Economic Cooperation and Trade Agreement between the Government of the Republic of India and the Government of Australia (signed on 2 April 2022) <https://commerce.gov.in/international-trade/trade-agreements/ind-aus-ecta/>.

8 Department for Business and Trade, 'Joint Outcome Statement: UK-India Round Eleven FTA Negotiations' (*Gov.UK*, 24 July 2023) <www.gov.uk/government/news/joint-outcome-statement-uk-india-round-eleven-fta-negotiations> accessed 24 July 2023.

9 'EU Trade Relationships by Country/Region: EU-India Free Trade Agreement, Investment Protection Agreement and Geographical Indications Agreement' (*European Commission*) <https://policy.trade.ec.europa.eu/eu-trade-relationships-country-and-region/countries-and-regions/india/eu-india-agreement_en>.

10 'Joint Statement of the 6th India-Canada Ministerial Dialogue on Trade and Investment' (*Ministry of Commerce & Industry*, 10 May 2023) <https://pib.gov.in/PressReleasePage.aspx?PRID=1922964>.

11 Kallol Bhattacharjee, 'Israel's Ministerial Visits to India Might Include FTA Talks' *The Hindu* (13 April 2023) <https://www.thehindu.com/news/national/israel-planning-big-ministerial-visits-to-india-fta-with-india-expected-to-be-discussed/article66730199.ece> accessed 9 August 2023.

12 'Bangladesh-India Free Trade Agreement' (*ARIC*) <https://aric.adb.org/fta/bangladesh-india-free-trade-agreement>.

economic bloc comprising Russia, Belarus, Kazakhstan, Kyrgyzstan, and Armenia),[13] South African Customs Union (a customs union comprising of Botswana, Eswatini, Lesotho, Namibia, and South Africa).[14]

Discussing these FTAs is vital because, as enunciated in the introductory chapter, India's investment treaty programme walked on two legs – BITs and investment chapters in FTAs. While BITs attract much focus, a fine-tooth comb seldom scrutinizes the FTA investment chapters. This is even though the investment chapters in India's FTAs contain substantive investment protection standards and ISDS provisions. As we saw in Chapter 5, the international arbitration claim that Nissan brought against India relied on the ISDS provision in the investment chapter of the India-Japan FTA. Moreover, given the lack of action on the BIT front, studying FTAs closely will illuminate India's recent treaty practice on investment protection and ISDS.

Therefore, this chapter focuses on India's FTAs to illustrate India's treaty practice on ISDS. The chapter is divided into the following parts to accomplish this task. Section 6.2 talks about India's see-saw approach toward FTAs. In Section 6.3, the chapter focuses on the investment chapters in India's FTAs by dividing them into two parts – from 2000 to 2014 and after 2014. The chapter attempts to theorize India's approach toward ISDS using the conceptual lenses of legalization and judicialization in Section 6.4. Section 6.5 concludes.

6.2 India's see-saw approach towards FTAs

India's FTA journey started in the early 2000s with the euphoria over multilateralism subsiding due to the delay in the trade negotiations at the World Trade Organization (WTO).[15] Till the late 1990s, India's trade policy was restrictive flanked by high tariff rates and quantitative restrictions.[16] Due to constraints imposed by India's precarious balance of payments situation, entering into FTAs was seen as politically challenging.[17] However, with the unleashing of economic reforms in 1991 and the subsequent improvement in trade volumes, India started negotiating FTAs, with the first being signed with Sri Lanka

13 Dipanjan Roy Chaudhury, 'Eurasian Economic Union Meets to Speed Up Proposed FTA with India' *Economic Times* (26 May 2023) <https://economictimes.indiatimes.com/news/economy/foreign-trade/eurasian-economic-union-meets-to-speed-up-proposed-fta-with-india/articleshow/100510786.cms> accessed 9 August 2023.

14 'India-Southern African Customs Union Preferential Trade Agreement' (*ARIC*) <https://aric.adb.org/fta/india-southern-african-customs-union-preferential-trade-agreement> accessed 9 August 2023.

15 Debashis Chakraborty and Dipankar Sengupta, 'Learning Through Trading? India's Decade Long Experience at WTO' (2005) 12 South Asian Survey 223; Debashis Chakraborty, Julien Chaisse and Xu Qian, 'Is It Finally Time for India's Free Trade Agreements? The ASEAN "Present" and the RCEP "Future"' (2019) 9 Asian Journal of International Law 359–91.

16 VS Seshadri, *Free Trade Agreements: India and World* (OUP 2023) 39–40.

17 ibid.

in 2000.[18] The UPA government that assumed office in 2004 continued the impetus the previous government gave to signing FTAs. Since then, till 2014, India signed several FTAs with important countries like Singapore, Japan, Korea, Malaysia, and the Association of South East Asian Nations (ASEAN). Many of these FTAs with the East Asian economies were also signed from the point of view of India's 'look east' policy (also known as the 'act east' policy).[19] This policy aimed at cultivating robust relationships with East Asian countries in all spheres including economics. From the perspective of trade balance, India benefitted from these FTAs.[20] India's FTAs with ASEAN, Japan, Singapore, Afghanistan, etc., boosted exports of India's manufactured products.[21]

Notwithstanding these gains, post-2014, India hit a pause button on FTAs. The chief reason for this was that the NDA government came to power, as some argue, on an anti-FTA plank.[22] The new government started critiquing trade liberalization and FTAs signed during the 2000s. These trade agreements were blamed for resulting in de-industrialization in some sectors.[23] They were slammed for being 'weak' and not serving India's national interest.[24] The National Institution for Transforming India (NITI) Aayog, the Indian government's apex public policy think tank, came out with a paper arguing that India's existing FTAs widened India's trade deficit.[25] This anti-trade rhetoric was not fully backed by empirical facts and contradicted India's gains under these FTAs.

18 Free Trade Agreement Between the Republic of India and the Democratic Socialist Republic of Sri Lanka (signed on 28 December 1998) <https://commerce.gov.in/international-trade/trade-agreements/india-sri-lanka-fta/free-trade-agreement-between-the-republic-of-india-and-the-democratic-socialist-republic-of-sri-lanka/>.

19 KV Kesavan, 'India's "Act East" Policy and Regional Cooperation' (*Observer Research Foundation*, 14 February 2020) <https://www.orfonline.org/expert-speak/indias-act-east-policy-and-regional-cooperation-61375/> accessed 12 August 2023.

20 Ministry of Finance, 'Economic Survey 2019–20' (January 2020) <https://www.indiabudget.gov.in/budget2020-21/economicsurvey/doc/echapter.pdf>; Sanjiv Shankaran, 'Foreign Minister Jaishankar's Views on FTAs and Trade Openness Are Not Supported by Facts' *Times of India* (20 November 2020) <https://timesofindia.indiatimes.com/blogs/cash-flow/foreign-minister-jaishankars-views-on-ftas-and-trade-openness-are-not-supported-by-facts/>.

21 Ministry of Finance (n 20).

22 JS Deepak, 'Give and Take: A Timely Book on Free Trade Agreement' <www.financialexpress.com/lifestyle/give-and-take-a-timely-book-on-free-trade-agreements-and-their-role-in-indias-economic-development/3140987/>.

23 Suhasini Haider, 'A Day After RCEP, Jaishankar Slams Trade Pacts, Globalisation' *The Hindu* (16 November 2020) <https://www.thehindu.com/business/a-dayafter-rcep-jaishankar-slams-trade-pacts-globalisation/article33110309.ece> accessed 9 August 2023.

24 'Modi Undid Damage Started by the Congress Govt, Says JP Nadda on RCEP' *ANI* (9 November 2019) <https://www.aninews.in/news/national/general-news/modi-undid-damage-started-by-the-congress-govt-says-jp-nadda-on-rcep20191109150626/> accessed 12 August 2023.

25 VK Saraswat, Prachi Priya and Aniruddha Ghosh, *A Note on Free Trade Agreements and Their Costs* (NITI Aayog 2019) <http://www.niti.gov.in/writereaddata/files/document_publication/FTA-NITI-FINAL.pdf> accessed 9 August 2023.

An impact of this anti-FTA rhetoric was that India walked out of the Regional Comprehensive Economic Partnership (RCEP) agreement negotiations just before the deal was to be signed, with the remaining 15 countries going ahead.[26] India's heavily skewed trade balance in favour of China, which would have worsened due to RCEP, was arguably an important reason for India not joining the trade pact.[27] However, other leading strategic and economic commentators like Sanjaya Baru disagree.[28] Baru argues that China was a mere camouflage while the real reason for India not joining RCEP was the pressure from India's cooperative dairy industry that apprehended cheap imports from RCEP countries.[29] While some commentators appear sympathetic to India's decision to pull out of RCEP,[30] others critique it because India has missed the opportunity to integrate with a dynamic global value chain hub like the RCEP.[31] The NDA government also declared its intent to review FTAs with Japan, South Korea, and ASEAN.[32]

Things started to change again from 2020 onwards. As Biswajit Dhar, India's leading trade economist, argues, when the Indian economy started emerging from COVID-19-induced pain, India's circumvention towards FTAs began to melt away.[33] India returned to being enthusiastic about FTAs and declared its intent to enter into new trade treaties. Economists argue that the following factors triggered a change of heart regarding FTAs. First, the Indian policy establishment started realizing that the lack of deep economic relations with countries like the UK, EU, Canada, etc., would come in the way of India becoming part of new global value chain arrangements that aim to reduce dependence on China.[34] Second, it also dawned on the policy establishment

26 For more on this see Rajat Deb, 'Is RCEP a Panacea for India?' (2020) 68(4) The Indian Economic Journal 659–66; Amrita Narlikar, 'India's Foreign Economic Policy Under Modi: Negotiations and Narratives in the WTO and Beyond' (2022) 58 International Politics 148–66 at 152 <https://www.tandfonline.com/doi/epdf/10.1080/10357718.2020.1725425?needAccess=true&role=button>.

27 See Akarsh Bhutani, 'India's Reluctance in Joining the RCEP – A Boon or a Bane in the Long-Run?' (*Observer Research Foundation*, 10 February 2021) <www.orfonline.org/expert-speak/india-reluctance-joining-rcep-boon-bane-long-run/> accessed 9 August 2023.

28 Sanjaya Baru, 'Amul and Dairy Co-ops: Milch Cows Get Political' *Deccan Chronicle* (17 April 2023) <www.deccanchronicle.com/opinion/columnists/160423/sanjaya-baru-amul-and-dairy-co-ops-milch-cows-get-political.html> accessed 9 August 2023.

29 ibid.

30 Seshadri (n 16) 301–2; Biswajit Dhar, 'India's Withdrawal from the Regional Comprehensive Economic Partnership' (16 November 2019) 54(45) Economic and Political Weekly.

31 Amita Batra, *India's Trade Policy in the 21st Century* (Routledge 2022) 157.

32 Biswajit Dhar, 'India's Renewed Embrace of Free Trade Agreements' (*East Asia Forum*, 21 February 2022) <www.eastasiaforum.org/2022/02/21/indias-renewed-embrace-of-free-trade-agreements/> accessed 9 August 2023.

33 ibid; Amitendu Palit, 'India's New and Robust FTA Engagements' (*Institute of South Asian Studies* at NUS, 5 October 2021) <https://www.isas.nus.edu.sg/papers/indias-new-and-robust-fta-engagements/>

34 Surendar Singh and Suvajit Banerjee, 'Is There Any Dichotomy Between India's New FTA Strategy and Its Trade Policy?' (2022) 57(24(11)) Economic and Political Weekly 25–28.

that India is not a party to mega FTAs – RCEP and the Comprehensive and Progressive Agreement for Trans-Pacific Partnership Agreement (CPTPP) – which might encumber India's ability to access more significant markets.[35]

Overall, looking at India's approach toward FTAs from the start of the millennia till date, it can be said that India's see-saw approach towards FTAs swung from enthusiasm (2000–2013) to disillusionment and skepticism (2014–2019) and then back to enthusiasm (2020 onwards). As a consequence of this renewed passion, as already pointed out, India signed FTAs with Australia, UAE, and Mauritius.

6.3 ISDS in FTAs

FTAs are comprehensive economic agreements that cover various issues such as tariff reduction, trade in services, intellectual property, competition policy, and investment. Several facets of investment form part of a broader economic agreement like an FTA. Protection of foreign investment is one of them. Substantive protection features like protection from unlawful expropriation, and ISDS shall form part of investment protection. Other dimensions of investment are liberalization, which regulates issues like the entry of foreign investment. Likewise, an FTA may also cover topics related to investment facilitation, such as regulatory transparency and predictability of investment measures, administrative procedures, information sharing, and exchange of best practices to bolster foreign investment inflows. The focus here is on FTAs containing ISDS provisions. We divide this discussion into two parts: FTAs from 2000 to 2013; and 2013 onward.

6.3.1 2000 to 2013

As enunciated, India signed several trade agreements during this period (see Table 6.1). Not all of these agreements were full-fledged FTAs, i.e., trade agreements that comprehensively cover trade in goods and services. Some of these treaties are 'partial scope agreements', i.e., they cover limited or select products.[36] These partial scope agreements do not qualify as an FTA aimed at covering substantially all trade between its constituents. India signed seven full-fledged FTAs, including five bilateral trade treaties with Sri Lanka, Singapore, Korea, Malaysia, and Japan and two regional or multilateral agreements – the South Asian Free Trade Area (SAFTA),[37] and Agreement and the

35 ibid; some commentators are sceptical of India's approach towards FTAs given the rising protectionism in India.

36 'Regional Trade Agreements Information System' (*WTO*) <https://rtais.wto.org/UserGuide/RTAIS_USER_GUIDE_EN.html>.

37 SAFTA is a free trade agreement signed between the eight nations of the South Asian Association for Regional Cooperation (SAARC) comprising Afghanistan, Bangladesh, Bhutan, Nepal, India, Maldives, Pakistan, and Sri Lanka.

India-ASEAN (Association of South East Asian Nations) FTA. Four of these seven FTAs (India-Singapore, India-Korea, India-Malaysia, and India-Japan) contain an investment protection chapter with ISDS. The India-ASEAN FTA does not include an investment protection chapter, but both sides have signed a separate investment agreement containing ISDS. These investment chapters survived India's backlash against international investment law because it is impossible to terminate a chapter from a treaty unilaterally.

India agreed to include investment protection chapters including ISDS, in these FTAs because economic literature supports a close linkage between trade and investment.[38] Transnational corporations look for ideal production sites to optimize market access possibilities for their products.[39] If a country is part of an FTA, it will be better suited to attract investment from other FTA member countries, which, in turn, will create conditions for more significant trade between these countries through the global value chains. Hence, we find several FTAs like the RCEP,[40] CPTPP, European Union-Canada Comprehensive Economic and Trade Agreement (CETA), the Common Market for Eastern and Southern Africa (COMESA), the ASEAN Comprehensive Investment Agreement (ACIA), and other critical bilateral FTAs like UK-Australia, UK-New Zealand contain a chapter on investment protection.

38 See Lee E Preston and Duane Windsor, 'Trade, Investment, and Enterprise Linkages' in *The Rules of the Game in the Global Economy* (Springer 2022) <https://link.springer.com/chapter/10.1007/978-94-011-5354-6_3>; Norbert Wilson and Joyce Cacho, 'Linkage Between foreign Direct Investment, Trade and Trade Policy' (*OECD Trade Policy Papers*, 2 March 2007) <www.oecd-ilibrary.org/docserver/152275474424.pdf?expires=1690530355&id=id&accname=guest&checksum=8070BBC36531AFD84270045A4EBC2FCB>; Simon Lester, Bryan Mercurio and Arwel Davies, *World Trade Law: Text, Materials and Commentary* (Hart Publishing 2012).

39 ibid.

40 Although RCEP contains a chapter on investment protection, it does not have an ISDS provision. Article 19.3(1)(b) of RCEP provides: "Unless otherwise provided in this Agreement, [the dispute settlement] Chapter shall apply when a Party considers that a measure of another Party is not in conformity with the obligations under this Agreement or that another Party has otherwise failed to carry out its obligations under this Agreement". Thus, it provides for only state-state dispute settlement (SSDS). However, the pertinent point is that RCEP's investment chapter does not rule out the possibility of including ISDS in the future. Article 10.18 provides: "*The Parties shall, without prejudice to their respective positions, enter into discussions on the settlement of investment disputes between a Party and an investor of another Party no later than two years after the date of entry into force of this Agreement, the outcomes of which are subject to agreement by all Parties*". Thus, the treaty gives a mandate to the member countries to enter into discussions on the possibility of including an ISDS provision in the RCEP in the future. See also Michael Ewing-Chow and Junianto James Losari, 'The RCEP Investment Chapter: A State-to-State WTO Style System for Now' (*Kluwer Arbitration Blog*, 8 December 2020) <https://arbitrationblog.kluwerarbitration.com/2020/12/08/the-rcep-investment-chapter-a-state-to-state-wto-style-system-for-now/> accessed 9 August 2023. On RCEP investment chapter see generally – Julien Chaisse and others, 'Drafting Investment Law: Patterns of Influence in the Regional Comprehensive Economic Partnership (RCEP)' (2022) 25(1) Journal of International Economic Law 110–28.

Table 6.1 India's FTAs, 2000 to 2013

Country	*Type of Trade Agreement*	*Whether Investment Protection with ISDS Is Part of It?*
Sri Lanka (2000)	FTA	No. But India-Sri Lanka had a BIT
Afghanistan (2003)	Partial Scope Agreement	No
Thailand (2003)	Partial Scope Agreement	No
MERCOSUR[41] (2004)	Partial Scope Agreement	No
Singapore (2005)	FTA	Yes
Chile (2006)	Partial Scope Agreement	No
Bhutan (2006)	Partial Scope Agreement	No
South Asian Free Trade Area (SAFTA) Agreement (2004)	FTA	No. But a separate SAARC Investment Treaty aimed at investment protection has been under negotiation for a very long time.
ASEAN (2009)	FTA	No. But almost simultaneously India and ASEAN signed an investment treaty with ISDS.
Korea (2009)	FTA	Yes
Nepal (2009)	Partial Scope Agreement	No
Japan (2011)	FTA	Yes
Malaysia (2011)	FTA	Yes

Source: Author's compilation from WTO, Regional Trade Agreements Database

6.3.2 2014 onward: FTA 2.0 and decoupling of trade from investment

Due to the pause button hit on FTAs from 2014 onwards, the pace of trade agreement negotiating and signing came to a grinding halt. It picked up speed again in 2020 with the result that India signed three new FTAs with Mauritius, United Arab Emirates, and Australia. However, unlike several FTAs that India signed from 2000 to 2013, India's recent FTAs do not contain a chapter on investment protection and ISDS (see Table 6.2). This can be called the FTA 2.0 approach of India because it marks a significant departure in India's trade treaty practice. Realizing the close economic linkage between trade and investment, India's past FTAs contained a chapter on investment protection along with ISDS. However, in the new generation FTAs, trade and investment protection linkage stands broken. The investment provisions in these FTAs

41 MERCOSUR or the Southern Common Market has the following countries as its members: Argentina, Brazil, Paraguay, and Uruguay.

Table 6.2 Explaining Decoupling International Trade Law from International Investment Law

Factual Situation	*Decoupling*
Countries A and B have signed an FTA covering all major economic issues minus investment protection and ISDS. Investment protection is part of another treaty signed by A and B, which co-exists with the FTA.	Partial
Countries A and B have signed a comprehensive FTA without investment protection and ISDS clauses. A and B have not signed a BIT covering investment protection and ISDS.	Complete

Source: Author's compilation

are limited to issues such as promotion and facilitation. For example, one of the objectives of the India-Australia FTA, listed in Article 1.2(d), is to expand trade and investment between the two countries. But there is no mention of investment protection.

India's new approach of divorcing investment protection chapters from the FTAs can be called decoupling international trade law from international investment law. Decoupling here means a phenomenon where a country dissociates trade from investment in its international law obligations *vis-à-vis* a particular country or a set of countries. It assumes international trade law obligations *vis-à-vis* one country or a group of countries. Still, it does not accept international investment law obligations *vis-à-vis* the same country or set of countries. Before taking this decoupling argument further, the following caveats are essential to ensure conceptual clarity. First, reference to not accepting international investment law obligations as part of decoupling means not being bound by international law on investment protection and ISDS. Assuming international law obligations on investment facilitation, promotion, etc., or anything less than investment protection is excluded from the purview of our discussion on decoupling. The reason is that international law obligations on investment protection with a binding ISDS, generally speaking, impose a far greater responsibility on countries in comparison to obligations imposed by facilitation or promotion measures.

Second, countries can undertake selective legalization of their international economic relations. Put differently, due to the benefits expected from trade, a country may prefer accepting international trade law obligations. If a country does not accept gains from investment and does not anticipate high investment flows, it may not show a penchant for legalizing investment relations. Countries might undertake to decouple trade from investment because they think it is in their national interest. Likewise, one may also come across situations where a country like India, in the past, preferred to legalize the whole gamut of international economic relations covering both trade and investment but now favours legalization of only trade relations, not investment. In short, a country could have several motivations to decouple trade from investment protection as part of a country's international law obligations. The purpose behind discussing decoupling is not to get into these motivations.

Third, there will also be situations where a country might have legalized only investment relations with another country (say by having a BIT) and not trade (say by not having an FTA). This too is a case of selective legalization of international economic relations between two or a group of countries. However, in the decoupling situation we discuss here, the focus is on FTAs not having investment protection obligations or a country having an FTA but not legalizing its investment relations with its FTA partner country. We generally find FTAs covering all economic issues including investment, competition policy, intellectual property, etc. On the other hand, investment treaties, by and large, do not cover international trade. Thus, the decoupling argument is strong when an FTA is without an investment protection chapter.

Moreover, even if two countries have signed a BIT and not entered into an FTA, the trade relations between them are still legalized if the countries are members of the WTO. Given that the membership of the WTO is more than 160 countries, a very high proportion of countries has already legalized their trade relations, even if there's no FTA between them. But the reverse will not be true since there is no multilateral treaty on investment protection as we have in trade. Thus, the legalization of investment relations either requires investment protection and ISDS as part of an FTA or as a standalone BIT co-existing with the FTA.

With these caveats in mind, let us understand at what levels decoupling can take place. The first level at which decoupling can take place is the FTA level. As part of an FTA or an economic agreement, a country may accept only international trade law obligations, not international investment law. This will show that this country is legalizing only its trade and not investment relations as part of the FTA or the economic agreement. For example, the UK signed an FTA with Singapore in 2020.[42] But UK-Singapore FTA does not contain provisions on investment protection. Thus, arguably, UK and Singapore have only legalized their trade, not investment, relations. We can call this partial decoupling (see Table 6.2).

But what happens if a country legalizes its investment relations with its FTA partner/s outside the trade agreement such as by signing a standalone BIT or if the country does not include investment protection in the FTA because a standalone BIT already exists? In such a situation, the FTA and the BIT will act in tandem and collectively constitute the legalization of the economic relations between the two countries. However, many a time, countries might include investment protection as part of the FTA despite a BIT. India did this with Malaysia and Korea when it signed the FTAs. Despite the presence

42 Free Trade Agreement between Singapore and the United Kingdom of Great Britain and Northern Ireland (entered into 11 February 2021).

of India-Malaysia[43] and India-Korea[44] BITs, the FTAs include an investment protection chapter.

Suppose a country has neither accepted international investment law obligations as part of an FTA nor outside the FTA, *vis-à-vis* its FTA partner/s country. In that case, it will make the partial decoupling complete. This is the second level of decoupling (see Table 6.2). In other words, complete decoupling means a country has accepted only trade law obligations, not investment protection obligations, *vis-à-vis* a particular country. Thus, in the UK-Singapore FTA example, the UK not having investment protection provisions in its FTA with Singapore is a case of partial, not complete, decoupling because the UK and Singapore have signed a BIT, which co-exists with the FTA.[45]

Circling back to India, let us apply this understanding to India's case. In the older generation of FTAs, India agreed to link trade and investment protection and thus accepted obligations on international trade law and international investment law as part of a comprehensive economic treaty. However, as part of FTA 2.0, international law obligations on investment protection are not part of an economic treaty (the FTA) containing other economic issues like trade in goods, services, intellectual property, etc. So, this surely qualifies as partial decoupling. But has India undertaken investment protection obligations with these countries outside the FTA? With Mauritius and Australia, India unilaterally terminated its BITs on 22 and 23 March 2017 respectively.[46] In other words, India's investment relations with these two countries were not legalized when they signed an FTA. Thus, India has completely decoupled international trade law from international investment law with Mauritius and Australia (see Table 6.3).

With the UAE, it is a case of partial decoupling because India signed a BIT with the UAE in 2013, which came into force on 13 September 2014,[47] and hasn't been terminated. There are two reasons for the same. First, Article 18 of the India-UAE BIT provides that the treaty shall remain "in force for a period of 10 years". Thus, the initial period of the validity of the treaty hasn't expired. Second, Article 18 also contains an interesting provision that imposes an obligation on countries to commence negotiations, no later than 1 January 2016,

43 Agreement between the Government of the Republic of India and the Government of Malaysia for the Promotion and Protection of Investments (entry into force 12 April 1997, terminated 23 March 2017).

44 Agreement between the Government of the Republic of India and the Government of the Republic of Korea on the Promotion and Protection of Investments (entry into force 7 May 1996, terminated 12 May 2017).

45 Agreement between the Government of the United Kingdom of Great Britain and Northern Ireland and the Government of the Republic of Singapore (entered into force 22 July 1975).

46 'Bilateral Investment Treaties (BITs)/Agreements' (*Department of Economic Affairs, Government of India*) <https://dea.gov.in/bipa?page=2> accessed 9 August 2023.

47 Agreement Between the Government of the Republic of India and the Government of the United Arab Emirates on the Promotion and Protection of Investments (signed 12 December 2013).

Table 6.3 2014 Onward (FTA 2.0)

Year	*The Country with Whom India Has Signed the FTA*	*Whether the FTA Contains a Full-Fledged Investment Protection Chapter?*	*Whether India Has Signed a Standalone BIT with This Country?*	*Decoupling*
2022	Australia	No	Yes (1999), but India unilaterally terminated it in 2017.	Complete
2022	United Arab Emirates	No	Yes (2013)	Partial
2021	Mauritius	No	Yes (1998), but India unilaterally terminated it in 2017.	Complete

Source: Author's compilation

to finalize a new agreement and replace the existing treaty with a new one. However, this deadline has been missed.

Although the India-UAE FTA does not contain a full-fledged investment protection chapter, it provides a fresh deadline to finalize a new BIT to replace the 2013 agreement. Article 12.1 of the India-UAE FTA provides:

> *The Parties note the existence of the Agreement Between the Government of the United Arab Emirates and the Government of the Republic of India on the Promotion and Protection of Investments, signed at New Delhi, India on 12 December 2013 (UAE-India Bilateral Investment Agreement). Further, the Parties renew their commitment to the ongoing negotiations between the Parties to replace the UAE-India Bilateral Investment Agreement, and agree to finalise a new agreement by June 2022.*

Thus, the new deadline was June 2022. But this deadline has also been missed. India and UAE have not completed their negotiations on a new investment treaty. The 2013 BIT continues to operate. The fact that the two sides are keen to replace the existing BIT with a new one also means that the India-UAE FTA will not contain an investment chapter even in the future. The two sides wish to keep investment protection outside the scope of the FTA.

It may well be argued that these few FTAs might not be a bellwether of India's future FTA practice, and one will have to wait and watch what India does in its other ongoing FTA negotiations before decisively concluding that India is indeed decoupling (complete or partial) international trade law from international investment law in its FTAs. As things stand today, the India-EU FTA will not contain a chapter on investment because the two sides are negotiating for a separate investment protection agreement (IPA).[48] The reason for this separate investment treaty, that is, keeping investment protection out of an FTA, is that the EU law requires that investment agreements containing procedures of ISDS have to be ratified not just by the EU but also by the EU member countries individually for them to come into force.[49] These treaties are called mixed agreements. Whereas a trade agreement falls under the exclusive competence of the EU and does not require individual ratification by the EU Member States. If investment protection is made a part of an FTA, it will have to go through a process of ratification by individual EU member countries, which might delay the treaty from coming into force.[50] Thus, the EU prefers an approach of keeping investment protection issues out of the FTA, as it did with countries like Singapore and Vietnam.

The EU believes that an IPA with India will "significantly increase the level of confidence among investors on both sides, thereby leading to further increases in foreign direct investment in both directions".[51] However, the IPA negotiations between India and the EU will not be easy for various reasons, including the two different stands that the two sides have on the dispute settlement between foreign investors and States. While India's Model BIT reflects a traditional ISDS arrangement, the EU wishes to create a multilateral investment court (MIC) for settling disputes between the investors and the State.[52] Until this international court is created, the EU has been negotiating to create a bilateral investment court system (ICS) in its bilateral IPAs. The EU has proposed to India to create a two-tier ICS with an appellate mechanism and tenured judges to resolve treaty disputes between investors and the State.[53] However, India's stand on establishing a multilateral investment court or a bilateral ICS is unknown.

As far as the UK is concerned, it now appears that investment protection will not be part of the FTA.[54] From the information publicly available, it surfaces that

48 See EU-India Free Trade Agreement, Investment Protection Agreement and Geographical Indications Agreement (n 9) <https://policy.trade.ec.europa.eu/eu-trade-relationships-country-and-region/countries-and-regions/india/eu-india-agreement_en>. India and EU are also negotiating a separate agreement on geographical indications.

49 See *Opinion 2/15 of the Court* [2017] C-2/15 (CJEU) <https://curia.europa.eu/juris/document/document.jsf?text=&docid=190727&doclang=EN>; Paola Conconi, Cristina Herghelegiu and Laura Puccio, 'EU Trade Agreements: To Mix or Not to Mix, That Is the Question' (2021) 55(2) Journal of World Trade 231–60 <https://respect.eui.eu/wp-content/uploads/sites/6/2022/02/to_mix_or_not_to_mix.pdf>.

50 ibid.

51 See 'EU and India Kick-Start Ambitious Trade Agenda' (*European Commission*, 17 June2022) <https://policy.trade.ec.europa.eu/news/eu-and-india-kick-start-ambitious-trade-agenda-2022-06-17_en>.

52 See 'Multilateral Investment Court Project' (*European Commission*) <https://policy.trade.ec.europa.eu/enforcement-and-protection/multilateral-investment-court-project_en>.

53 ibid.

54 See Shivangi Acharya, Aditi Shah and Aftab Ahmed, 'India, UK Still Far Apart on Free Trade Deal' *Reuters* (19 May 2023) <https://www.reuters.com/world/india-uk-still-far-apart-free-trade-deal-sources-2023-05-18/> accessed 9 August 2023.

India and the UK are currently negotiating a separate investment treaty parallel to the FTA negotiations.[55] This situation is different from when the UK set out its objectives of signing an FTA with India. UK was keen on having an investment chapter in the FTA, thus re-legalizing its investment relationship with India.[56] The UK's Department for International Trade (DFIT) listed the protection of British investment in India as a key objective of the investment chapter in the proposed FTA.[57] Specifically, the investment chapter is supposed to "provide sufficient protections to UK investors and guarantee that they receive fair and non-discriminatory treatment, ensuring access to adequate remedies in the event that these obligations are breached".[58] This is an apparent reference to having investment protection provisions in the FTA such as protection from illegal expropriation, assuring FET, and non-discrimination. The International Agreements Committee (IAC) of the House of Lords has also expressed concerns over the protection of British investment in India.[59] The IAC recommends that given the substantive challenges that British investors may face in India, there is a justifiable reason to include an ISDS provision in the investment chapter.[60]

It appears that on India's insistence, the UK agreed to move out investment from the FTA and negotiate it as a separate treaty. This might look like a concession that the British might have made to India. But it may not be such a big concession if the British can manage to bind India to provide investment protection to the English investors with an ISDS, if not as part of an FTA, then as a separate BIT. However, these negotiations will be challenging because of the variance in the position of the UK and India on the issue of investment protection and ISDS.[61] On ISDS, the UK is uncomfortable with India's position that

55 See Shreya Nandi, 'India-UK FTA: Next Meet Looks to Build Consensus on Rules of Origin, IPR' *Business Standard* (28 July 2023) <https://www.business-standard.com/economy/news/india-uk-fta-aim-to-build-consensus-on-investment-pact-ipr-in-next-meet-123072800716_1.html> accessed 9 August 2023.

56 India signed a BIT with the UK on 14 March 1994 which it unilaterally terminated on 22 March 2017; Agreement between the Government of the United Kingdom of Great Britain and Northern Ireland and the Government of the Republic of India (entry into force 6 January 1995).

57 Department for International Trade, 'UK – India Free Trade Agreement: The UK's Strategic Approach' (2022) <https://assets.publishing.service.gov.uk/government/uploads/system/uploads/attachment_data/file/1046839/uk-india-free-trade-agreement-the-uks-strategic-approach.pdf>.

58 ibid 13.

59 International Agreements Committee, *UK-India Free Trade Agreement: Scrutiny of the Government's Negotiating Objectives* (HL 2022–23, Sixth Report, HL 53) (hereinafter 'IAC Report').

60 ibid. See also Rt Hon Kemi Badenoch MP, 'Response to International Agreements Committee's Report "UK-India Free Trade Agreement: Scrutiny of the Government's Negotiating Objectives"' (18 October 2022) <https://committees.parliament.uk/publications/30415/documents/175532/default/>.

61 See Prabhash Ranjan, 'India-UK Investment Relations and "Global Britain"' (2023) 34(1) King's Law Journal 120–44.

a foreign investor must exhaust local remedies for five years before commencing international arbitration.[62] Thus, it is anyone's guess whether India and the UK will agree to a BIT. The two sides may end up with an FTA minus the BIT, leading to what we describe as complete decoupling.

From these trends, can it be said that the pattern that seems to be emerging is that India is not too keen to include an investment protection chapter in FTAs? Seemingly India wishes to have a standalone investment agreement outside the ambit of the FTA. The advantage of having a separate investment treaty could be that it is easy to terminate it unilaterally after the expiry of the initial period for which the treaty is signed, as India did with most of its BITs. Suppose investment protection provisions are part of an FTA as a separate chapter. In that case, it is not possible to terminate just one chapter while retaining the remaining treaty without the consent of the treaty partner/s, as discussed earlier. At the same time, the fact that a country can unilaterally terminate the investment treaty poses grave risks for foreign investors. This reduces the certainty and predictability foreign investors always crave while investing in an alien land.

Moreover, India's approach of not including investment protection within the ambit of FTAs is mystifying for several reasons. First, India's rationale for signing FTAs with several countries is to be part of the global value chains. Trade and foreign investment are central to creating these global value and supply chains.[63] Therefore, decoupling trade from investment in these FTAs defies economic sagacity. Second, if investment protection is a part of these FTAs, India will have a better bargaining position to negotiate balanced investment chapters than a standalone investment treaty. When several related issues are part of the same deal, there is a superior likelihood of 'give and take' and reaching a win-win compromise.

With Australia and Mauritius, little evidence supports that India is interested in signing even a standalone BIT. This coupled with the fact that India has barely signed a few BITs in the last seven to eight years, reveals that India is not interested in accepting international investment law obligations with ISDS. This observation takes us to the next set of arguments that India appears to be indulging in what is known as the de-legalization and de-judicialization of international investment law. We discuss this next.

6.4 Toward de-legalization and de-judicialization

The collapse of communism in the late 1980s and the triumph of liberalism created a germane ground for embracing the Washington Consensus[64] – a

62 See Nandi (n 55).

63 Christine Zhenwei Qiang, Yan Liu and Victor Steenbergen, *An Investment Perspective on Global Value Chains* (World Bank 2021).

64 Paul B Stephan, *The World Crisis and International Law: The World Crisis and International Law* (CUP 2023) 21–25. See also Dani Rodrik, 'Goodbye Washington Consensus, Hello Washington Confusion? A Review of the World Bank's *Economic Growth in the 1990s:*

term coined by English economist John Williamson that codified a philosophy of neoliberalism based on privatization, liberalization, and globalization.[65] In this neoliberal order, markets and competition came to occupy a central role,[66] and so did the role of the State.[67] Many countries, including several developing nations, adopted neoliberal policies to boost international trade and foreign investment. Ernst-Ulrich Petersmann explained the role of law in creating this neoliberal order. He argued that the 'invisible hand' of market competition must be necessarily complemented by the 'visible hand' of the law.[68] This visible hand of law was to operate both nationally and internationally. Thus, an important element of the neoliberal international order has been its legalization – countries accepting international legal obligations on economic matters. New international organizations like the WTO were created, which legalized the trade relations of countries. Likewise, as pointed out earlier, countries entered into scores of investment treaties that legalized their international investment relations. India is one such country that legalized its international trade and investment relations significantly in the 1990s and 2000s by participating in the WTO and signing close to 80 investment treaties and investment chapters in FTAs. To discuss how India is de-legalizing and de-judicializing, it's first essential to look at the concepts of legalization and judicialization briefly.

6.4.1 Legalization

Legalization is defined as a form of institutionalization with three characteristics: obligation, precision, and delegation.[69] Obligation here means that the State is bound by international legal rules or commitments.[70] Precision means that international rules imposing obligations on countries specifically and explicitly define State conduct.[71] Delegation means the extent to which countries delegate the power to a third party (such as an international court or an international tribunal) to interpret the rules, apply them, and also to resolve

Learning from a Decade of Reform' (2006) XLIV Journal of Economic Literature 973–87 <https://drodrik.scholar.harvard.edu/files/dani-rodrik/files/goodbye_washington_consensus_.pdf>.

65 John Williamson (ed), *Latin American Adjustment: How Much Has It Happened?* (Institute for International Economics 1990).

66 See Stephan (n 64) 35–37.

67 Quin Slobodian, *Globalists: The End of Empire and Birth of Neoliberalism* (Harvard UP 2018).

68 EU Petersmann, 'International Economic Theory and International Economic Law – On the Tasks of a Legal Theory of International Economic Order' in J Macdonald and DM Johnston (eds), *The Structure and Process of International Law* (Martinus Nijhoff 1983) 237.

69 Kenneth W Abbott and others, 'The Concept of Legalization' (2000) 54(3) International Organization 401–19.

70 ibid 401.

71 ibid.

disputes that may arise under these rules.[72] While dispute resolution is vital in delegating power to a third body, it is not the only component.[73] States can delegate legal authority to others, such as individuals, by giving them direct access to the international courts or tribunals or the bureaucracies of international organizations for the application of the rules.[74]

Abbott *et al* argue that all international legal regimes will not show the same level of legalization.[75] Some cases will be of 'hard legalization', where all the three characteristics or at least the 'obligation' and 'delegation' bits are high.[76] An excellent example of 'hard legalization' is the Trade-Related Aspects of Intellectual Property Rights (TRIPS) Agreement under the WTO.[77] The TRIPS Agreement imposes binding obligations on WTO member countries, which are precise in nature, unambiguously delineating the State's conduct. Furthermore, the disputes between two WTO Member States under the TRIPS Agreement are resolved by a two-tier WTO dispute settlement body, whose rulings are final and binding on member countries. This shows that the third characteristic of delegation is also satisfied. It is argued that 'hard legalization' imposes significant sovereignty costs on States because they lose control over several matters, which move from national to international.[78]

Contrary to 'hard legalization', one may find 'soft legalization' instances where States control more items within their jurisdictions and transfer fewer powers to international forums, bodies, or institutions.[79] This way, States manage to retain greater sovereignty.

The relevant question for us is what kind of legalization investment treaties demonstrate – 'hard', 'soft', 'high', 'low', or something else? Investment treaties impose obligations on States that require them not to discriminate against foreign investment, to treat them fairly and equitably, not unlawfully expropriate foreign investments, etc. These provisions clearly mean that the State is bound to act in a particular way as per the international norms. Thus, it qualifies as a 'high' obligation. Coming to the next characteristic, precision, the question is whether these norms unambiguously define State conduct. This is a difficult question to answer. Quite a few standards in investment treaties, like

72 ibid.
73 ibid 417.
74 ibid. See also Robert O Keohane, Andrew Moravcsik and Anne-Marie Slaughter, 'Legalized Dispute Resolution: Interstate and Transnational International Organization' (2000) 54(3) Legalization and World Politics 457–88.
75 Abbott and others (n 69) 401–3.
76 ibid.
77 ibid 406.
78 Nicole Deitelhoff, 'The Discursive Process of Legalization: Charting Islands of Persuasion in the ICC Case' (2009)63(1) International Organization 33–65, 40. See also Barbara Koremenos, Charles Lipson and Duncan Snidal, 'The Rational Design of International Institutions' in Barbara Koremenos, Charles Lipson and Duncan Snidal (eds), *The Rational Design of International Institutions* (CUP 2004) 1–40.
79 ibid.

fair and equitable treatment, are not defined with any precision. The fair and equitable treatment standard is quite vague and ambiguous. Likewise, while investment treaties expressly prohibit countries from unlawfully expropriating foreign investment, these treaties do not define expropriation, especially the old-generation ones. On the other hand, some of the provisions in investment treaties, like monetary transfer clauses, are explicit in that they specifically require the State not to impose restrictions on the investors' rights to transfer funds. Thus, one can say that investment treaties are a mixed bag regarding the characteristic of 'precision'. It is moderately satisfied.

Regarding delegation, the third characteristic, most old-generation investment treaties delegate the legal authority to arbitration tribunals to settle disputes. As we know, these arbitrators are ad hoc and appointed by both the investor (the claimant) and the State. The arbitration tribunal has considerable judicial power to interpret the broad and equivocal provisions.[80] Some investment treaties allow investors to access international arbitration without exhausting local remedies, thus showing 'high' delegation. On the other hand, some treaties require the exhaustion of local remedies before resorting to international arbitration, which would fall under the 'moderate' delegation category. Given the ad hoc nature and the lack of an independent institutional resource and memory, ISDS has been described as a quasi-judicial dispute settlement mechanism.[81]

Overall, one can say that investment treaties demonstrate a moderate to high degree of legalization (see Table 6.4). This means that the investment relations between the countries were mediated by international law and subject to compulsory third-party adjudication. Of course, the actual degree of legalization will vary from one investment treaty to another. Some BITs that do not contain ISDS (such as the BITs signed by Brazil[82] or the investment chapter in RCEP, as mentioned before) but only SSDS imply that they will have a 'low' delegation characteristic. Likewise, those BITs that have heavily restricted or curbed ISDS of the kind one finds in the United States-Mexico-Canada Agreement (USMCA), also imply a 'low' delegation characteristic. Canada is not a party to the USMCA's chapter on ISDS (chapter 14).[83] ISDS

80 See LR Helfer and AM Slaughter, 'Why States Create International Tribunals: A Response to Professors Posner and Yoo' (2005) 93(3) California Law Review 899–956, 945.

81 Johann Robert Basedow, 'Why De-Judicialize? Explaining State Preferences on Judicialization in World Trade Organization Dispute Settlement Body and Investor-to-State Dispute Settlement Reforms' (2022) 16(4) Regulation & Governance 1362–81, 1374. See also J Bonnitcha, L Poulsen and M Waibel, *The Political Economy of the Investment Treaty Regime* (OUP 2017) 33–59.

82 See Geraldo Vidigal and Beatriz Stevens, 'Brazil's New Model of Dispute Settlement for Investment: Return to the Past or Alternative for the Future?' (2018) 19(3) The Journal of World Investment & Trade 475–512.

83 Kiran Nasir Gore and Esmé Shirlow, 'The USMCA/CUSMA/T-MEC's Entry into Force: Introducing a New Era in Regional ISDS with NAFTA 2.0' (*Kluwer Arbitration Blog*, 22 June 2020) <http://arbitrationblog.kluwerarbitration.com/2020/06/22/

Table 6.4 Legalization of Investment Treaties

Characteristic ⇒	Obligation	Precision	Delegation
Degree ⇒	High	Moderate	Moderate to High
Degree (for Indian BITs)⇒	High	Moderate	High

Source: Author's compilation

provisions between the US and Mexico have a restricted scope in terms of the kinds of disputes that can be submitted for arbitration.[84]

India's investment treaties signed during the 1990s and 2000s will fall in the category of a 'high' degree of legalization (see Table 6.4). As part of international normative order, these treaties imposed obligations on India regarding foreign investment. Most Indian investment treaties fall in the old-generation category and thus contain broad and ambiguous provisions that are not precise enough. On the point of delegation, all investment treaties contain broad ISDS provisions that investors could resort to without exhausting local remedies and often for all kinds of disputes between the investor and the State.

6.4.2 Judicialization

An important component of the legalization of international relations has been the creation of new international courts and tribunals. This has led to the judicialization of international politics.[85] Judicialization refers to the increasing roles of international courts and tribunals in global governance and international politics.[86] Judicialization can diminish the sovereignty of States and reduce their regulatory autonomy.[87] It results in the shift of power from domestic governments and domestic legislatures to international courts and tribunals.[88]

---

the-usmca-cusma-t-mecs-entry-into-force-introducing-a-new-era-in-regional-isds-with-nafta-2-0/> accessed 9 August 2023.

84 For a detailed discussion on the ISDS provisions in USMCA see Jerry L Lai, 'A Tale of Two Treaties: A Study of NAFTA and USMCA's Investor-State Dispute Settlement Mechanisms' (2021) 25(2) Emory International Law Review 259 <https://scholarlycommons.law.emory.edu/cgi/viewcontent.cgi?article=1256&context=eilr>.

85 See Michael Byers, *The Role of Law in International Politics* (OUP 2000); Karen Alter, 'Delegation to International Courts and the Limits of Re-Contracting Power' in Darrell Hawkins and others (eds), *Delegation and Agency in International Organizations* (CUP 2006) 312–38; Alec Stone Sweet and Thomas L Brunell, 'Trustee Courts and the Judicialization of International Regimes: The Politics of Majoritarian Activism in the European Convention on Human Rights, the European Union, and the World Trade Organization' (2013) 1(1) Journal of Law and Courts 61–88.

86 See KJ Alter, EM Hafner-Burton and L Helfer, 'Theorizing the Judicialization of International Relations' (2019) 63(3) International Studies Quarterly 449–63.

87 ibid.

88 John Ferejohn, 'Judicializing Politics, Politicizing Law' (2002) 65(3) Law and Contemporary Problems 41–68.

Out of the three characteristics of legalization discussed earlier, it can be argued that judicialization partly falls in the category of delegation. Partly because, as pointed out earlier, delegating legal authority to international courts is one part of the delegation characteristic. It also contains other parts such as access to courts and other actors to whom the power to apply rules may be delegated.

As pointed out in the introductory chapter, ISDS is an example of the judicialization of international investment relations between two countries. By accepting ISDS as part of an investment treaty, States transfer the power to an arbitration tribunal to interpret the treaty clauses and hold the host State to account. This way, several issues pertaining to regulating foreign investment that they could have controlled domestically are now in the purview of these international tribunals. For example, if the host State enacts a law favouring national enterprises more than foreign ones, and if a foreign investor challenges it on account of a breach of national treatment, the ISDS tribunal will have the power to review the host State law judicially.[89] Given the proliferation of investment treaties and thus of the ISDS tribunals and the number and range of disputes that these tribunals have decided, as discussed in the introductory chapter, the judicialization of international investment relations is all-pervasive.

6.4.3 Moving away from investment treaties and ISDS

Anthea Roberts *et al* argue that the rise of China and the narrowing of the gap between the American and the Chinese economy has triggered a geoeconomic competition between the great powers.[90] This geoeconomic competition, in turn, has several consequences, including the de-legalization of international economic law.[91] In other words, it is argued that the levels of obligation, precision, and delegation associated with the international economic law regime will decline.[92] De-legalization in the context of international economic law is described as having two parts, first, vertical redirection of the decision-making authority, that is, the decision-making authority moving from international law to domestic law; and second, horizontal redirection of the decision-making authority, that is, the decision-making authority moving from the adjudicatory sphere to executive determination.[93] In short, de-legalization will result

89 Doreen Lustig and JHH Weiler, 'Judicial Review in the Contemporary World – Retrospective and Prospective' (2018) 16(2) International Journal of Constitutional Law 315, 326–28 <https://academic.oup.com/icon/article/16/2/315/5036485>.

90 Anthea Roberts, Henrique Choer Moraes and Victor Ferguson, 'Toward a Geoeconomic Order in International Trade and Investment' (2019) 22(4) Journal of International Economics Law 655.

91 ibid 672.

92 ibid.

93 ibid.

in the relegation of issues decided as per international law to the domestic framework.

In the context of international investment law, this can be understood with the help of a simple example. There are quite a few instances of countries terminating BITs, either unilaterally or mutually. In such an eventuality, it means that issues pertaining to their bilateral foreign investment inflows that countries had decided will be mediated as per international law, will now come under the purview of domestic law. Thus, if countries wish to give preferences to domestic investments over foreign ones, they will be able to do so as per their domestic policy requirements. Put differently, the de-legalization of international investment law will mean that the decision-making authority will shift from the international to the domestic level. Putting an end to BITs also implies the termination of third-party adjudication for investment claims, that is, de-legalization is accompanied by de-judicialization. The walking away of countries from ISDS[94] is part of what Daniel Abebe and Tom Ginsburg called the de-judicialization of international politics: the "complete removal from judicial cognizance of a policy issue that had previously been subject to judicialization".[95] De-judicialization, the opposite of judicialization, is often a question of degree. When something is completely removed from the international judicial cognizance and put back within the purview of domestic courts or domestic executive authorities, it would be a case of complete de-judicialization. On the other hand, when specific or select issues, not all, are pulled out from international judicial cognizance, or when countries selectively judicialize, it can be called a case of partial de-judicialization.

Important to note, it is not necessary for countries to de-legalize and de-judicialize international investment law simultaneously. There are quite a few instances where States have not de-legalized international investment law but have only de-judicialized it. The investment chapter of RCEP, which is without an ISDS, is an excellent example of this. Likewise, the investment chapters in UK-Australia and UK-New Zealand FTAs that do not contain the ISDS provision are also examples of de-judicialization without de-legalization.

The motivations of countries behind de-judicialization may vary, but by and large, it is argued that countries may want to de-judicialize to regain regulatory space.[96] The same argument can be made in the context of international

94 This does not mean that the ISDS system does not exist or that all countries have walked away from the ISDS mechanism. Nonetheless, some countries have surely terminated BITs and ISDS and thus have indulged in the de-legalization and de-judicialization of international investment law.

95 Daniel Abebe and Tom Ginsburg, 'The Dejudicialization of International Politics?' (2019) 63(3) International Studies Quarterly 521–30, 521.

96 See Todd Allee and M Elsig, 'Why Do Some International Institutions Contain Strong Dispute Settlement Provisions? New Evidence from Preferential Trade Agreements' (2016) 11 The Review of International Organizations 89–120. See also Robert Basedow (n 81) 1362–81.

Table 6.5 Signing and Termination of International Investment Agreements, 2018–2022

Year	*Number of IIAs Signed*	*Number of IIAs Terminated (unilaterally and mutually)*
2018	40	24
2019	22	34
2020	21	42
2021	13	86
2022	15	58

Source: UNCTAD's World Investment Reports, 2019 to 2023

investment law as well. As discussed in Chapter 1, one of the major criticisms the ISDS system has attracted is that it unduly encroaches on the regulatory space of the host State. Thus, States want to break free from the shackles imposed by the ISDS regime to adopt policies and laws as per their domestic needs. However, one author argues that it is not necessary that de-judicialization may always be done to augment regulatory space.[97] He gives the example of the European Union (EU) to show that the EU's judicialization effort in international investment law by creating a bilateral ICS and trying to establish a MIC relates to preserving the regulatory space.[98]

It is necessary to ask how widespread the phenomenon of de-legalization in international investment law is. Of course, countries continue to sign investment treaties and accept ISDS. So, the argument is not that all countries have de-legalized their international investment relations. However, if we look at UNCTAD's data (see Table 6.5), one can see that the trend of de-legalization in international investment law seems to be catching up. From 2019 to 2022, one can see that the number of International Investment Agreements that have been terminated outnumbers the ones that have been signed. It is important to mention some caveats. In some instances, new treaties may replace the ones that have been terminated. Further, several examples of European countries terminating their BITs, which might appear in these numbers, are primarily due to reasons specific to the EU. It might be misleading to construe these numbers as instances of countries walking away from ISDS.

Nonetheless, the BIT termination numbers capture the general mood of disenchantment of some countries with international investment law. Terminating BITs also implies walking away from the ISDS mechanism, and, thus, de-judicializing international investment relations. It is quite possible that countries might enter into new BITs in place of the terminated ones. Nonetheless, it demonstrates that several countries are contesting the ISDS regime.

97 Robert Basedow (n 81).
98 ibid.

6.4.4 India's case

Based on these concepts, it can be safely said that while India in the 1990s and 2000s legalized and judicialized its international investment relations, it has embarked on a process of de-legalization and de-judicialization of international investment law in the last few years. The most striking example of this is the decision to terminate BITs and, thus, ISDS unilaterally, as discussed in Chapter 1. As a result, India has redirected decision-making from international (treaties and ISDS) to national (executive, legislature, and municipal courts). Such redirection will give greater regulatory control to India to deal with foreign investments and investors, including investor-state disputes that may arise.

In this regard, there have been proposals that, in place of investment treaties and ISDS, India should enact a domestic law to safeguard foreign investment.[99] The avowed purpose of the proposed law seems to be twofold. First, it offers legal protection to foreign investors from abrupt policy changes; second, keeping in mind the slowness of the Indian legal system, to provide speedier dispute resolution. More details of this law are still not available. However, even in the absence of such a law, the termination of BITs and, thus, ISDS means greater power and reliance on domestic laws and authorities. True, India has adopted a Model BIT and signed a few BITs based on it. Moreover, India has not formally walked away from the ISDS system. The Indian Model BIT contains an ISDS mechanism, although heavily skewed in favour of the State. Additionally, India formally remains committed to signing new BITs based on the Model. However, as discussed, the number of new BITs signed has been too tiny in the last several years. The absence of investment protection chapters and ISDS in India's new FTAs is the most significant proof of de-legalization and de-judicialization. This new practice is a break with the past.

Collectively, this indicates moving away from investment treaties and ISDS. Laws and policies regulating foreign investment or that affected foreign investment are being withdrawn from the competence of international law and international adjudication. Like several countries that have practised de-legalization and de-judicialization, India is doing this to regain the regulatory space it believes it had lost to international law and international adjudicatory bodies like the ISDS. But can one conclude that India has lost its regulatory space simply because of several ISDS claims brought against it? As we have seen, many of these claims were brought against India due to poor regulation or abuse of power. So, the jury is still out on whether India's regulatory space has been constrained due to India's BIT obligations and ISDS.

99 Rajeev Jayaswal, 'Long-Awaited FDI Protection Provision Expected in Budget' *Hindustan Times* (31 January 2020) <https://www.hindustantimes.com/india-news/long-awaited-fdi-protection-provision-expected-in-budget/story-0V3o1e6SvvfS8ZcPyAUAIL.html> accessed 9 August 2023.

6.5 Conclusion

In this chapter, contrary to the previous chapters, the discussion has been on identifying the macro trends in India's investment treaty practice. Given the absence of new BITs India has signed in the last seven to eight years, the chapter uses India's FTAs as a proxy to understand the macro trend. Unlike the past practice, the chapter finds India does not include investment protection provisions and ISDS in its newly signed FTAs. This demonstrates an attempt on India's part to decouple international investment law from international trade law. From the three recent FTAs that India signed with Mauritius, UAE, and Australia, it becomes apparent that while India is willing to accept obligations on international trade under international law, it is not inclined to accept international law obligations on foreign investment.

The chapter also uses this trend to ask more significant normative questions on India's overall approach to ISDS and international investment law. Given the rise in debates on de-legalization and de-judicialization in international law, including international investment law, it becomes imperative to ask whether India's investment treaty practice is moving in that direction. Although India formally remains committed to ISDS, it hasn't signed many BITs and has stopped accepting investment protection and ISDS in its new FTAs. This gives credence to the argument that India is walking down the road of de-legalization and de-judicialization of international investment law. These early trends may be reversed depending on the outcome of India's ongoing negotiations with the UK and the EU on an investment treaty. But if India fails to sign a BIT with the UK and an IPA with the EU, it will further cement the de-legalization and de-judicialization hypothesis.

7 Conclusion

7.1 Introduction

This book is not an unabashed cheerleader's account of the ISDS mechanism. Its goal is not to try to defend the ISDS regime against the valid criticisms levelled against it. There is no gainsaying the fact that ISDS indeed suffers from several systemic lacunas, which the regime's critics have correctly pointed out. Many fundamental problems currently plague the system, including the lack of transparency in the process, incoherent and inconsistent jurisprudence, lack of an appellate mechanism to correct the errors in legal interpretation, broad and expansive interpretations of the substantive guarantees that foreign investors enjoy under investment treaties, a systemic arbitral bias that raises questions about the independence and impartiality of the arbitrators, awarding extensive damages to the foreign investors, the failure of ISDS tribunals to duly incorporate human rights concerns and interests of indigenous communities, the chilling impact that ISDS claims may have on a host State's right to regulate, etc. Additionally, there have been instances of foreign investors trying to abuse the system. States have faced claims that threatened their sovereign regulatory measures to protect public health, combat climate change, address fiscal imperatives, and the like.

For these reasons, many scholars and civil society find the ISDS system disconcerting, to the extent of being deemed precarious.[1] However, opposition to the system extends beyond academia and activism. Several countries, especially those at the receiving end of the ISDS system in terms of facing an avalanche of treaty-based claims, have also contested the system, triggering a backlash. Consequently, countries like Australia,[2]

1 See IEL Collective, 'COVID-19 and the Precarity of International Investment Law' *Medium* (6 May 2020) <https://medium.com/iel-collective/covid-19-and-the-precarity-of-international-investment-law-c9fc254b3878> accessed 22 September 2023.

2 Luke Nottage, 'Australia's (Dis)Engagement with Investor-State Arbitration: A Sequel' (*Kluwer Arbitration Blog*, 21 December 2022) <https://arbitrationblog.kluwerarbitration.com/2022/12/21/australias-disengagement-with-investor-state-arbitration-a-sequel/> accessed 23 September 2023. Also see Senator the Hon Don Farrell, Minister for Trade and Tourism, 'Trading Our Way to Greater Prosperity and Security' (Speech at the Australian APEC

DOI: 10.4324/9781003324379-7

South Africa,[3] Canada,[4] New Zealand,[5] the European Union,[6] Ecuador,[7] etc., have opposed the ISDS mechanism, with some choosing to exit the system completely. Numerous examples of countries terminating their BITs have fuelled the debates on de-legalization and de-judicialization of international investment law.

While being cognizant and incorporating this perspective on ISDS, often referred to as the 'Philip Morris narrative', championed by the virulent critics of the system, it is essential to understand one narrative cannot do justice to the complexities of the ISDS mechanism. One may have to analyse meta-narratives to integrate different perspectives to understand a system entirely. This book elucidates the other narrative to understand ISDS, based on the premise that not all sovereign action is bona fide or for the protection of genuine public interests. States often abuse their power, and they need to be held accountable under international law when they do so. This is the 'Yukos narrative' that is indispensable for a holistic understanding of the ISDS system.

This book illustrates this point by taking India as an example and examining ISDS claims that India has lost. The genesis of all the high-profile ISDS claims

---

Study Centre, RMIT, Melbourne, 14 November 2022) <https://www.trademinister.gov.au/minister/don-farrell/speech/trading-our-way-greater-prosperity-and-security> accessed 23 September 2023.

3 Section 13 of the Protection of Investment Act, 2015 (South Africa) <https://investment-policy.unctad.org/investment-laws/laws/157/south-africa-investment-act>. See also Tafadzwa Pasipanodya and Javier García Olmedo, '21st Century Investment Protection: Africa's Innovations in Investment Law Reform' (*International Bar Association*, 24 November 2021) <https://www.ibanet.org/africas-innovations-in-investment-law-reform#_edn8> accessed 22 September 2023.

4 Government of Canada, 'Investment Chapter Summary' <https://www.international.gc.ca/trade-commerce/trade-agreements-accords-commerciaux/agr-acc/cusma-aceum/investment-investissement.aspx?lang=eng> accessed 22 September 2023. Also see, Government of Canada, '2021 FIPA Model – Summary of Main Changes' <https://www.international.gc.ca/trade-commerce/trade-agreements-accords-commerciaux/agr-acc/fipa-apie/2021_model_fipa_summary-2021_modele_apie_resume.aspx?lang=eng> accessed 22 September 2023.

5 New Zealand, Foreign Affairs and Trade, 'Investment and ISDS' <https://www.mfat.govt.nz/en/trade/free-trade-agreements/free-trade-agreements-in-force/cptpp/understanding-cptpp/investment-and-isds/> accessed 22 September 2023.

6 Clause c (xv) of European Parliament resolution of 8 July 2015 containing the European Parliament's recommendations to the European Commission on the negotiations for the Transatlantic Trade and Investment Partnership (TTIP) (2014/2228(INI)). See also European Commission, 'Multilateral Investment Court Project' <https://policy.trade.ec.europa.eu/enforcement-and-protection/multilateral-investment-court-project_en>.

7 Juan Carlos Herrera-Quenguan, 'Explaining Ecuador's Shifting Position on FDI, Investment Treaties, and Arbitration' *Investment Treaty News* (5 October 2020) <https://www.iisd.org/itn/en/2020/10/05/explaining-ecuadors-shifting-position-on-fdi-investment-treaties-and-arbitration-juan-carlos-herrera-quenguan/> accessed 22 September 2023. Also see ICSID, 'Ecuador Ratifies the ICSID Convention' *ICSID* (4 August 2021) <https://icsid.worldbank.org/news-and-events/news-releases/ecuador-ratifies-icsid-convention> accessed 23 September 2023.

that India lost lay in the slackness of the system, the abuse of public power, or poor governance. In short, these cases reflect numerous dimensions of the Yukos narrative. For instance, The *White Industries* claim arose due to the Indian judiciary's failure to get its act together. When a country's courts take nine years to decide on a commercial arbitral award, what is the foreign investor supposed to do? Surely, the investor can't be expected to wait endlessly! In such a situation, it can't be held against a foreign investor if she initiates an ISDS claim. Instead of normalizing and rationalizing this inordinate delay in deciding the fate of a commercial arbitration award, and acting as apologists for the system, it should be seen as an alarming sign of profound systemic problems in India's judicial governance. Indeed, the Law Commission of India took cognizance that exorbitant judicial delays triggered the *White Industries* claim and used it to make a case for reforms in India's arbitration law to minimize judicial intervention in the arbitral process. However, the ongoing interpretation of the Arbitration and Conciliation Act by Indian courts, including the assertion that it does not apply to ISDS and the inconsistent amendments to arbitration laws, shows that perhaps the lessons of the White Industries fiasco have not been fully learned.

The two Devas cases and India's dealing with them, before and after the disputes, share several dimensions with the Yukos narrative. These cases arose due to India's decision to abruptly cancel the contract without following any due process. This triggered one commercial arbitration claim against Antrix and two treaty-based arbitrations against India. If there was a suspicion of corruption or wrongdoing in the Devas-Antrix deal, the decision to rescind the contract should have been based on these reasons. However, India did not cancel the agreement on the grounds of corruption, investor misconduct, or fraud but advanced a cocktail of other reasons ranging from social objectives to national security. But these reasons were primarily a veil to mask the contract cancellation motivated by political reasons. In 2014, India launched a criminal investigation into the Devas-Antrix deal. India lost both cases and did not comply with the awards. In fact, after the issuance of awards, India followed an aggressive litigation strategy, internationally and domestically, raising the fraud argument against CC/Devas and Deutsche Telekom. The objective is to get these awards set aside. While most international tribunals and foreign courts have rejected India's contention, domestic judicial institutions have lent an ear to the Executive.

Hence, the National Company Law Tribunal and the National Company Law Appellate Tribunal agreed that the establishment of Devas was for fraudulent purposes – a ground recognized by Indian company law to allow for the winding up of the company. The Indian Supreme Court subsequently endorsed these decisions. Consequently, this led to the annulment of the commercial arbitration award favouring Devas over Antrix by an Indian court, prompting Devas to initiate a second BIT arbitration under the India-Mauritius BIT. In response, India amended the Arbitration and Conciliation Act retroactively, making it difficult to enforce awards borne out of contracts tainted by fraud, which would directly affect Devas's commercial and treaty-based awards. Furthermore, India convinced Mauritius to adopt a Joint Interpretative Statement (JIS) regarding the India-Mauritius BIT, which was terminated in 2017. This JIS is a curious development for multiple reasons. This is the only instance of India's involvement in adopting a JIS for a terminated BIT.

Moreover, unlike the other two JISs involving India-Bangladesh and India-Colombia BITs, this JIS includes a provision on corruption. As discussed in Chapter 3, this JIS provides that investors against whom judicial or administrative fraud proceedings are pending cannot enjoy protection under the BIT. Arguably, this has been done to thwart Devas's attempt to bring the second BIT termination. In a nutshell, India left no stone unturned to ensure that Devas cannot bring claims, including by amending domestic and international law. It is worth noting that Devas's criminal liability or involvement in corruption has not been conclusively established. If India has evidence about Devas's involvement in corruption or fraud, this must be submitted to the newly constituted ISDS tribunal, which should decide the matter. Should Devas be found to have engaged in corruption or fraudulent practices, its investment would not qualify for treaty protection, as Article 1(a) of the India-Mauritius BIT requires investments to be made lawfully. If an investment is made through fraudulent means or if Devas got the contract by bribing officials, it will be a case of unlawful investment. Thus, Devas's investment will not enjoy protection under the BIT. But changing laws to create procedural bottlenecks in the path of an investor to file an ISDS claim is not something that a liberal democracy like India should be doing.

The two retroactive tax cases against India exemplify the Yukos narrative. These disputes arose when the central government, unhappy with an unfavourable Supreme Court decision, got the income tax law retroactively amended. This overturned the Supreme Court of India's favourable decision towards Vodafone in one stroke. So, a foreign investor challenges a governmental action and takes the legal battle all the way to the highest court of that country, which, based on the existing law, decides the case in the investor's favour. Instead of complying with the decision, the government changes the law to overturn the judicial decision. India's objective was not only to compel Vodafone to pay taxes that the country's apex court believed were not owed but also to revisit previously closed transactions, such as Cairn Energy's business restructuring.

In such a situation, what should the foreign investor do? Accept the new law as its fate or use ISDS to hold the State action accountable? Clearly, Vodafone and Cairn Energy opted for the second option. The decision to amend the tax law retroactively attracted widespread criticism, globally and nationally. It rattled the foreign investors. It spooked the market sentiment because even the Supreme Court's decision was not final. Only in 2021, when the government recognized the mistake in retroactively imposing taxes, India repealed it. However, the damage had already been done by then, and India had lost two mega ISDS claims.

The *Nissan* case is not just a grim reminder of one more Yukos moment – the State luring investors by offering incentives and then going back on these promises to the detriment of investors without any policy justification – but also how the actions of sub-national governments could land India in trouble under international law. India needs to strengthen the internalization process of BITs and bolster the capacity of the 28 provincial governments to understand BITs and consider India's international obligations while formulating policies and laws.

The Yukos narrative, rather than the Philip Morris perspective, overarchingly dominates India's ISDS story. None of the disputes discussed in the book were an affront to India's sovereignty. They were an indictment of India's regulatory capriciousness. India could have avoided all these claims if it had acted with circumspection and employed better regulatory governance. Rattled by these ISDS claims, India reviewed its investment treaties and took drastic actions such as terminating BITs. Unfortunately, the blame for these claims was attributed to the ISDS mechanism without honest introspection of the reasons that triggered them. India tried to brazen it out while defending these claims, such as continuous assertions that tax-related issues are not subject to the jurisdiction of ISDS tribunals or amending the laws to foil the attempt of foreign investors to bring claims, etc. As the book showed in Chapter 6, India has doubled down on the road of de-legalization and de-judicialization of international investment law by not including investment protection and ISDS in its three latest FTAs.

India should draw right lessons from its experience in these six ISDS claims. Instead of moving towards the de-legalization and de-judicialization of international investment law, India should conduct a self-introspection exercise to analyse the real reasons for these claims. The need is to focus on domestic governance issues with necessary administrative reforms so that such disputes do not crop up in the future.

It is not the contention that foreign investors never abuse the system to their advantage. But litigants using the judicial system to their vantage should not be a surprise as one sees that happening in the domestic legal systems all the time. However, this does not mean one should shut down the judicial system. The abuse of the system by the litigants should alert us towards plugging the lacunas, not throwing the baby out with the bathwater. Moreover, it is also a fact that States abuse their public powers to the detriment of foreign investors. Foreign investors should have the right to defend themselves against any inconsistent use of regulatory power by the States without relying on their home States. This is a crucial element of a rule-based global economic order.

7.2 Future of ISDS and India

Reforms within the ISDS framework are currently being pursued at various levels. The second-generation or the new-generation investment treaties endeavour to overcome the deficiencies in drafting old BITs by including detailed substantive and procedural provisions. The ambition is to reduce arbitral tribunals' discretion while interpreting investment treaties. A significant arena for brainstorming sessions for possible ISDS reforms is the United Nations Commission on International Trade Law (UNCITRAL).[8] In 2017, an UNCITRAL Working Group III was created to assuage criticisms against ISDS and find workable reforms.[9] The Working Group III is focussing on a number of reform measures focussing on issues like concerns regarding the consistency and coherence of ISDS awards;[10] costs and duration of ISDS cases;[11] code of conduct for arbitrators;[12] third party finding;[13] possibility of introducing a permanent investment court;[14] or an appeal mechanism.[15] Much has already been written on these ongoing reform attempts.[16]

Where does India stand on the issue of ISDS reform? A sizable deterrent to understanding India's views on ISDS, including on possible reform, is the unavailability of public documents or interventions. Barring the 2016 Model BIT, no public document enunciates India's stand on ISDS. Several countries have submitted their views on ISDS to UNCITRAL Working Group III, expounding their perspectives, challenges, and reform ideas. These countries

8 Malcolm Langford and others, 'UNCITRAL and Investment Arbitration Reform: Matching Concerns and Solutions: An Introduction' (2020) 21 Journal of World Investment and Trade 167–87.

9 UNCITRAL, 'Working Group III: Investor-State Dispute Settlement Reform' <https://uncitral.un.org/en/working_groups/3/investor-state> accessed 20 September 2023.

10 UNCITRAL, 'Draft Report of Working Group III (Investor-State Dispute Settlement Reform) on the Work of Its Thirty-Sixth Session' (6 November 2018) <https://uncitral.un.org/sites/uncitral.un.org/files/draft_report_of_wg_iii_for_the_website.pdf> accessed 20 September 2023.

11 UNITRAL, 'Working Group III, Possible Reform of Investor-State Dispute Settlement (ISDS) – Cost and Duration' <https://documents-dds-ny.un.org/doc/UNDOC/LTD/V18/057/51/PDF/V1805751.pdf?OpenElement> accessed 20 September 2023.

12 UNCITRAL, 'Working Group III: ISDS Reform, Codes of Conduct' <https://uncitral.un.org/en/codeofconduct>.

13 UNCITRAL, 'Working Group III: ISDS Reform, Third-Party Funding' <https://uncitral.un.org/en/thirdpartyfunding> accessed 20 September 2023.

14 UNCITRAL, 'Working Group III: ISDS Reform, Multilateral Permanent Investment Court' <https://uncitral.un.org/en/multilateralpermanentinvestmentcourt> accessed 20 September 2023.

15 UNCITRAL, 'Working Group III: ISDS Reform, Appellate Mechanism' <https://uncitral.un.org/en/appellatemechanism> accessed 20 September 2023.

16 See Anthea Roberts, 'Incremental, Systemic, and Paradigmatic Reform of Investor-State Arbitration' (2018) 112 American Journal of International Law 410; Sergio Puig and Gregory Shaffer, 'Imperfect Alternatives: Institutional Choice and the Reform of Investment Law' (2018) 112 American Journal of International Law 361; Anthea Roberts and Tylor St John, 'Complex Designers and Emergent Design: Reforming the Investment Treaty System' (2022) 116 American Journal of International Law 96; Chiara Giorgetti, 'The Transformation of International Organizations – Specialization, New Initiatives, and Working Methods – Some Observations on the Work of UNCITRAL Working Group III' (March 2023) 26(1) Journal of International Economic Law 40–50.

are Indonesia, Morocco, Brazil, South Africa, China, Colombia, Turkey, Ecuador, Costa Rica, Korea, Bahrain, Kuwait, Kazakhstan, etc.[17] These submissions dovetail various critical issues on ISDS, ranging from doing away with the current ISDS mechanism to championing its reform. However, India's proposals or statements are unavailable on the UNCITRAL Working Group III website on ISDS.

India's statement at the United Nations General Assembly is one document where India mentions the UNCITRAL Working Group III process.[18] This statement states:

> *We [India] commend the progress of the work of Working Group III on Investor–State Dispute Settlement Reform. We note that the two possible reforms include reforming the current system in a step-by-step process and a structural reform which includes the creation of a World Investment Court with an appellate body. It has been agreed to pursue both work streams simultaneously, in order to give ample opportunity and accommodate all the parties and have consensus on the way forward.*[19]

But this general statement welcomes the Working Group III process without delineating India's stand or concerns on ISDS and the various attendant issues. Consequently, one does not know where India stands on the various reform issues flagged for discussion, including the proposal to create a multilateral investment court.

Reportedly, India opposes the idea of establishing a multilateral investment court to resolve disputes between investors and States.[20] The issue of creating an investment court system that would replace the traditional arbitration-based ISDS mechanism is a sticky issue between India and the EU in the ongoing investment protection agreement (IPA) negotiations. The EU's position on this issue is well known. The EU in its recent FTAs and IPAs contains what can be called a bilateral investment court system (ICS). In its treaties, the EU provides for creating an investment tribunal that would hear

17 The submissions made by countries to UNCITRAL Working Group III are present here: UNCITRAL, 'Working Group III: Investor-State Dispute Settlement Reform' <https://uncitral.un.org/en/working_groups/3/investor-state>.

18 UNGA, 'Report Of The United Nations Commission On International Trade Law' (10 November 2020) 75th Session (2020) <https://pminewyork.gov.in/IndiaatUNGA?id=NDA5NA>.

19 ibid.

20 Special Correspondent, 'India Rejects Attempts by EU, Canada for Global Investment Agreement' *The Hindu* (23 January 2017) <https://www.thehindu.com/business/India-rejects-attempts-by-EU-Canada-for-global-investment-agreement/article17083034.ece>; Jayshree Sengupta, 'Future of EU-India Free Trade Agreement' (*ORF*, 13 July 2017) <https://www.orfonline.org/expert-speak/future-of-eu-india-free-trade-agreement/>; Investment Treaty News, 'European Union and Canada Co-Host Discussions on a Multilateral Investment Court' (*IISD*, 13 March 2017) <www.iisd.org/itn/en/2017/03/13/european-union-and-canada-co-host-discussions-on-a-multilateral-investment-court/>.

the disputes between investors and States. This tribunal will have 15 members. For instance, Article 8.27(2) of the EU-Canada Comprehensive Economic and Trade Agreement (CETA) provides that

> *the CETA Joint Committee shall, upon the entry into force of this Agreement, appoint fifteen Members of the Tribunal. Five of the Members of the Tribunal shall be nationals of a Member State of the European Union, five shall be nationals of Canada and five shall be nationals of third countries.*

Thus, out of the 15 members, five each will be nationals of the EU and Canada and the remaining five will be nationals of third countries. These members shall be appointed on a five-year term. In order to ensure the availability of the members, they would be paid a monthly retainer fee. Thus, this system is a departure from the establishment of ad hoc arbitration tribunals for settling disputes between investors and States.

Article 8.28 of the EU-Canada CETA provides for the establishment of an appellate tribunal. The function of the appellate tribunal is to

> *uphold, modify or reverse a Tribunal's award based on:*
>
> *(a) errors in the application or interpretation of applicable law;*
> *(b) manifest errors in the appreciation of the facts, including the appreciation of relevant domestic law;*
> *(c) the grounds set out in Article 52(1) (a) through (e) of the ICSID Convention, in so far as they are not covered by paragraphs (a) and (b).*

Thus, the appellate tribunal, as the name suggests, will have the power to correct the errors in law made by the tribunal or the court of the first instance. The EU has made a similar proposal to India, which involves creating a two-tier court-like system with an appellate mechanism and tenured judges to resolve treaty disputes between investors and the State.[21] The EU says it is still waiting for India's response to its proposal to create an investment court system.[22] It is widely reported that India has decided to move away from its 2016 Model BIT given its ongoing investment treaty negotiations with the United Kingdom and the EU.[23] Allegedly, India is no longer insisting on the

21 CIRCABAC, 'EU Textual Proposal – EU India IPA Negotiation' <https://circabc.europa.eu/ui/group/09242a36-a438-40fd-a7af-fe32e36cbd0e/library/13cb61e4-79d4-42e0-942e-28156a3cd815/details>.

22 Kallol Bhattacherjee, 'Waiting for India's Counter Proposal on Investment Court System: EU Trade Commissioner' *The Hindu* (26 August 2023) <https://www.thehindu.com/news/national/waiting-for-indias-counter-proposal-on-investment-court-system-eu-trade-commissioner-valdis-dombrovskis/article67238278.ece>.

23 Ravi Dutta Mishra and Gulveen Aulakh, 'Waiting for India's Counter Proposal on Investment Court System: EU Trade Commissioner' *Mint* (27 August 2023) <https://www.

requirement for investors to exhaust local remedies. However, there has been no official confirmation of this change in India's stance on ISDS.

India should shed its caginess on ISDS and take part in its reform process with aplomb. As a liberal constitutional democracy that has always championed a rule-based global order, India should not shy away from being held accountable under international law. A reformed and improved ISDS, whether it takes the shape of an investment court or any other mechanism with an appellate review, can be a valuable tool to haul up States for their whimsical and abusive behaviour towards foreign investors. India should play a proactive role in building this new global order premised on international rule of law.

In conclusion, the Yukos dimension of ISDS is as much a reality as the Philip Morris version is. While the flaws in the ISDS system should be plugged to ensure that a country's sovereignty is not affronted, ISDS should be available to foreign investors to defend themselves from State arbitrariness. The endeavour to reform the ISDS mechanism, bearing in mind only the Philip Morris narrative, will result in the existing imbalanced system being replaced by a new variety of unevenness where the scale tilts towards the State's regulatory power to the detriment of foreign investment protection.

---

livemint.com/news/india/india-may-revise-bilateral-investment-treaty-template-amidst-negotiations-for-free-trade-agreements-with-uk-and-eu-11693155107441.html>; Aanchal Magazine, 'India UK Bilateral Investment Treaty Likely to Be Finalised Soon, to Differ from 2016 Model' *Indian Express* (28 August 2023) <https://indianexpress.com/article/business/india-uk-bilateral-investment-treaty-free-trade-agreement-2016-model-bit-european-union-8912276/>.

Index

Note: Page numbers in *italics* indicate a figure and page numbers in **bold** indicate a table on the corresponding page.

FSC
www.fsc.org
MIX
Papier | Fördert gute Waldnutzung
FSC® C083411

Kolibri 360 GmbH
Ferdinand-Jühlke-Straße 7
99095 Erfurt, Deutschland
produktsicherheit@kolibri360.de